WOMAN IN THE WILDERNESS

Woman in the Wilderness

LETTERS OF HARRIET WOOD WHEELER, MISSIONARY WIFE, 1832–1892

NANCY BUNGE

MICHIGAN STATE UNIVERSITY PRESS — *East Lansing*

♾The paper used in this publication meets the minimum requirements
of ANSI/NISO Z39.48-1992 (R 1997) (Permanence of Paper).

Michigan State University Press
East Lansing, Michigan 48823-5245

Printed and bound in the United States of America.

16 15 14 13 12 11 10   1 2 3 4 5 6 7 8 9 10

LIBRARY OF CONGRESS CATALOGING-IN-PUBLICATION DATA
Bunge, Nancy L.
Woman in the wilderness : letters of Harriet Wood Wheeler, missionary wife, 1832–1892 / Nancy Bunge.
p. cm.
Includes bibliographical references and index.
ISBN 978-0-87013-978-9 (paper : alk. paper)
1. Wheeler, Harriet Wood, 1816–1894. 2. Wheeler, Harriet Wood, 1816–1894—Correspondence.
3. Wheeler, Harriet Wood, 1816–1894—Family. 4. Women pioneers—Wisconsin—Biography.
5. Missionaries' spouses—Wisconsin—Biography. 6. Ojibwa Indians—Missions—Wisconsin—History—19th
century. 7. Frontier and pioneer life—Wisconsin. 8. Wisconsin—Ethnic relations—History—19th century.
9. Women—Education—United States—Case studies. I. Title.
F584.W47B86 2010
977.5'03092—dc22
[B]
2010003505

Cover and book design by Sharp Des!gns, Lansing, Michigan
Cover art: Harriet Wood Wheeler, Courtesy of the Wisconsin Historical Society, WHi-36771.
The gorge on the Bad River, where the Wheelers established their mission in 1845, they named
the community Odanah, used courtesy of the Wisconsin Historical Society, WHi-66597.

g green
press
INITIATIVE
Michigan State University Press is a member of the Green Press Initiative and is committed to developing and
encouraging ecologically responsible publishing practices. For more information about the Green Press Initiative
and the use of recycled paper in book publishing, please visit www.greenpressinitiative.org.

Visit Michigan State University Press on the World Wide Web at www.msupress.msu.edu

For Jon, Will, and Katie

———————

Contents

———

Acknowledgments

---

*F*irst and foremost, I thank Keith Widder for suggesting this book and for generously sharing the expertise he has developed through decades of working as a historian of the Great Lakes. He graciously offered advice not only as I worked on this manuscript, but from the very beginning of my obsession with the Wheelers. Thanks to Michigan State University for giving me the sabbatical I needed to focus on this project and to the Harvard Divinity School for giving me the chance to develop some expertise of my own by spending my sabbatical as a visiting scholar there. This meant I not only could audit Harvard classes, but I also had access to the amazing collections in the Harvard libraries. I am especially grateful to Ann Braude and Brian Delay for allowing me to attend their seminars. I could not have taken advantage of these opportunities without a place to stay in Cambridge, so I thank the Episcopal Divinity School and especially Margaret Thorpe for supplying me with convenient, affordable housing, which I shared with kind people from all over the world.

I also thank Anne Dubuisson Anderson, who helped me figure out how to shape the manuscript and made very helpful comments about the portions she reviewed. And I owe a debt of gratitude to friends and family who expressed enough interest in and enthusiasm about the project to keep me going: Bob Cary and Janet Nussmann, Jerome Gundersen, Agnes Widder, Sylvia Watanabe, Sybil Eakin, Patti Mueller, Judy Jensen, Sigurd Midelfort, Catherine Cook, my brother Jon Bunge and his family. Thanks also to Bonnie Zahn and Nan Hutton for their research help.

Of course, professional validation also helps, so I am grateful to Waldemar Zacharasiewicz for inviting me to speak about the Wheelers at the University of Vienna and to Alexia Kosmider and William D. Howden, the editors of the *ATQ* issues where my first work on the Wheelers appeared.

Thanks to the many librarians who helped me locate relevant materials in their collections, especially Patricia Albright of the Mount Holyoke Archives and Special Collections; Martha Mayo, director of the Center for Lowell History; and Elizabeth J. Delene, archivist for the Bishop Baraga Association in Marquette, Michigan. I also learned a lot from Jim Daumpier of the Baraga County Historical Museum, from Sharon Manthei of the Ashland Historical Society Museum, and especially from Timm Severud, who describes himself as a "regional amateur historical researcher who helps people."

I am lucky to have Michigan State University Press as my publisher, in part because dealing with the Press has been extremely pleasant. Julie Loehr has not only been enormously helpful, her enthusiasm for the project motivated me to try my best. And thanks also to Travis Kimbel for patiently answering my endless questions as I grappled with the details of getting this book ready for publication, to Robert Burchfield for his expert copyediting, to Annette Tanner for producing such an attractive book, and to Kristine M. Blakeslee for cheerfully overseeing the entire project.

This collection would have been completely impossible if Steve Cotherman, director of the Madeline Island Historical Museum, and Linda Mittlestadt, archivist at the Northern Great Lakes Visitor Center, had not collected and preserved the Wheeler Papers. Thanks especially to Steve Cotherman and Linda Mittlestadt for their persistent cheer and helpfulness as my visits to their collections multiplied and the years passed. I also appreciate Pam Ekholm's help at the Ashland archives. Unless otherwise indicated, all the documents come from the Wheeler Family Papers, Northland Mss 14, Part I, Box 1, Folders 6–11, and Box 2, Folders 1–5, at the Wisconsin Historical Center and Archives, Ashland.

Preface

The basic plot of a story my father told when I was a child went like this: long ago, an ancestor in my family walked from Wisconsin to Washington, D.C., helped the Indians, and then died as a result of his efforts. As I aged, this tale seemed more and more improbable, but also persistently fascinating. By 1995, when I stopped overnight in Marquette, Michigan, while driving to Duluth, Minnesota, I had learned the identity of its hero: my great-great-grandfather, a missionary to the Ojibwe named Leonard Wheeler. On the way back to my hotel that evening, I realized that I had nothing to read, so I went into a bookstore, discovered Edmund Danziger Jr.'s *The Chippewa of Lake Superior* on a shelf labeled "Regional Books," looked up Leonard Wheeler, and realized that the following morning I would drive through the town he founded with Ojibwe volunteers: Odanah, Wisconsin. Just west of Odanah, I encountered a highway marker praising Leonard Wheeler for standing with the Ojibwe when they successfully resisted the government's attempts in the early 1850s to remove them from northern Wisconsin.

Anxious to find out more, I headed for La Pointe, the place where Leonard Wheeler's mission work began. The ferry to Madeline Island leaves from Bayfield, Wisconsin, and as I walked toward the dock, I happened on the Bayfield Historical Museum. The young woman there told me that I would find information about Leonard Wheeler at the Madeline Island museum and mentioned that his daughter might interest me since she had written novels using the history of the region. At the Madeline Island Historical Museum, a young man pointed out pictures of Leonard and his wife, Harriet; told me that Leonard had tried to make "gentlemen farmers" of the Ojibwe; and added, "I suppose you've seen Wheeler Hall at Northland College." It turns out that one of Leonard Wheeler's sons, E. P. Wheeler, served as the first president of the North Wisconsin Academy when it was founded by the Congregational Church in 1892 and guided its transformation to Northland College in 1907. When I stopped in the public library at Ashland, Wisconsin, I found J. N. Davidson's book, *In Unnamed Wisconsin*, and devoured its biography of Harriet Wheeler.

This information satisfied me for a time, but by the next summer I felt compelled to find out more and went back to Madeline Island, where I discovered several boxes of Wheeler documents, including Leonard's letters to his father in Vermont. The following spring, I gave a paper at the American Culture Association in San Antonio, Texas, based on my research and followed it with two articles published in *ATQ*. I hoped these events would end my fascination with the Wheelers. This did not happen.

When I had a sabbatical in 2003–2004, I returned to the Wheeler documents, this time focusing on Harriet because teaching a course on women in America had impressed on me how few early documents survive from the lives of American women. So, I photocopied all of the correspondence for Harriet Wheeler held by the Wisconsin Historical Society in Ashland, Wisconsin, and spent the year as a visiting scholar at Harvard Divinity School, where I had access not only to the Harvard libraries but also to the Lowell Historical Library, the New England Genealogical Society, the Boston Public Library, and the Mount Holyoke College archives; I found invaluable materials in all of these places that filled out Harriet's early life in New England. Meanwhile, I attended Harvard courses to enrich my knowledge of American religious history, American Indian culture, and the interactions between American Indians and various Euro-American nationalities.

I believe the letters proved irresistible to me because I love people's voices. Much of my research has involved interviewing writers, so I have spent hundreds of hours transcribing words and then doing my best to edit them into compelling sequences. I approached these letters like a very long interview. I first transcribed all of them and then went through the 560-page initial manuscript, repeatedly, cleaning out dull or repetitive material until the letters fell into a fascinating narrative.

That my interest in the Wheelers had lured me into territory outside my area of expertise concerned me, but my history as an interviewer helped me here, too: interviewing requires that one remain curious and open enough to accompany the subject wherever he or she chooses to go. Assembling Harriet Wheeler's letters into a harmonious whole and researching the names and events that appeared in them provided me with a similar education. Following the letters' leads, I traveled vast distances both geographically and intellectually. I found myself listening to Shaker songs and eating Shaker food when I searched for documents at the Canterbury, New Hampshire, colony where Harriet's sister Mary lived from 1850 until 1852, probably as a member of the North family. I learned much about Father Frederic Baraga's role in northern Michigan history as Jim Daumpier of the Baraga County Historical Museum helped me identify the Mr. Smith who traveled from L'Anse, Michigan, to visit Harriet's daughter Julia in Houghton, Michigan. These searches, along with many others, afforded a continual and broad lesson in nineteenth-century American culture. Fortunately for me, filling out the Wheelers' references also involved spending time in beautiful places; I will especially miss "having to" do research in the magical Lake Superior region.

Since digesting the letters provided me with a rich and pleasant education, I hope reading them will have the same impact on others. Since they focus on a single person, they invite sustained sympathy for the characters surfacing and resurfacing in them, particularly for Harriet Wood Wheeler. So few documents survive from the pre–twentieth century lives of women that even the many excellent books about pioneer women necessarily piece together fragments that convey information, but leave readers outside these women's experiences. In the exceptional case of Harriet Wheeler, 260 letters endure, covering the years 1832–1892. Her letters offer particular interest because her life touched upon institutions that played pivotal roles in the history of American women, such as the first schools for women teachers like the Ipswich Female Seminary Harriet attended; the beginnings of a well-paid, literate female workforce at the mills in Lowell, Massachusetts, where Harriet grew up; the establishment of women's associations, especially in churches; and the close and enduring ties that characterized women's relationships in the late nineteenth century. Harriet's sympathetic attitude toward the Indians as well as her concern with her family and her husband's rants about the Indians and worries about their conversion reflect the defined gender roles of the period, but both Harriet and Leonard evolve. He soon comes to share her more empathetic view of the Ojibwe, and when illness incapacitates Leonard, Harriet takes over his responsibilities.

But the letters taught me about much more than American women's history. Reading them makes one sharply conscious of the difficulties pioneers endured. Their daily struggle with scarcity and isolation helps explain the Wheelers' intense focus on the boxes of goods Massachusetts relatives send them. The references to illness seem constant; not surprisingly, longing for the relative ease and comfort of New England life often accompanies these accounts, and when sickness overwhelms them, the Wheelers travel back to Massachusetts for respite. I discovered when researching names mentioned in the letters that tragedy stalked others on the frontier even more virulently than it did the Wheelers: they survived their twenty-five years in the far north, but many with whom they came in contact did not.

Harriet's experiences in Wisconsin helped me understand more fully the history of Wisconsin and United States during the period the letters cover. The government's attempts to remove the Ojibwe from northern Wisconsin stand out, as do the various Indians, Indian Agents, and missionaries who played central roles in this drama. Harriet's letters provide a more intimate and later version of the relationships between Indians and Euro-Americans in the Great Lakes that Richard White examines from a political perspective in his groundbreaking study *The Middle Ground: Indians, Empires and Republics in the Great Lakes Region 1650–1815*. While White characterizes Yankees as generally indifferent or hostile to American Indian culture, the Wheelers develop enormous sympathy for the Indians after living with them for twenty-five years: Julia Wheeler even writes a 1864 newspaper article blaming government officials for the 1862 Sioux uprising in Minnesota.

Despite their remote location, the Civil War also touched the Wheelers in a variety of ways. They paid for someone to replace their son Leonard in the

Union army so that he could continue to help the family. But Benjamin Smith, whom Harriet's sister Hannah met and married while staying with the Wheelers at their mission, died of typhoid he contracted at Shiloh. And although the Wheelers' second son, William, participated in the war for only a short time, from May until September 1864, he returned home severely emaciated and virtually blind.

When the war ended, the Wheelers entered the energetic economy of the Gilded Age. Julia Wheeler tried, briefly, to make a living selling her artwork in Chicago. Like Carrie Meeber in Theodore Dreiser's *Sister Carrie*, Julia soon discovered that even during the Gilded Age, a poor woman from Wisconsin had little chance of rising in Chicago through hard work and talent. While Carrie found other ways to ascend the social ladder, Julia pursued a more ordinary life, supporting herself by performing domestic services, such as sewing in people's homes. After surviving the Chicago fire on October 8, 1871, Julia returned to her mother's house in Beloit, Wisconsin, in 1873, where she died of consumption in July of that year.

Her brothers, on the other hand, thrived, thanks to their father's legacy. Although publicly the Wheelers claimed that Leonard Wheeler's health forced him to leave his mission in 1866, in fact both his letters and letters to him from the American Board of Commissioners for Foreign Missions show he had to leave because the board refused to continue supporting his work: he had not converted enough Ojibwe. Finding himself jobless with a houseful of children to support, Leonard Wheeler moved to Beloit and patented a windmill he had invented. After his death in 1872, unnamed people tried to wrest its patent from his widow, Harriet. So, a son, William, went to Washington, D.C., and fought successfully to retain it. The patent became the foundation of the Eclipse Wind Mill Company, which thrived. Versions of the windmill won a gold medal at the Philadelphia Centennial Exposition in 1876 and first prize at the Paris Exposition of 1878. In 1890, Fairbanks Morse assumed control of the company the Wheelers established and developed.

Harriet herself offers the final judgment on the Gilded Age. At the end of her life, she found herself ensconced in a huge Victorian house, longing for the Bad River Reservation in northern Wisconsin. It cheered her to realize that one of her sons, E. P. Wheeler, had returned to the area to continue the work she and her husband had to abandon in 1866. Visits to the Lake Superior region revived her spirits; in fact, she died in Ashland, Wisconsin, close to Odanah where she and her family had their mission, because she had returned to the area in an attempt to restore her health. Even her businessman son William declared at the age of eighty-four that the period he spent with the Indians in northern Wisconsin supplied his most vivid memories. Indeed, the Wheelers' sustained affection for the time they spent with the Ojibwe and for American Indian culture complicates the view of missionaries as terminally righteous agents of cultural imperialism. As Harriet's letters show, missionary life offered severe physical and psychological challenges, but the Ojibwe's gratitude convinced the Wheelers that their work in Odanah mattered. They deeply regretted having to leave it unfinished despite the relative comfort and ease of their subsequent lives in Beloit.

The Wood/Wheeler Family

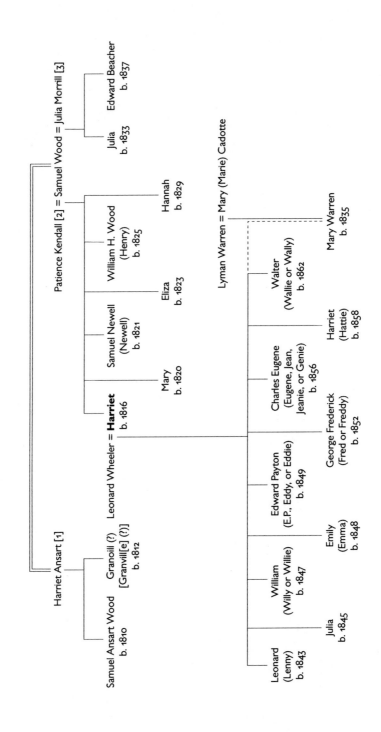

1.

Preparation
for the Journey

———

Harriet Wood was born in Dracutt, Massachusetts, to Patience and Samuel Wood on December 4, 1816. Her ardently religious parents named her after the missionary Harriet Newell. Her mother gave birth to three more daughters, Mary, Eliza, and Hannah, and two sons, Newell and Henry, before dying of typhus when Harriet was fourteen years old. Even though her father was a marginally literate sales clerk, in 1832 he sent Harriet to the Female Seminary in Ipswich, Massachusetts run by Zilpah Grant[1] and Mary Lyon.[2] The seminary was one of a handful of schools in the United States where women could receive teacher training. Grant and Lyon aspired not only to educate their charges but also to cultivate their religious dispositions and their commitment to social change. According to a pamphlet produced by the school covering the years 1830–1835, Lyon and Grant thought that their students must "have their views and feelings drawn away from self and beyond the family circle—they need to act as members of a large community—they need to learn by practice, the true Christian philosophy of sacrificing private interest to public good."[3]

More specifically, Lyon and Grant hoped their students would become missionary wives or missionaries like Harriet's namesake. A fragmentary letter that survives from Harriet's sojourn in Ipswich shows her beginning to learn this lesson. On July 27, 1832, she writes from school to her father and her stepmother, Julia, that "for a few weeks past I have begun to look around and consider what I must become when I leave here, and the more I think of it, the more I am bewildered. I very much wish to form a character that will do some good; one that will be useful; not one that will live only for the gratification of selfish principles."[4]

A letter written by another Ipswich student, Maria Cowles, on March 29, 1831, to her family, describes the specific form this education took.[5]

𝒲ould you be interested to know something of the history of this school the past term? We have had 123 scholars, from the age of 12 to some 35 or 40 years. One minister's widow, one of the children of the forest, from Mackinaw, Mich. Ter. Her father is an Englishman, her mother a native. She is very respectable, intelligent, accomplished, & pious. She is as much respected as any of our N. England ladies, & as worthy of respect.

Not far from one half of the young ladies have been engaged in teaching; several of them have been preceptresses of academies etc. These teachers with several others who were desirous of preparing to teach, have met weekly to receive instruction upon the subject, from Misses Grant & Lyon, to present their difficulties, & to mention plans which have proved successful by experiment. The course of instruction pursued this winter, was designed to promote the object of preparing teachers for their responsible office. A course of familiar lectures on conversation, & another course of intellectual philosophy have been given by Miss Grant, which are valuable not only to teachers, but to all in whatever station. Miss G. has given a course of instruction on Monday mornings, on the doctrines of the gospel.

The young ladies are much interested in the cause of benevolence. Miss Lyon has given a course of lectures on this subject, which in connection with the state of religious feeling existing in the school, has produced a most powerful, & we hope, salutary effect. Many of the young ladies seem resolved henceforward, to spend their time, money, & influence in the way which shall effect the most possible good. The design & effect of these lectures were to affect the heart, the main spring of action. Probably something of a revolution will be the result of these lectures: a revolution in the manners of spending time, in dress, furniture etc. etc. The several courses of lectures mentioned, have all seemed to aim at one point, to converge to one focus,—that of stimulating minds & hearts to action in promoting the happiness of mankind in general. One division seemed to be this, to rouse to action in influencing mind so as to prepare it for greater enjoyment & usefulness.

One evidence that the desired effect of these lectures is producing is that several are now willing to devote their time to teaching, who have hitherto been averse to it. Another is that several young ladies are willing to sacrifice home, friends, & New England privileges, for the sake of doing good to minds in the Valley of the Mississippi. Some have actually set out for that Valley & others are only waiting for the wind and tide, & will probably launch in a few days. Some are bound for Edwardsville, Illinois; one for Chillicothe, Ohio. Three young ladies who were members of this seminary, have been laboring for several months in Chillicothe, Ohio. One left us some six or eight weeks since for Marietta, Ohio. These have all gone in answer to applications which have been sent to this seminary. Since it is understood in that part of the country, that there is a seminary in N.E. to which applications may be made for teachers, the way is open for doing much good.

Probably Misses Grant & Lyon can be much more useful here than in the Valley of the Mississippi. Hence, in comparison, they have only to polish & refine the stock, or, as it were, give the finishing touch; while there they must take the raw materials. The valley of the Mississippi is not the only field for which Misses G. & L. can prepare teachers. They receive applications from various parts of N.E. & from Canada. Their sphere of usefulness is as large as that of any females on the stage of action.

The religious state of our school has been very interesting this winter. Nearly one half entertained the hope that they had passed from death onto life, before they entered the school. Many of these have been alive & active this winter. The Lord, in infinite mercy, perhaps in answer to their earnest requests, has been pleased to appear among us, by his Spirit. Some 18 or 20 give evidence of having been born again. Several others have been deeply solicitous for their soul's salvation. Not more than six or seven have remained unaffected. At the commencement of the school, the invitation was given to those who were decided to seek religion, & were anxious to learn the way of salvation, to meet at Miss Grant's room for the purpose of receiving instruction, & for personal conversation, if they desired it. At first, few attended. At one of the last meetings the number was increased to 50. Those who indulged hope previous to this winter, have met weekly with Misses G. & L. for prayer and religious instruction. These meetings have been held on the same evening of the meeting for those who were enquiring. Meetings for prayer have also been held on Sabbath morning in the several boarding houses. We have had 34 boarders in our family this winter; about 20 belonged to this circle. Our religious privileges exalt us to heaven, but dreadful would be the shock should any of us fall from such a height.

We have had a class of about forty young ladies, in vocal music. About half never tried to sing before. Several had before considered it impossible for them to learn. Not more than eight or ten had attended a regular singing school, & all felt that they were very deficient in this brand of science. Some voices were manufactured by patient practice. Six or seven hours in a week were spent for five or six weeks. Some practiced as long as this before they could sound all the notes in the octave.

We practiced singing as much as would average an hour a day, for five or six weeks, before we commenced singing tunes at all. All this time was spent in cultivating the voice, viz, its tone articulation, & pronunciation, swelling & accent. Instead of singing syllables as is usually practiced, only a sound was emitted, resembling aw prolonged. For variety, however, we used to sing the syllables do, ra, mi, fa, sol, law, si. We endeavored to improve articulation by singing these syllables. Our object was to sing the vowels & articulate the consonants. This exercise assisted in gaining a proper pronunciation, but to become acquainted with the art more thoroughly, we practiced singing phrases like the following. "Praise ye the Lord," "Hosanna." We thought this plan recommended itself to common sense, "One thing at a time is our motto." If we had attempted to cultivate the voice in connection with learning written music, the mind must have been divided between different objects; & it is an acknowledged fact that if the attention is thus divided, great improvement cannot be made as might otherwise be. It seems to be the most natural order that the voice should be first cultivated. We should first learn what is natural before we proceed to that which is artificial. We have proved by experiment greater improvement will be made in a given time. We learned a whole hymn, & could sing it pretty well. When written music was introduced upon the blackboard, the young ladies seemed prepared to understand it, & in a few days, most of the class were able to read music with a considerable degree of facility. Within six weeks after they commenced reading written music, they actually excelled common choirs of singers in readiness and accuracy.

It is truly surprising—at first thought, but when we consider what a rapid improvement the mind is capable of making, when instructed on natural principles, it is no longer a subject of surprise. For the last two or three weeks of the term, we were able to sing a hymn at the opening of the school in the morning. The effect was favorable. The words were generally sung in such a manner as to give the sense to express the sentiment & we trust, many sang with grace in their hearts unto the Lord, while others listened with the most solemn attention. This seemed to prepare the mind in some degree for the religious instruction which immediately succeeded, though many minds were very solemn before.

Yesterday, being the close of school, we had an exhibition of music & composition, interspersed. It was truly interesting to see the propriety with which every thing was conducted & the order that prevailed. All were able to retain their self-possession although placed in a trying situation. Something of a specimen of a course of composition, which has been prose, tried here for a few months past, was exhibited. No young lady read her own composition, but some members of the school who had good voices & could read pretty well, were appointed. The compositions were very acceptable. I was called to bear my part on the piano, which, as you may judge, places me in a trying situation, inexperienced as I am in the art of fingering. But I was supported through it. I realized the promise, "As thy day is, so shall thy strength be." We have abundant cause for gratitude for all the mercies we receive, especially for the support we experience in the performance of trying duties.

The course of composition which we are endeavoring to bring to perfection, promises a rich harvest. It is made a subject of every day study & recitation as much as geography & arithmetic. By making it an every day study, instead of sitting down alone to write, as a task, once in two or three weeks, by taking subjects that are in themselves interesting, & conversing familiarly upon those subjects in the class before writing, the scholars are interested in it & learn to love it instead of feeling it to be an insupportable burden. With emotions of pleasure & gratitude, we have witnessed most wonderful improvement, in the minds & characters of several of the young ladies; probably the effect of this course of composition. In the first part of the course we take the most familiar objects to describe, such as plants, trees, animals etc. & proceed to historical sketches, Bible scenes, & at length, to traits of character etc. Composition might profitably be pursued in connection with almost, if not every branch of study taught, & not only pursued in connection, but subjects might be taken from the study itself. For instance, in geography descriptions of towns & countries, etc. In history, any anecdote or historical fact; biography of historical characters, etc. In botany, descriptions of plants etc. etc. We find abundance of interesting & profitable subjects, without being under the necessity of taking such subjects as education, memory, improvement of the mind etc. which are enough to puzzle a wise metaphysician.

Perhaps you will not thank me for filling this sheet in such an egotistical strain, but judging you by myself, I thought you would like to know what I was doing.

I want to know more of the state of society among your people. I hope you will both of you be useful & faithful to them. Your affectionate sister Maria Cowles.

Like many of the seminary's students, Harriet Wood only stayed at Ipswich for a brief time. One of the few students to complete the course was the woman to whom Cowles refers, Mary Holiday,[6] *whose father was English and mother was Ojibwe. Holiday was one of only nineteen students in the 1834 senior class. Harriet's early exposure to the intelligent, cultivated Holiday there may help explain why, from the start of her mission work, she regarded the Ojibwe more tolerantly than her husband, Leonard. Perhaps motivated by learning that music can enhance grace, she instructed both the Ojibwe and her own children in singing; her daughter Julia also became an accomplished pianist. Harriet Wheeler's early introduction to composition as an important means of exploring one's daily life while improving character may help explain why two of her daughters, Julia and Harriet, became writers who produced work about the Ojibwe.*

After Harriet Wood left Ipswich, she returned to her family in Lowell, Massachusetts, where she taught school, both in the public system and at her church, the Appleton Street (Orthodox) Congregational Church. During this period, the establishment and growth of the Lowell textile mills increased the size and wealth of the city exponentially. Harriet undoubtedly had many contacts with the New England girls who did most of the mill work during this time. Mill workers earned higher incomes than any other American women: they could make six or seven more times than a schoolteacher.[7] But they refused to let their demanding jobs obstruct their educations. The mill girls not only read avidly during their scant free time, they wrote, producing journals, including the well-known Lowell Offering. *Its prominent contributors included Betsey Chamberlain, an American Indian woman.[8] Lowell became a prominent stop on the Lyceum lecture series, which meant intellectual luminaries like Horace Greeley, John Quincy Adams, and Ralph Waldo Emerson gave talks there throughout the winter, often with mill girls in attendance.[9] They also joined the Lowell churches where all who had been saved, including mill girls, enjoyed respect. Reverend U. C. Burnap, the minister of Harriet's church who recommended her for mission work, regularly visited his other parishioners in the mills.[10] And the author Lucy Larcom,[11] the most famous and distinguished mill alumna, reports that the mill girls saved their money in the hopes that they could one day attend the Female Seminary in Ipswich. Indeed, the list of students attending the Ipswich seminary in 1828 includes the name Betsey Chamberlain. Thus, Harriet Wheeler returned to Lowell, where she circulated among other young women quietly shaping larger and more powerful lives than American women had ever before led.*

The diary of her best friend, Susan Wetherbee, gives a sense of Harriet's daily life from 1836 until May 20, 1841, when Susan reports that her friend Harriet has left Lowell with her new husband to do mission work at Ojibwe reservations in northern Wisconsin.[12] Susan, who corresponds with Harriet until Susan's death in 1881, describes a gentle life of church, lectures, teas, and parties interrupted with surprising frequency by death. The entries also suggest the religiosity and passion of Harriet's friends and

9

family for both abolition and temperance. In her few florid entries, Susan also displays a romantic fondness for nature that persists throughout her lifelong correspondence with Harriet.

1836

MAY 1. I attended on the preaching of Mr. Lewis a Coloured Man who discoursed at the Free Will Baptist's Chapel, his subject the Graces of the Spirit. His discourse really edifying.

MAY 15. Our family all attended a Temperance Lecture this eve at the City Hall by Mr. Graham—a very powerful one.

21. What a lovely evening is this! The moon shining in brightness yet surrounded by fleecy clouds, the bright stars twinkling around. Dark clouds repairing far off in the West, suggesting to the mind the salutary thought that all bright things here decay—A horn from a neighboring dwelling pours its sounds on the enchanted ear! Is this not a joyously sad hour?

JULY 5. This morning is delightful the sky clear, the Sun bright the fields green after the rain the streets still from dust and listen yonder little bird pours his carol of praise upon the ear. Let our hearts rise in gratitude to the kind author of the scene.

AUGUST 21. Father took Mr. Wood's [Harriet's father] chaise and sister C [Catherine, who has been very sick] and myself rode several miles. She is not much fatigued. How delightful, how heart cheering the face of nature; oh how many alleviations for every cup of woe. Let us not overlook these.

MARCH 12, 1837. Catherine dies. JANUARY 29, 1837. In the eve she sang the verse commencing "A glorious hour; O blest abode." Grandmother said, "Your voice will be stronger soon." "O yes," she said, "When I appear in yonder cloud with all the throng, then shall I sing more sweet, more loud, and Jesus be my song" (Dear little sister Catherine).

JUNE 1. Another summer has returned "Bringing to earth her lovely things again: All save the loveliest fare! A voice, a smile, a young sweet spirit gone"

NOVEMBER 16. Sister Nancy, Margaret myself, accompanied by Mr. Russell, visited friend Harriet and this even I passed the night, returned 17th. A large party we collected and politely entertained.

20. Mr.Knowles kindly presented our family with two tickets to attend Mr. Emerson's lectures.

December 26. Friend Harriet and Mary Wood spent this eve with us.

February 21, 1838. Sister Nancy and myself and Friend Harriet Wood went into the High school. Harriet took tea with us. We hear of revivals of religion in various places. An unusual time of interest in many places. Our family are gone to Lyceum with Harriet.

May 18. Mr. Wood just called for Mother to go and assist at their house as their little suffering Babe[13] is at length at rest.

April 27, 1839. For two Sabbaths past I have had Miss Wood's Sabbath School class.

December 1839 1. A lecture this evening by Mr. Boutwell[14] a Missionary from a tribe of the North American Indians—65 dollars collected for the cause of missions. Last Eve November 30 he addressed the Missionary Society recently formed. The friends of Missionary have great cause of joy for the transactions of these days.

January 1840

18. A week to the day since I rode to Andover with Harriet Wood [Leonard Wheeler, Harriet's future husband, studied at Andover Theological Seminary[15]].

March 24. There has been considerable talk among one or two individuals about the propriety of females speaking in our meetings. Poor Brother Wood [Harriet's father] has made special effort concerning this matter. Our Poor Minister too has felt some anxiety. I think they won't be stunned with Female effort.

August 2. A meeting of the missionary society at 5 o'clock, an address by Mr. Wheeler [Harriet's future husband].

27. Sister Mary had gone to work in the Boot Cloth room [at the Lowell Mills] for a time.

On August 30, 1840, Harriet Wood writes to her parents reporting on a dinner she attended in Newburyport, Massachusetts, presumably with Leonard Wheeler. She seems a typical young woman, more interested in the table settings than in politics and utterly devoted to her home and family. But her concluding reference to her sister Hannah's willingness to get along without her suggests that Harriet already knows that she may leave her family to begin mission work as Leonard Wheeler's spouse.

I received your kind letter yesterday + was very glad to hear that you were all better. I do hope that should our family all recover and we all be permitted to meet again, we shall be grateful + shall rightly improve this affliction. I suppose you have attended meeting + Sabbath school today. I have thought of you often although I do not think I should have heard better sermons had I been at home. This morning a minister from Deerfield preached. This afternoon the services have been very interesting. All the children that could sing well requested to sit in the orchestra. They sang very sweetly and reminded me of our little ones at home. This eve good Mr. Meigs[16] preached. Now don't you think I am a very obedient good girl to stay at home. I did want to go *very much indeed*; but I remembered your injunction dear Father "not to run about too much and get excited." Be assured I will try not to.

Mond. morn

I think I shall start for home tomorrow. I want to see you all very much; I am not homesick but I do find that home is the dearest, sweetest spot on earth to me. Friends here are *very, very* kind. Newburyport is a beautiful place. I suppose you have heard of the [Caleb] Cushing dinner.[17] The speeches were very interesting, particular Mr. [Leverett] Saltonstall.[18] Mr. [Daniel] Webster[19] spoke last. I was so tired that I could not hear much. I went to see the tables. They were set for a thousand people and a gentleman who dined with them told me that he did not see a vacant seat. Every thing that would gratify the eye or the taste was there. I shall not attempt to give you a description now. In the eve Mr. Cushing gave a great party. I went and after trying an hour to get into the room where he was returned without seeing him. Such a crowd I never was in before + I hope never to be again. There were over five thousand present, but more of this when I see you.

Hannah is very well + happy—thinks she shall be contented when I am gone. Your affectionate daughter,

Harriet

Susan Wetherbee's journal continues to document Harriet Wood's social life, along with her own:

OCTOBER 15. Our Sewing Circle met at Mrs. Reed's. Semiannual meeting. Choice of officers. President Miss Miles. Vice President Harriet Wood. Nov. 2. A party here this Evening, Miss Fox, Julia Wight and Margaret, Harriet Wood. . . . A singing party, quite a pleasant party.

Leonard Wheeler's letter to Harriet of November 30, 1840, certifies their intention to marry as well as their short acquaintance. Women who aspired to missionary work frequently married missionaries whom they did not know well with the understanding Leonard delicately hints at in this letter, that their shared commitment mattered more than romantic passion.

Dear Friend,
You will perceive from the date of this letter that I did not leave town for Vermont as I contemplated. I take this opportunity to inform you of the

fact and moreover to add a word about our *affair.* In conversation with Brother Hanks[20] today he asked me positively whether I were really engaged to Miss Wood. I told him I supposed we were engaged so far as we *could* be for ought I knew. He said he found the feeling pretty fast circulating among his people that this was the fact and some as might be supposed would infer without a particular knowledge of the facts a little haste in our proceedings. When he is inquired of about it, he very justly defends any appearance of precipitating by informing such inquirers of our previous acquaintance. Now as we remarked last evening, I shall be out of the *storm* and that you may not be *overwhelmed* by the *Breakers,* I will drop a perhaps needless hint that if any of your friends are disposed to censure you for any haste in the affair, you can mention the fact of our previous acquaintance; this probably more than any other one circumstance, will satisfy the minds of enquirers. A previous and rather intimate acquaintance + knowledge also of the particular field where I am expecting to go—together with the interest we have both felt for a long time in the Missionary work, and if not that *strong attachment* which, as some think, can only result from long and very intimate acquaintance, we doubtless share that *preference* for each other, at the time of our engagement, which cast no cloud of doubt over our prospects of happiness in the marriage state.

Now I have not written this because I apprehend any serious objections on the part of your friends in regard to the course we have pursued, nor because I have not perfect confidence in your wisdom and discretion, in any statement you make of the reasons of our apparently sudden engagement. I merely write to inform you that our friends this side of the river will appreciate our motive and approve the course we have taken.

In regard to the *Lady* I mentioned in my letter in a neighboring town, it would be well perhaps to say nothing about it. I don't suppose you intend to say anything but you know my expectation to see her was one prominent reason why I wished to have the business decided as soon as possible. While this would be a reason in the minds of some of our immediate friends sufficient to justify our conduct, it would not be so well to make it very public.

This however is as needless as my other caution. But if we never do each other any greater injury than that which results from a *superfluity* of well meaning cautions we have certainly not much to fear from that source.

My pen has run somewhat after the manner of a locomotive; it has sometimes run off from the *track*. Thus, I have filled out a sheet. Tomorrow morning I shall start about 9 o'clock in the stage. Now let me instruct you not to give yourself any undue anxiety in regard to our affairs. The exhortation of the Apostle in II Phil—"Be careful for nothing"—expresses what I feel to be peculiarly applicable to us. My kind regards to your parents, any other members of your family you may see fit to inform of the reception of this letter.

Yours affectionately, L. H. Wheeler.

Susan Wetherbee records news of the engagement.

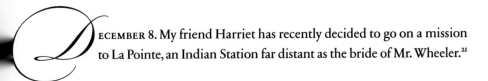

ECEMBER 8. My friend Harriet has recently decided to go on a mission to La Pointe, an Indian Station far distant as the bride of Mr. Wheeler.[21]

January 1841

5. A call from Harriet this P.M. She is expecting in a few months to go on a mission.

On January 13, 1841, the minister of Harriet's church, Rev. U. C. Burnap, writes to the American Board of Commissioners for Foreign Missions, the group proposing to send Leonard Wheeler to northern Wisconsin to serve as a missionary to the Ojibwe, explaining why Harriet Wood would make an exemplary missionary wife.

She is a member of our church, and from her devotedness and activity we have been more familiar with her than almost any other one.

In her natural temperament she is ardent and sympathetic and she is very easily excited by objects of compassion and kindness. She will be in danger of effort beyond her strength when those passions predominate. Her ardor, however, is not connected with stubbornness or self-will. She is docile and very ready to receive council. Tho' very active and persevering she seems always to prefer to be guided by others; and we think she has a peculiar aversion to contention, and everything connected with the morose. She will always be a peace maker, unless the counsils of those in whom she confides should lead her to the opposite course.

She has been trained under circumstances which rendered her own efforts necessary for her support, and is probably as well acquainted with domestic duties as almost anyone of her age. Altho' she has been engaged most of the time for several years as a teacher, she had boarded at home and taken a responsible part in the toils of the family.

As a *teacher*, she is eminent. Having a great fondness for children and a peculiar facility to secure their affections, she has been highly esteemed in every place where she has taught. Until recently she has been employed for a considerable time in the public schools and in a number of the school committees in this city. I could safely imploy the names of all my associates in giving her the most unqualified recommendation.[22]

In his own January 14, 1841, letter to the American Board of Commissioners for Foreign Missions, Leonard Wheeler explains how his fiancée's background has prepared her to serve as a missionary wife.

I will simply say Miss Wood has been favoured with pious parents who early taught her the principles of the Christian religion and the importance of personal attention to the salvation of her soul and at the age of nine years she thinks she became a subject of renewing grace. At the age of ten, she made a public profession of religion and united with the first congregational church in this place under the care of the Reverend George W. Beckwith and subsequently united with the second congregational church in this city, with which she is now connected.

In regard to her "views and motives in desiring the missionary work" Miss Wood informs me that her mind has been interested upon the subject of missions for a number of years. As early as the age of fifteen when a member of Miss Grant's school at Ipswich, her attention was particularly called to the subject and she was led to examine the question of her personal duty to the heathen and has several times since had serious thoughts of offering herself to the board.[23]

Susan Wetherbee's diary documents the bond between Harriet and Leonard as well as Leonard's growing presence in both their lives.

[JANUARY] 20 [1841]. Mr. Wheeler lectured last evening before the Missionary Society and others on the State of the Indian nation in general, and the station at La Pointe in particular.

FEBRUARY 14. Preaching this Sabbath by Rev. Mr. White from Andover. Mr. Wheeler in the desk in the morning prayed and read the hymn.

FEBRUARY 22. Father, mother and myself spent the evening socially at Mr. Wood's. Mr. Wheeler was present.

[FEBRUARY] 24. Mr. Wheeler came to board with us for a while.

MARCH 27. I heard the great [William Lloyd] Garrison[24] lecture in the evening.

APRIL 6. Ladies met at Mrs. Fox's[25] to sew for Harriet.

26. I attended friend Harriet's wedding today. She left immediately in the cars[26] for a journey of a week.

M<small>AY</small> 5. The Reverend Mr. Wheeler is ordained this Eve at John Street church.[27]

The Missionary Herald *reports Leonard and Harriet's certification as missionaries on May 12, 1841.*

A missionary meeting as held at Lowell, Mass., May 12th, at which the instructions of the Prudential Committee were read by one of the Secretaries of the Board to Rev. Leonard H. Wheeler and Mr. Woodbridge L. James, and their wives, and Miss Abigail Spooner, who are to proceed immediately to join the mission to the Ojibwa Indians, on Lake Superior. The exercises on the occasion were held in the John Street Church. The Rev. Messrs. [Amos] Blanchard,[28] [U. C.] Burnap, and [Stedman W.] Hanks, let in the devotional part of the services.

Susan Wetherbee's journal reaches its bittersweet conclusion.

[M<small>AY</small>] 16. Preaching this morning by the Reverend Mr. Wheeler.
[M<small>AY</small>] 20. Mrs. Wheeler, my Harriet, left Lowell to return no more.

On May 30, 1841, Mary Wood writes her sister Harriet, expressing both the emptiness her sister's departure has left and her family's understanding that their sadness is the necessary accompaniment of a greater good. The letter articulates for the first time the

religious consolation that Harriet draws on repeatedly during her twenty-five years
in northern Wisconsin.

ear Sister Harriet,
    I cannot let so favorable an opportunity of writing you pass unimproved and it is with peculiar sensations that I now attempt to address a few lines to a dear sister with whom I have spent so many happy hours; but with whom I never expect to commune again. But I esteem it a great pleasure and privilege that I can hold converse with you by the medium of pen and paper. And ought we not to be thankful for this blessing. It is the Sabbath, and I am now seated in the room you occupied before you left us. It seems a dear spot to me, and I spend much of my time in it. I often reflect on the many times I have heard your voice importuning the throng of Grace no doubt for the perishing multitude in heathenish darkness without one ray of light to guide them to the feet of Jesus which taketh away the sins of the world, and I have felt that I too would pray to the Lord on their behalf. I also have felt much for those dear Missionaries already in the fields and I hope and trust that I may do something for the heathen though I may dwell by my own peaceful fireside.

Be assured Sister you have our prayers and sympathies, at the family altar and in the closet. Not only by our family, I trust by the many dear friends you have in this place and in other places; I suppose your thoughts are more with us on the Sabbath than any other day. There are particular times I think you are with us in heart and perhaps despondency would brood over your spirits did you not look to the Lord. It is then I pray that the Lord will give you grace according to your day and prepare you for all the trials of future life and fit and qualify you for the station you are now in.

We had a very lonely day the day you left. Everything seemed to wear a gloom. And I felt as though I could not have it so; when I reflected that it was for the cause of God you had left I felt that it was all right. So, dear sister I would not call you back from your glorious work, although it is trying to our natural affections; but I would bid you Godspeed. I see many things I might

19

have done to render you more happy when you were with us. I feel that I need a great deal of grace and wisdom to direct me aright. My mind is often cast down in view of the responsible duties that now rest upon me, and my unfitness for the place I now hold in the family. Perhaps you know something about such feelings. Therefore, you will know how to sympathize with me. Give my love to Leonard and tell him I want him to write me a long letter if it will not be too much trouble—do not let him see this and excuse all the mistakes yourself. Do write me soon, and give me some good advice.

Your affectionate Sister,

Mary-Maria

P.S. Mother has sent you some old linen thinking they might be of service to you when you are sick on board the boats.

M. W.

2.

The Reality of Mission Life

Harriet and Leonard Wheeler arrived at the mission at La Pointe, Wisconsin, in July 1841.[1] In a sermon dated July 15, 1841, Leonard Wheeler presents a version of the prodigal son appropriate to his new parishioners. He explains that the son sought to leave home and join the heathen because of their excessive tolerance for emotion. Wheeler proclaims passion dangerous to Christianity and civilization: "How readily the propensities of the human heart are developed whenever the restraints and religion are taken away."[2] His bride, Harriet, on the other hand, learned at the Ipswich Female Seminary that true religious sensibility grows from the heart. Her letters reveal that her emotions continue to guide her despite her marriage to someone who suspects them. On November 20, 1841, she writes her parents expressing her compassion for the Ojibwe and their situation, although she quickly moves to a theological position compatible with her husband's more pessimistic view of the Ojibwe.

*Y*ou can hardly imagine how much this poor people suffer in sickness. They have no comfortable houses, no soft pillows to recline their aching heads upon and no palatable food. I have felt for some time that I could not rest satisfied until God should come by the influence of His Holy Spirit and convert this people. Pray, my dear parents, that we, who are sent here to be as light to this dark people, may be, indeed, bright and shining ones; that our hearts may be purified and sanctified, and made meet for this service.[3]

Harriet again writes her parents on November 25, 1841, the anniversary of her last Thanksgiving at home, when she contemplated marrying Leonard Wheeler and becoming a missionary wife. Now that she has spent four months at the La Pointe mission, she wonders whether she can endure her new life. She turns to God for the necessary strength and, once again, pledges herself to Him.

This has been an interesting, though somewhat trying, day for me, a day which I have looked forward to with interest and dread. The power of association in my own mind is so strong, and past scenes, looks and tones come rushing upon me with such overwhelming force, that I dread anything that has a tendency to remind me of them. You will, I think, remember the occurrences of that day. Oh, what a day of anxiety and trial it was to me. With what fearfulness and trembling did I come to the final decision. Never can I forget the anxious looks of my dear parents. The enquiring ones of my little sisters have come up before me to-day with a vividness and a freshness that has been very painful. The scenes of that evening have all been lived over again,—our parlor, the bright fire, my dear parents, that happy group of brothers and sisters.

When I seated myself in my chamber this morning, the thoughts of home, and the scenes of last year, came rushing upon me with such force as almost to overwhelm me. For a few moments I could do nothing but weep, but soon I was enabled to cast myself on the blessed Redeemer, to look to him for strength.

And so, on this day, she writes a covenant that, again and again, reveals her belief that in order to do God's will, she must cultivate humility and compassion, remembering always her frailty. Harriet even declares herself a "prodigal child."

Almighty and most merciful God, the author of my being and the preserver of my life, I desire at this time, with the deepest reverence, humility and self-abasement to present myself before thee, sensible of my utter unworthiness to appear in thy majesty's presence, especially on such an occasion as this; even that of entering into a solemn and everlasting covenant with the King of Kings and Lord of Lords. But this gracious proposal is from thee. Thine infinite mercy and condescension have opened the way, and thy grace, I trust, has inclined my heart to accept the terms of that gracious covenant according to which I would now heartily surrender and consecrate myself wholly to thee, to be thine forever. I acknowledge myself a great sinner and, with a penitent heart, beseech thee to be merciful to my unrighteousness, and forgive all my sins through the atonement and mediation of thy dear Son, in whom are all my hopes of acceptance. I beseech thee to pardon and receive thy prodigal child, who desires nothing so much as a place in thy family, and to be entirely devoted to thy glory. And yet such is the exceeding sinfulness of my heart and life that I cannot approach this solemn transaction without trembling. But convinced that it is but a reasonable service, I do this day, in the presence of witnessing angels, make an entire and hearty surrender of myself to thee. I yield to thee my mortal body and all its members, faculties and sense to be henceforth wholly employed in thy service and resigned to thy will. To thee I also surrender my rational and immortal soul with all its intellectual and moral powers, to be sued, directed and disposed of, according to thy holy and sovereign pleasure. I also surrender and consecrate to thee all my time, property and influence, accounting myself thy servant bound to improve all to thy glory, and submit all my interests and desires to thy management and direction. At the same time, I renounce all other Lords which have had dominion over me and choose and avouch the Lord Jehovah, Father, Son and Holy Spirit to be my God and portion forever. I take and own God, the Father, as my Father in heaven, engaging thus the aid of his grace to love and obey him as such, and humbly pray to be owned and blessed of him as a daughter of the Lord Almighty. The Lord Jesus Christ I accept as my only Redeemer and Saviour, beseeching him to wash my polluted soul in the fountain of his blood and make me a meek, exemplary follower of him till death and then receive me to his everlasting kingdom. The Holy Ghost I also avouch as my Enlightener, Guide, Sanctifier and Comforter entreating him to make my heart the temple of his residence, to shed abroad a Savior's love there, to leave and enliven all my devotion and bring every thought and desire into subjection to the divine will.

And now, O Lord, behold I am thine; oh make me a faithful servant, a willing and obedient child. Use me for thy glory as seemeth good in thy sight. Put me among thy children and number me among thy peculiar people. Feed and nourish my soul from thy bounteous table and clothe me with the robe of salvation prepared by the labors and sufferings of thy dear Son. While I live enable me to live wholly to thee, performing the duties and fulfilling the obligations of this solemn covenant, or if at any time, through indwelling sin, I violate my covenant vows, oh, let not thy loving kindness depart from me nor thy covenant of peace be removed; but grant me evangelical repentance and faith in Christ, and then save me from all my backslidings and by every fall make me more humbly watchful and prayerful, that my path may be as the rising light, which shineth brighter and brighter to the perfect day. And when my warfare shall be accomplished, my work on earth finished, receive me to thyself in that time and way which shall be most for thy glory. Only grant, I beseech thee, that amid the struggles of dissolving nature, I may enjoy thy gracious presence, have the peace of God ruling in my heart and be enabled to employ the last breathings of morality in thy praise. And when this clay tabernacle shall be returned to the earth from which it was taken, and this immortal soul, now engaged in covenant with its Maker, shall have entered on the retribution of eternity, should this memorial meet the eye of survivors, may it prove an instrument in the hands of the Spirit of awakening and saving such as are impenitent and of quickening to greater care, diligence and zeal such as have taste that the Lord is gracious, that they may be prepared to join with the covenant people of God, who are before the throne, in ascribing blessing and honor and glory and power unto him that sitteth on the throne and to the Lamb forever and ever. Amen.[4]

A report in the Missionary Herald *written by Sherman Hall[5] on February 2, 1842, indicates that at La Pointe, Harriet meets regularly with Ojibwe women, passing on lessons she had learned at the Ipswich Female Seminary.*

*M*rs. Wheeler has also met a class in the evening for some time past, composed of Indian women and girls, for the purpose of teaching them to read and sing. These schools have apparently excited considerable interest in the people.[6]

While Harriet deals with her difficulties by embracing humility and dedicating herself, once again, to God, on February 2, 1842, Leonard Wheeler writes from La Pointe to someone identified only as "Respected Friend," revealing a much more negative view of the Ojibwe than Harriet's. He apparently addresses a class interested in helping with the Wheelers' work.

*C*ould you stand here with us and see the ignorance and degradation of this people, especially their deadness to spiritual things, you would not long doubt the absolute necessity of some power beyond that of man to awaken this people from the deep slumbers of sin into which they have fallen. There is no hope of ever essentially changing the temporal condition of this people only so far as they are brought under the power of the gospel. They will continue to live in their dirty lodges, wear their filthy garments and follow the superstitious customs and wicked practices of their fathers, till their hearts are changed by the spirit of God.

My dear young friends, could I look in upon you as you sit and listen to your teacher while she reads to you I now see a great many little boys and girls sitting in a good room with a warm clean clothes and happy countenances nearly all of them able to read. And what must we meet together for? To be told about God, about the Savior, and a great many things in the Bible. Should you come here where I blessed all these people on the Sabbath, you would see very few children in the Sabbath School. Some of the parents and children do attend meeting and the Sabbath school, but the great mass of the Indians don't think much about the Sabbath and many of them don't know when the Sabbath comes. They will be at play or sitting in their smoky lodges at home wearing hardly anything to cover their nakedness or keep off the cold but a dirty blanket—and sometimes they have nothing to eat from morning to night because their fathers do not kill any game or catch any fish. They are growing up in ignorance. They can neither read or write and know nothing about the word of God. They have all of them souls that will live forever; many have all wicked hearts too and need to be born again or they cannot go to the Kingdom of God. Now it was for just such poor ignorant wicked people that the Savior came into this world and died. And it is to tell them about this Savior that the Missionaries came to live among them. And it is because a great many years ago missionaries came to teach our fathers and because we enjoy the light of the Gospel what we are made by differs from the heathen. Had God not given us his word we might have been as ignorant and miserable as the Indians. I am glad to know that you give something to send the gospel to the heathen. This is what our Savior wants us to do. Let me instruct you all to love the Savior yourselves and give him your hearts, then when you come to die you will go to dwell forever with God.

Yours truly,

L. H. Wheeler

Florantha Sproat, the wife of the missionary Grenville Sproat, reports in a letter to her family the birth and death of Harriet Wheeler's first child.

March 23, 1842

Last night Mrs. Wheeler gave birth to a dead child. She has been confined to her bed for two months previously, on account of convulsions and other difficulties. Again I must speak of the great necessity for women missionaries to this country, to be of good and firm health. None should come but of strong and rugged constitution if they wish to be of use.

March 25

A beautiful evening although it was a stormy morning which prevented me from washing, so I have been doing a lot of little things and sitting with Mrs Wheeler.

March 30

I came home at noon, to stay with Mrs. Wheeler that Miss Spooner might go in the afternoon. Mrs. W. is getting along well. She is frail in the extreme but her spirit is of the best kind.

April 1

Husband is in Mr. Wheeler's chamber singing with him and his wife, and it sounds as if they were enjoying it much.[7]

News of this death traveled to Lowell, and a number of Harriet's friends wrote, including Julia Wight, who composed the following letter on May 16, 1842.

My very dear Harriet,
        I have never before written you because you have so many other friends who have greater claims upon your attention, but you have been very dear to me during this long silence. My heart has ached for you many times

27

during this winter + I have longed to see you + to share your suffering with you, but you suffer for Jesus' sake + I trust count it all joy. Yet there are times when we need our best friends with us to comfort + cheer us. I heard with sorrow that your dear babe was taken immediately from your arms to Jesus', but you will meet it again in that world where the beautiful increases in beauty + the perfect loses none of its perfection.

I have spent most of the last year at Fall River with some friends of ours. I have been studying; I expect to return next month. I do not feel at home in Lowell as I formerly did: it seems almost like a deserted city. All that I loved are married + away. Deacon Wetherbee's family alone remain. You probably know that Amanda resides in New York and Lizzie in Boston. They are both expecting to become mothers soon. Stephen Goodhue preaches Millerism traveling round the country.[8] Last Sabbath I went into your former Infant Sabbath School. 80 children were present. Miss Alice Brown their present superintendent told me that they felt great interest in contributing for the objects of their charity seem so definite, for you can tell them all about the little Indian. How I do hope, dear H, that you will come back to us again if only for a visit. I have never given up the hope of seeing you ever in this world. I often think of our happy ride to Andover—the Missionary Meeting + the ride home by Moonlight.[9] We stop'd and listened to the Music of the waves breaking against the shore. I sang to you the "Messenger Bird." It is all vividly before me as if it occurred last night. I received a letter from H. D. Perry today; he is still at Amherst; thinks something of studying theology at Lane Seminary Cincinnati. He has recently become deeply interested in the valley of the Mississippi.

God bless you + your husband in your attempt to cause the wilderness to blossom as the rose. It appears to me that your trials + suffering must be very great—sometimes amounting to agony. I pray for you dear Harriet + May God comfort you + bless your labors abundantly. May Jehovah be to you as "the shadow of a great rock in a weary land."

I cannot ask you to write me for your labors are so very great, but I am always delighted to hear from you. Your dear sister Hannah, I had not seen her for a year till the other day + the resemblance was very striking.

I send you a few raisins. I wish I had something which I knew you would like but I had only the evening to write + send so I have no time for anything.

Mother, Abby + Margaret send love to you + your husband. My love to your husband + dear Harriet receive my love, for you + your cause are very dear to me.

Ever your affectionate friend,

Julia Wight

By July 20, 1842, Harriet recovered and returned to mission work. She writes a letter from Fond du Lac[10] to her parents that reveals that, unlike her husband, she seems anxious to hear what the Ojibwe have to say.

The meetings to-day have been very solemn and interesting, this evening especially so. It was a prayer and confessional meeting, and I have been very much interested in hearing these Spirit-taught children speak and pray.

The first one who spoke had been a medicine man until within a few weeks. When the war party fitted out for the Sioux country this spring, he called on Mr. Ely,[11] the missionary, shook hands with him, and told him if the Lord spared his life to return again, he would go to war no more, but would live differently. He went. Towards the close of a battle, the Chippeways [Ojibwe] were obliged to flee. The Sioux took another route and came out directly in front of them. The balls of the enemy were flying about his head on every side. Death stared him in the face. He says that he then promised the Lord in his heart, that, if he would spare his life, he would listen to his word. When he returned he told Mr. Ely his promise, came and settled down with his people, and ever since has been an attentive listener to the preaching of the gospel. This evening he has publicly renounced his heathenism and expressed his determination to become a Christian. He told the Indians that they must not invite him again to their *metawa* (religious) dances or their feasts. He appears to be sincere.

This afternoon Mr. Wheeler visited him at his lodge and, after conversing with him, turned to his wife and asked her how she felt. "She," said he, "will go with me. When I travel, she generally sits in the stem of the canoe, and I forward. She is not quite as far along as I, for I am the length of the boat before her, but she will follow."

A number of the Indians spoke this evening; one of them had recently united with the church at Sandy Lake.[12] Before he commenced speaking, he went round and shook hands with the missionaries. This he did, he said, to keep up his fellowship with them. He expressed a strong desire that all the natives should become Christians. He said that he wished they would all be like little children, who, when any danger was near, would run to their mother and cling to her. So he wished all would flee to Christ and cling to Him. In his address to the Indians he told them to look about upon this world and see the works of God. "But," said he, "where are the tracks of our gods; we cannot see anything that they have made." Some of the Christian Indians exhorted each other to live more holy; and to renew their consecration to the service of God. It was a solemn and interesting session. All without was calm and still. The bright moon cast its silvery rays into our little tabernacle, and here were a people recently sunk in all the horrors and degradation of heathenism; now singing the praises of God and calling upon his name. I remarked to L. this evening, that it was enough to repay us for all the privation we were called to endure to witness such a scene.

Sabbath evening: This has truly been an interesting day. This afternoon the sacrament was administered, and two Indians were admitted to the church. One of these was an old man. He is the head chief of the band. He is very tall and dignified in appearance. It was an affecting sight to see him come and kneel before the desk, and receive the ordinance of baptism. Mr. Wheeler baptized him and gave him the name of David. Two of his children were baptized also. The other person admitted was a young woman, wife of one of the native members. I cannot describe to you my emotions, as I celebrated the dying love of Jesus with this little band in the wilderness.[13]

When Harriet learns that her sister Hannah may join her at La Pointe, she cannot hide her delight, but her responsibility as an older sister obliges her to warn Hannah of the difficulties she will encounter. Harriet reports her reaction in a letter written at La Pointe on September 18, 1842.

My very dear Sister Hannah,

You cannot imagine my feelings when they informed me that you wanted to come and live with me. I have often wished you were with me; but have never said anything about it; fearful that you would not be happy here; or that Father would be unwilling to part with you. It would indeed be a great comfort to me to have you with me, but I have felt that it would not be right for me to consult my own feelings without any reference to your good.

The principle objections to your coming here are the following. First, your *health*: I have suffered so much from sickness myself since I came here that I never can advise any one who has not good health to come. We have no experienced physician, no nurses and are deprived of many of the comforts and conveniences that we have been accustomed to at home. We all of us have as much labor to perform as we can do when we are all well, and when we are sick we cannot expect much care. Do not think by what I have said that I should consider it a burden or a trial to take care of you when sick. No, my dear sister, I have often felt that I should love to be at home to assist in taking care of you when I have heard of your sickness.

Another thing which I have thought might be an objection was your age. You are just getting your education, just forming your habits and manners, and I suppose that here you would not have as many advantages as you would at home. There are the two principle objections which presented themselves to my mind and I suppose are the same which father has thought of.

With regard to the first you have written me that your health at present is good. After consulting with Mr. W [Wheeler] we think that the second need not prove a hindrance to your coming. Should you come, we should wish you to bring on your school books and pursue a course of studies with us; one of us would be your teacher as far as moral and religious influence is concerned;

it should be, to say the least, as good in a mission family as at home. You would probably have no intimate friends out of the family. Should we remain here or go to Bad River you would have opportunities to mingle in good society as often as would be profitable for your age.

But there is another question which I have often asked myself, "Could Hannah be happy here?" Do you think you could? Much as I want you with me, I will not deceive you. This is a dreary desolate country. Nothing but the presence of the Saviour can make us happy here and nothing but the hope of doing good would induce us to stay a single day. Do you think, my dear sister, that you love the Saviour and do you desire to honor him in this way? If you do, let me assure you that you can be *happy*, yes, *very happy here*. I have a good many things I want to say about this subject, but I have not time now; but one thing I must say is do not come without Father is *perfectly willing*. Did I know certainly that you would come I am afraid I should be almost impatient to have the winter pass away. Let us both my dear sister ask direction of our Heavenly Father who knows what is best for us. Please write soon and tell me all how you feel about coming.

Your aff. Sister

Harriet Wheeler

In May 1843, a friend named Helen E. Bancroft, another woman from Lowell who studied at the Ipswich Female Seminary longer than Harriet, reports to Harriet that Harriet's family misses her, but urges her not to let that impede her important work. Still, she cannot resist telling Harriet a horror story about another of Mary Lyons's students who became a missionary wife.

I should not be surprised if you were unable to recognize the handwriting of the superscription or this sheet. I trust your kind feelings will excuse me, + readily perceive my reasons for writing you now, when I tell you that I have recently spent several weeks in *our once beloved city* + of course made a long visit at your *Father's house. The loved, the absent one* was thought of & talked about yet & prayed for too, morning + evening around the family altar, supplication was made for *that child* far away, for the "red people of the forest"— + more than this, tears often moistened the eye + frequently found their way down the cheek of *that Father* as he spoke of his darling daughter whom he had given to the Lord to do his work + of whom he seems to fully believe that she is useful. I *could not feel* that those tears *were tears of regret* that he had consented to part with his child.

You perhaps sometimes think of me, + will recollect that I made occasional visits to Lowell & just before you left, Miss Fox wrote me respecting your leaving, + I did hope to have had the pleasure of seeing you once more + made an effort to that effect but it was so ordered + undoubtedly for wise reasons. I did not arrive in the city until the evening of the day you had taken your final department, but to make sure of securing an opportunity of seeing you I went directly to Dea. [Deacon] Bancroft's when to my great grief + disappointment I learned that you had gone. I could have wept heartily but it was useless.

In a day or two I called at your house; it seemed lonely. Your mother the only member I recollect of seeing looking pale and anxious, but appeared cheerful during these two years that have rapidly passed away. I have often thought of you + with eagerness have turned over the pages of *Missionary Herald* to learn something of those I have known & loved, now in distant lands, but still loved. I had a real feast perusing your letters + enjoyed it to a charm.

Dear Harriet, I am glad that you are a missionary. I hope + trust you will make yourself very useful + will be permitted to behold the fruits of your labor, + never have occasion to regret the very solemn + important steps you have taken. It is certainly a matter of deep + heartfelt rejoicing to find any who are willing to forsake parents + home + almost every thing dear + social + to take their lives in their hands + go forth among the heathen, with the prospect of laying their bones in a land of strangers. Is it not a sacrifice, is it not a great self denial thus to do? Did you not find it so dear friend! How fondly the heart clings to our home + all its joys + to every object that clusters around it. But when we think of our Blessed Savior, who went about doing good + after the toils and labor of the day had not a pillow on which to repose his aching head,

+ at last groan under the weight of our transgressions in connection with those of a guilty world, + when we look over poor fallen human nature in its misery + wretchedness, with missions floating down to perdition, does it not almost seem as if our very souls would burst within us?

I believe that in days gone bye I professed *a little bit* of a missionary spirit, + a thousand times I wished that spirit had been cherished, that glimmering spark had been fanned into a brilliant flame, which would have illuminated at least a little spot in some dark + benighted corner of the earth—and I think too the time is near, when *parents* will be more willing to make an entire *consecration* of *their children* to this blessed cause. Do you not sometimes think of what Miss Lyon at Ipswich used to say? "It isn't of much matter *where we are*, if we are where we can do *the most good.*"

Do you recollect Prudence Richardson of Dracutt? You know she labored hard to obtain an education + the last school she attended was at Mt. Holyoke Seminary. There she was unfortunate, fell down stairs and broke both her arms, but after her recovery, she went to the state of Va., taught a school of colored children two years, then married a missionary + went to Africa—either south or West Africa, I have forgotten which, was immediately taken sick and laid within her *lowly grave* in three months after her arrival there. How suddenly her plans of usefulness were frustrated.

I find my pen almost on the last writing point of the sheet + my time too for writing has expired & yet I have hardly commenced saying what I wish. I suppose through your many friends you get all the Lowell news which would interest and cheer you. For a few weeks I am visiting, but shall soon commence once again my occupation of Schoolteacher.

Whenever my thoughts roam away, far over the "*Superior*" I shall think of you as being happy with a *kind husband* + I hope very many of the comforts of life, although surrounded with superstition, ignorance + moral death. May the smiles of Heaven ever rest upon you. The Blessed Savior can stand by to uphold you, the Holy Spirit can direct + lead you through all your toils + trials up to the Mansions of everlasting bliss is the constant prayer of your affectionate friend H. E. Bancroft.

On May 31, 1843, Harriet's stepmother, Julia Wood, reports a visit from a missionary at La Pointe, William T. Boutwell, and his wife, Hester Crooks.[14] *The fact that Hester Crooks has American Indian blood may help explain Julia Wood's reaction to her. Julia Wood's stern warning to Harriet about spoiling her new child reflects the Puritanical atmosphere that must have pervaded Harriet's Lowell home.*

I cannot express the feelings with which I received a call from Dr. Boutwell and wife. While I was grateful for a call, I felt very unpleasantly to think the time they spent with us was so short. They came just at dinner time. It was our washing day and we had a picked up dinner and their stay was to be so short that we had no time to do anything more as they wished to go into the mills. I suppose you would like to know my opinion about them and I can tell you in very few words we were all delighted with them. Mariah [Harriet's sister-in-law] and myself almost fell in love with him. He was very attentive to his wife. I was very glad to see it, but she does not look much like him. Your Father thinks she is a *noble* looking woman. I did not say half as much to her as I wanted to the time was so short that it confused me so that I hardly knew what to say.

We shall send you a small box of things which came too late to go in the other. The Dr. thought you would like some extract of lemon and we shall send you some and some more figs. He says you are too benevolent with the good things that we sent to you, that you ought to keep them for your own good.

May the Lord give you strength to be a faithful mother. Do be very careful and not love it more than you ought; if you do, you will not keep it long. Idols we must not have. I hope that you and your Husband will have a system and be united in it and bring up the little one aright. I think you will be very much in danger of too much indulgence, particularly as it is sickly; but I can tell you if you ever wish him to be obedient, you must commence young and carry a decided steady hand.

I must now close for the box must go. I wanted to send Mrs. Boutwell something and I did not know what. You know I have not much money to spend. Good bye J M Wood

---

On June 19, 1843, Susan Wetherbee writes much more passionately and positively about Harriet's new child.

My Dear Harriet,
I was very happy in receiving your kind little note and the precious little package which accompanied it. You spoke of your dear little Babe. How I should love to see it. Does it resemble yourself Harriet? I think it will occupy much of your time, and be another object around which your affections may fondly cling. I suppose you will say you know not the power of a Mother's Love. True, but we all know it is a fountain of blessedness and joy, yet often troubled, and even overshadowed by the dim specter *Fear*—"For in our prescient breast are lyre strings quivering with prophetic thrill, to the footstep of each coming ill." Perhaps you will say Susan is sad, yet I know in thy bosom is an answering echo to mine. Well H. give my best love to the little fellow and tell him I love him sincerely for his mother's sake.

How is Mr. Wheeler? And Hannah? I should love to see you all very much, but most of all your own dear self, my *precious friend*. Harriet may we not sometime hope to see you here? People travel back and forth so often of late that the distance seems in a great measure annihilated. It seems almost to bring our friends to our doors to have messages from them.

I called at your Father's a few evenings since; he says he should like to see the little Babe, and I presume he is not the only one of the family who wishes to see it. Your Mother showed me a lock of his hair.

I know of nothing of particular interest of which to inform you. Our City has this day received a Visit from the President of these United States.[15] Of course, there was a mighty gathering of the good people of the City and some others. Daniel Webster was also present, and his Excellency Governor Morton. But these days have not very peculiar charm for me. I suppose the character of your public days are somewhat different from our own: the rude or half civilized Indian is so unlike the educated refined new Englander; but perhaps I am touching a tender chord in your heart in bringing the comparison before you. Still, you have a constant demonstration of it.

Oh H, I wish I could walk with you this beautiful June evening, and talk over the many scenes through which you have passed since you left us. But this may not be. Oh, may we together walk the streets of the New Jerusalem, together spend a blest Eternity. Dear H, I suppose you find enjoyment in Christian intercourse there with a few who possess some refinement of soul, some of the women of the Gospel. May you ever have the light of God's countenance shining on your pathway to illumine your descent to the tomb. There has been no particular interest in Religion, in our city for a long time past. I understand things are encouraging at La Pointe. I'm happy to learn that fact. I hope we shall still hear more encouraging news from you.

We like our place of worship much. Mr. Hancock sends us many excellent preachers besides giving us good Sermons but it is not in the Preaching alone that the Christian must find good to his Soul; in the retirement of his closet, in his own heart, he must have resources of enjoyment.

Well, Christ will one day make his appearing and every eye shall behold him. May we be prepared to welcome his coming. Those very trials which we have here deplored may if ever understood in their bearing upon our character be reckoned among our richest blessings. And now dear H Adieu. May you be happy in your Maternal relation, happy in the Love and confidence of your dear Mr. Wheeler, happy in the home and favor Of your God. Write me when you can, and believe me as even your dearest Friend, Susan M. Wetherbee

Our family all wish to be remembered to you and yours. Mother sends her love to you and your little Babe. Says, "Tell Harriet I would give much to see them" and is glad you possess the gift for she thinks it will make you more contented in your solitude. May it be long spared you. Does Mr. W love it? Please tell him I ask the question. Though on heathen ground may it early be brought into the gold of the good Shepherd.

The following letter, written in Lowell on July 26, 1845, shows that people at home continue to take an interest in Harriet's efforts and want to help.

*D*ear Mrs. Wheeler—

Do you remember before leaving your home in New England, meeting occasionally a juvenile sewing circle in vestry of the John Street Church? You may perhaps think of it sometimes now, and the pleasure you gave those little girls by visiting with them, and particularly after you decided to give your all to the dear cause for which we plied our needles so and with so much pleasure too. Among the names you may remember that of Charlotte Russell, though in your multiplied duties it would not be strange if you had forgotten me. Be that as it may, she remembers you with a great deal of pleasure, and has listened to accounts of your labors, written by yourself and your husband, with great interest. And, always, Mrs. Wheeler when I have heard of you, and about you, I have remembered how happy you were in the prospect of going and have thought how happy you must feel too, in being able to accomplish so much good and in being so useful—even though it be so far from your own kindred and friends.

We can know comparatively nothing of the trials and cares to which you are subjected, and of the self denial which you must practice, neither can we know anything of that happy feeling which you must have, often accomplishing your labors of love to those placed under your influence. I believe besides promising not to forget you (and that promise has not been a difficult one to keep,) I also promised with others of that sewing circle, that you should hear from us. This I intended to do, but have not, as there were many ways whereby we heard from you, and presumed you might hear from us, through others.

But let me tell you what has particularly induced me to write at this time. "A young people's missionary society" has recently been formed in the John St. Church for the purpose of obtaining and collecting missionary intelligence, relating to foreign home missions, and also to include other objects of interest such as Seamen's Friends Society,[16] and the Sabbath School.[17] Beside the common office of such a society, this is a corresponding committee, consisting of two gentlemen and two ladies, whose duty it is to correspond with missionaries and others from whom they can obtain missionary intelligence, which is to be read at the meetings, which are to be on the fourth Sabbath of every month. At a meeting of the officers, it was thought that there was no station in which our society would be interested more than the one where you and Mr. Wheeler are laboring.

Although I know you slightly yet as I knew you at all, they wished me to be the one to ask you if you will occasionally send a communication to the society—and was very happy to be the one to ask of you the favor as I have now the opportunity of telling you that even the labors you performed while meeting in a circle of little girls are remembered by them with a great deal of interest and I have no doubt, that they love the cause of missions more, and are much more interested in those little Indian children, now that they know who is teaching them, and laboring with them daily. If it will not be too much of a tax upon your time, nothing would give us more pleasure, than occasionally, as often as is convenient for you, send us some account of your labors and of anything of interest which is occurring at your Station.

You must be happy in the consciousness of being able to do much good and you are sure we hope for the love, and kindly remembrance of all your friends you have left behind in New England. As soon as you can conveniently write a letter, it will be most gratefully received by the members of the society, and particularly by your young friend Charlotte R

When she reports on her activities to the Young People's Missionary Society, Harriet cautions against romanticizing the Indians.

This whole subject is invested with such sacredness and encircled with such a halo of romance, that it is impossible for others to get the subject

39

before their minds in a true light; to obtain a correct impression. They have often heard so much of the poetry of Indian character, of his proud and lofty bearing, of his gratitude for favors, and of the beautiful simplicity of nature's children, that they entirely lose sight of the darker shades of the picture. Perhaps few have had more of this feeling than I had myself when I first came to this country; but I can assure you that it did not require many weeks of actual experience on the ground, to put to flight all such ideas. I found it was sober, prose business; a stern reality, but yet a most precious, a most blessed work.[18]

She offers a critical description of her American Indian students' appearance, admitting that, nonetheless, she loves some of them.

Some of them came with their long black hair streaming over their shoulders. Others with it braided with thimbles and potato balls attached to the ends. Others with it tied up with a string of red flannel, and others again, still more exquisite in their tastes, had a bunch of wild flowers tied in. Their hands and faces look as if they were perfect strangers to the blessings of cold water. However, I could not help loving some of them at least; and I spent many happy hours with my wild, bright-eyed Indians children in the shanty.[19]

And Harriet reports that she and her husband plan to relocate, with some Ojibwe, to the Bad River, where they hope to help the Ojibwe establish farms and a more settled way of life.

We feel that there is but little prospect of doing the Indians permanent good, while they are wandering about from place to place. Nothing can be done for their civilization under such circumstances; and we find that Christianity and civilization go hand in hand. They are inseparable.[20]

The letter Harriet wrote to her stepmother on May 7, 1845, makes the practical difficulties of her own life clear: she apparently has worn the same heavy dress for four years, and now needs to have it dyed and quickly returned to her. The challenge of trying to maintain a domestic life while dealing with such basic needs may help explain why Harriet easily appropriates Ojibwe items that she finds useful and even conveys them to friends in Lowell who would not realize, for instance, that moccasins allow one to travel with relative ease through the snow.

Dear Mother,

I have sent my dress to have it dyed jet-black. Perhaps you will think it very soon to be sent now but it was almost ruined before we reached here. I had no thin dress and I was obliged to wear it in very warm weather. If it could be dyed in 3 or 4 days and sent immediately to the Missionary House, I should probably get it this summer.

We have sent a few articles to friends. I have sent each of the clergyman's wives a pair of moccasins they were made by Indian women and are such as are worn here. I am sorry that the pair I sent you is not made of better leather, but I thought that the others would be too small for you. I think you will find them comfortable in winter particularly when there is snow on the ground. I intended to write notes to each of the ministers' wives, but baby has had a sore mouth and has required so much attention that I could not possibly get time. Please give my regards to them. And tell them to accept the moccasins as a slight token of affection.

I have sent the little ones sugar. They were made by Indians and I hope it will taste as sweet to them as the kisses they sent to me did. Those little painted sticks are called sho shi mancy and are such as the Indians boys play with in winter.

They made a narrow path in the snow have it somewhat descending and the boy whose sho shi man goes the furthest claims them. All the minerals where found on the shore of this lake. Some of them will admit a very fine polish, and were formerly very much used by jewelers. I had a beautiful stone given me and was intending it for a watch seal; but a gentleman visiting here saw it + asked Abba[21] for it. She, not knowing that I intended it for any particular purpose, gave it to him. One of the handsomest watch seals that I ever saw was made from one of these stones. I was very sorry that we had not a pair of Moccasins for dear Father. Husband was intending to send him a pair but we have none large enough now. Hope to be able to get a pair made this summer and send them by Mr. [Sherman] Hall.

Aff Your Daughter

On July 27, 1845, Harriet's father, Samuel Wood, writes to each of his daughters in Wisconsin, adamantly instructing them. Samuel Wood's grammar and spelling suggest that he left school at an early age. They have been corrected here to make his letters readable, but the awkward phrasing survives.

Dear Hannah,

I have not received a letter from you for a long time. I read your letter that you sent to Henry[22]—you tell him that you are growing tall & fleshy; I want to know if you grow good. I often think about you & feel very anxious to know that you are doing any good where you are; if you have your health you can be of much service to your dear sister. I hope you are not disobedient to her but do all you can to help her. Mr Charles Oakes & Wife[23] & his son Greg & Grandpa Oakes called to the store yesterday about two o'clock. Mr. Oakes told us you was very large & that you could run with any of them. I want you to write me as soon as you get this & tell me how you get along. Tell me dear child if you love the Savior. If you do not, give yourself no rest till you have an Interest in his Precious Blood. I want to hear from you.

From your Affectionate Father
Sam L. Wood

Dear Harriet, I received your letter that you wrote us in June & was very glad to hear from you but I was disappointed not to hear one word about my dear little grandchildren, not a word about Hannah only that she was well. I want to know if Hannah is a good girl & is any help to you. You told me in your later letter about your house you was building at Bad River. I don't like the idea to have you go any further off. If I should come to La Pointe, it will take me a day longer to come to see you. I have written to H [Hannah] how Mr. Oakes called upon us; I was very much pleased with the appearance of Mr & Mrs Oakes; I should think them excellent Friends. Mrs. Oakes says that Mr Wheeler said he should not come again; I want to know what he has done that he does not come. He must have done some thing very bad to have an excuse from coming. I want you to write me as you seen this. If I can't see you I want to hear from you. Tell son Wheeler to write me & if he will come on here, I will discuss with him original sin. Perhaps we should not be so far apart as when he left.

As for the health of the family, it is pretty good. The Lord has been kind to us; we have not had the doctor for a year & I hope these lines will find you enjoying the same blessing. Give My Love to Brother Hall & family + tell him I hope he will write me also A. Spooner— + all the Mission Family

From your Affectionate Father
Sam L. Wood

On August 1, 1845, Harriet's stepmother, Julia, writes to announce the birth of Harriet's nephew. As she recalls the labor she just witnessed, Julia cannot help imagining how much more difficult the whole process of giving birth must be for Harriet at La Pointe. While others refer to the difficulties of childbirth during this era, Harriet remains silent on the subject, and gives birth to one child after another.

*B*rother Newell was last night made the *happy Father of a fine little boy*. Perhaps to a sister who knows by experience *the trials of such an hour as this*, it will not be considered improper for me to give some particulars. Your Brother came for me at half past one in the morning M [Mariah] having been sick all the evening. Before getting her up to the room, we sent Mrs. North and soon after for Boot Groves. He said although she was suffering so much she should not be sick at present. When we went home, he told us she would not probably get through until tonight; he called again at noon and told us the same story. At five we sent for him; she had suffered almost without cessation during the whole time: she could keep nothing in her stomach and wearing herself out without making any progress. He came and gave her Morphine to quiet her. She soon after went to sleep and for a little time was able to rest. About seven, her sickness came on again regularly and continued to until half past eleven at which time she became a joyful mother. I have not seen her but a moment today but the Doctor says she is doing as well as could be expected. They see no reason why she should not do well.

Dear Harriet, when I was standing by that bed of suffering I could not but contrast it with yours on such occasions. Here was Mother and Sisters, an experienced nurse and Physician and other friends all around ready to do any and everything that could be done for her while my poor Harriet must be a stranger in a strange land surrounded by those who on account of different training and circumstances were but poorly prepared to sympathize with her—*not that they would not do all that they thought necessary*, but you know very well what I would say probably better than I can tell you.

Our family are well although we have had some extreme hot weather and we all feel the affects of it somewhat. Mary [Harriet's younger sister] has gone out in the eve to Boston with some of the sisters; she expects to see Eliz Heady. She and her mother go to the advent meeting where they keep Saturday instead of Sunday and where they wash one another's feet. Mary has had hers washed and has washed others. She says, "To the pure all things are pure" and says Adam and Eve had no shame until they had sinned and when we are in heaven, we shall have none of these feelings. I told her I did hope she would be redeemed in this world.

I was not able to finish my letter yesterday on account of a nervous headache caused probably by being up most of two nights. I have just come from Mariah's chamber; she seems very comfortable and the little boy is very quiet and well; I do not know what they will call it. Mrs Sanborn says they cannot find any name pretty enough for it. I have been afraid they would not keep it long; they are so happy about it. Julia [Harriet's stepsister, the child of her father and her stepmother Julia] is so delighted she hardly knows what to do with herself she thinks she shall want to go and live with Mariah now & I should love to have little Leonard [Harriet and Leonard's first child] here for her to take care of. Why did not you send him on by Mr. Oakes or do you mean to train him up in the field? Perhaps Hannah could not do without him; well, I will consent to let you keep what you have and I do hope that it will suffice for the present at least until you are better able to have and take care of them. I do not think it would be wicked for you to wait a little now, but suppose you will think I am talking rather strangely; but the scenes I have been through the last days make me dread the thought of your going through them every year.

But I must stop as my sheet is fully written.

Julia

In a letter to her parents written on January 4, 1846, from La Pointe, Harriet announces her intention to keep her children with her as well as her hope that her family life can serve as a model to the Indian families. Missionary wives typically focused on influencing Indians by running successful households, rather than through direct conversion. That they saw themselves as living with the Indians rather than preaching to them helps explain why they often took a more pragmatic and empathetic stance toward their Indian neighbors than did their husbands.

*T*hey call me here an over-anxious mother. Be this as it may. I cannot help it. Perhaps you would like to know what we intend to do with the children, should they be spared us. My present opinion is that we shall not send them away from us; at least, not until they are able to take care of themselves. I can not yet see the consistency of missionaries neglecting their own children or of throwing them upon the care of others, that they may be at liberty to devote themselves exclusively to the heathen. Besides, the heathen need the influence and example of a well-regulated household. They need to see the great principles of the gospel embodied. A missionary's family should be a model one, exhibiting to the heathen all that is lovely and desirable. The poor, dark-minded heathen want something more than a good theory. Will you not pray, my dear parents, that your children may be enabled to emit a steady, unwavering light in this dark land? Oh, never did I know the crushing weight of responsibility, until I had the charge of a family on missionary ground.[24]

The tone of Leonard's letter to Harriet of March 12, 1846, contrasts sharply with her father's reprimanding note. Moreover, Harriet has married a man who admires letters written by a female missionary, while Susan Wetherbee's diary indicates that the notion women might preach troubles Harriet's father. In brief, Harriet seems to have married a man amazingly free of gender bias for the time period. Leonard's remark about expressing his emotions so fully that Harriet cannot complain suggests that she not only has even challenged the commitment to reason and suspicion of emotion that he articulated in his first sermon, he has listened to his wife. Despite the Wheelers' pragmatic decision to marry, their bond has grown: the woman whom Leonard addressed as "Dear Friend" before their marriage is now "My Dear Harriet."

*T*he wind is now howling fearfully about our little dwelling but we are safe, quiet and comfortable. It commenced snowing yesterday about three o'clock continued through the day, and evening, but before morning there was a change from rain to snow. It has continued to snow all day and the storm still rages. We have done little today except stay in our house. Brother J [Johnson] has a tight cough settled upon his lungs and has felt unable to work. Tomorrow, if it is pleasant, we hope to commence work again. Yesterday afternoon we received by the hand of Shibagizhik notes from yourself, Mrs J—Abbe and Mr. Sproat. We were very happy to hear from you and learn that you were all well. I perceive that what I said about being gushkendum and unwell elicited much sympathy and interest.[25] Mrs. J says she sympathizes with me in my feeling of loneliness. Abba says I looked sad and care-worn the morning I left. You say you noticed the same. But I hope you will not chide yourself, as though anything you had said or done was the cause of any of my ills. No, far from it. I am always happy at home, and find my highest earthly happiness in the bosom of my own family. But did however feel somewhat burdened with care and anxiety the morning I left home.

I felt doubtful about the ice, I knew we must have a fatiguing day and I felt that my business was approaching such a crisis, as to require for several successive weeks my whole time, strength and much of my thoughts. But I did not think my countenance exhibited any peculiar marks of sadness. I wrote from my shanty, as I felt, so you will give me the credit, for once, of giving full expression to my feelings.

I have not yet read the life of Mrs. Bright, but I have that of Mrs. Grant,[26] with great interest, and I trust some profit. Her letters are quite interesting, plain, and written doubtless without the remotest expectation that they would ever be published. She wrote without reserve, noticing scenes and incidents, upon the journey, just as they occurred; and these intermingled with her own impressions and experiences give a remarkable sprightliness and life to her letters. While we see pictured out before us the lofty mountain, the rugged cliff and waterfall and sea. Spread before us again the fertile plain, with all the marks of busy industry. We see also her own mind as it is affected by the varied objects and scenes she is called to witness; we see how she appreciates kindness; how cheerfully she submits to little privations and disappointments. The field of her anticipated labors, we see how zealously, systematically and effectively, she prosecutes her labors. Her remarks upon the missionary circle are highly interesting—her minute notice of several Mission families: how happily they lived together, their means of mental, moral and social improvement, the systematic manner in which they addressed themselves to the various departments of missionary work, present us with the internal life of missionary operations, in a way we do not often see described, and while we read along, our interest increasing as we advance, we are suddenly stopped with these expressive words, "Thus far had our beloved Judith written on the second, and they are her last lines!" The curtain of life is suddenly dropped. From her little ones she so fondly loved, from her work in which she was so orderly engaged, she is suddenly snatched away. Just one year from the time of her death, one of her three little ones was buried by her side. Since then her husband has ceased from his active and interesting labors! What a call to be diligent! How soon will our labors be ended.

Friday evening March 13

It has snowed today almost without interruption, but it seems to have ceased this evening. We have got along so far with our work as to lay down three planks for the house. It is so stormy this week, we do not expect to see any one from La Pointe; tomorrow afternoon, I intend to go to the sugar bush[27] and spend the Sabbath. I have been very well this week—have rested well nights and had a good appetite. In my last letter I forgot to send for another pair of pants. These I have now will soon be in rags. Tell Stedman we shall be happy to see him here, as soon as he is able; we do not wish to have him come however until he gets well. If we had him here now we could make a cook of him if he were not able to labor much out of doors; but perhaps you need him more than we do.

Remember me to the little ones—tell Leonard I shall send him and Julia some new sugar as soon as I can get some. Much love to Hannah and a kind remembrance to all the household.

Your husband

The head of the mission at La Pointe, Sherman Hall, reports to David Greene²⁸ at the
American Board of Commissioners for Foreign Missions that the missionary Grenville
Sproat has been relieved of his post. Hall says that Sproat has been said to comment
that "love between man and man is purer than between husband and wife." Moreover,
another missionary staying at Sproat's house awoke in the middle of the night to find
Sproat in his bedroom; Sproat claimed that he had been sleepwalking and left. The
unnamed missionary reported to Hall that another evening while he slept at Sproat's
house, "To my utter astonishment, he seized my privates, put them into his mouth.
. . . Horrible to tell, the night was spent in efforts to keep my privates from him."²⁹
Florantha Sproat, Grenville's wife, wrote this letter to Harriet on May 26, 1846, as
she and her young daughters headed home to Massachusetts after the scandal broke.

We are now on Lake Huron pleasantly situated on a propeller. We are all well save Lucy; she has been quite unwell for two or three days with fever owing, I think, to an apple that she ate at Mac tho' Elvira ate one larger which did not hurt her at all. She is robust and in high spirits. They both often speak of Leonard and little Julia; every little thing that they get that pleases them, they say they will carry some to Lenny and sweet little Julia; when hearing them, a feeling of sadness comes over me, a feeling that they will never see them more. In their sleep they often call upon them and want to see them.

Mr. W. has told you I presume something of our leaving, as we went in a hurried manner, my things were thrown in confusion into boxes I know not how or what, and we hurried away. My feelings you may imagine a little what they were, but never can know or I hope you may never feel the full extent or never know the deep agony of heart and perfect wretchedness of heart that I experienced at that time, and a week after. I now feel different; I feel calm in the thought that God permitted all, and that he sees not as man sees, and I hope and pray that in his tender mercies will so apply this dispensation that it will be for our eternal good. I pray that whatever afflictions God sees fit to put upon us, that he will save our souls entire and Glorify himself.

My friends at La Pointe were kind and assisted me as much as they could. Mrs. H [Betsey Parker Hall] particularly so at last. She said something that

49

injured my feelings exceedingly soon after my return from your place, but she was highly excited and I should not think of it. I had a talk with Abbie the night before we left; I told her in some measure how I had felt with regard to her. She justified herself in the steps she had taken, that all had advised her to do so, or some of the mission had, and the others did not blame her. I feel sorry that she told me that, for I had placed the same confidence in her that I had in you, but God I feel is teaching me to put my trust in no one but himself. But aside from this Mrs. J [Johnson] has been very kind and I love her very much. I think there are few like her in excellence and if it were for nothing else, I should love her for the sympathy she manifested for me. With regard to Abba I have no hard feelings, and can appreciate her goodness, tho' I do not like to think of things transpired, for if I do I cannot help but feel that she acted not according to the precepts of the gospel. My husband (I write to one who I feel that I can trust) I feel has been left by God to fall into a dreadful sin, but I do not feel that he has been as guilty as the people at La Pointe think, and if he is, God sees things in their true light; this is my comfort as well as his. May God forgive in him his transgression, and lead him to himself. I know it is impossible for every one to see the thing as it is. You, I feel, will live honestly as far as needful, and for the next, you will act instead of talk, for I never in one instance doubted your faithfulness as a friend, or your principles as a Christian. Your kindness shown to me in that deep darkness was the only ray of light which broke in upon my agonized heart, for which I in some measure feel grateful.

I had some little conversations with Miss Gates with regard to the people at La P. while on Lake S [Superior]. She said she wished Mrs. W. [Wheeler] knew a little something about the speeches that are made at La P. with regard to Hannah wearing a ring which they say was given her by Peter Loonsfoot; she asked me if I knew when she got it. I told her I knew not. She wished you to know so if possible to prevent further remarks. She said that people were very ready to make remarks especially about missionaries and those that belong to them.

June 19

We are now in New York and have been here a week. Lucy, after having written the above, got much worse when at Detroit. We employed a physician; he thought her a very sick child, thought we had better stop in Detroit until she was better. It being so warm and unhealthy, we chose to take her to Cleveland. The night after we left Detroit she grew so very much worse that we put plasters made of the clear mustard wet in brandy over her stomach and bowels. I had frequently put her into a salutary butter (a great remedy for inflammation in Detroit) after which she sank to sleep in the morning, awoke better, inflammation gone, a very sudden change for the better. I had begun to be afraid that we should have to leave our darling child in Cleveland or its mortal remains. Its disease was inflammation of the mucus membrane. She has since been pretty well. Elvira remained quite well until the day before we arrived here; she was taken something with but not as sick. She has now got better.

If Hannah has the little ones, my little ones are often talking about them and are going to take them a great many things that they see here. They often say, "Come, let us go home" and then mention all whom they knew and loved while at La P. saying they want to see them. Love to all the friends at La. P. I want to hear from you very much.

Monday. My bonnet is all out of date; all old + young wear hats; they now do up their hair on the top of their heads + wear high fashions. I shall leave NY in 2 or 3 days.

Mrs. Sproat.

3.

Building a Home
Alone in the Forest

In 1845, Leonard Wheeler moved to the Bad River with Ojibwe volunteers to establish a farming community. Although this seems consistent with the benighted attempts of Euro-Americans to make American Indians mimic them, when the Ojibwe of Bad River recollect their treaties with the whites, they complain that in 1825 they were promised "a farm . . . at every one of their Villages."[1] A bit later, the government promised but failed to provide them with "Beef and working cattle," as well as "School Teachers, Black Smiths, Farmers and Carpenters."[2] The Wheelers tried to meet these requests.

Since this new community was Wheeler's project, his family put Lake Superior between themselves and the other missionaries collected at La Pointe. Thus, the Wheelers become pioneers, and the letters from this period make clear that they have fallen into the patterns typical of a pioneer family. Leonard, like other pioneer fathers, welcomes the opportunity to explore new territory, while his wife, Harriet, looks longingly toward her Massachusetts home, asking her mother to send wallpaper, presumably so she can create a parlor.

The move to Odanah sets off a new round of anguish in Harriet, which she resolves the same way she quieted the despair that overwhelmed her during her first Thanksgiving at La Pointe: she turns to God. She confesses her depression in a letter written to her parents from Bad River on July 26, 1846.

*J*t has been a long time since we have received a letter from you. The last one contained the melancholy intelligence of dear Mariah's death. I felt very anxious to learn more of the particulars and also how brother N. [Newell] was supported under this heavy affliction. Dear brother, my heart bleeds for him. I presume he feels that *this* is his *first affliction*. May it be sanctified to him. I would like to write him, but I do not think it would be prudent for me to attempt it at present, as my health has not been good for a few weeks past and I find it necessary to avoid everything of an exciting nature.

I have suffered somewhat from depression of spirits, and have thought more seriously of a return home than I have ever done before since I came into the country. Perhaps in the course of a year or two you may see me in L [Lowell].

Mr. W [Wheeler] wrote some sometime since, and informed you that we were at last settled in our new home. Our house is not yet finished, although we find it very comfortable and convenient. Mr and Mrs Johnson are living in our family. Mrs. J has been sick this spring and summer, part of the time unable to turn herself in bed. Her difficulties are such as to make it dangerous for her to exert herself in the least. Mr. W has two hired men who board with us, which makes our family quite large. I have a young Indian girl who is also to assist H [Hannah] very much, and I find it a relief. Our house is not very large, yet arranged as to make the most of the room, and when it is finished will be very convenient. The location is very pleasant, being on a point where the river branches off in two beautiful streams.

Our prospects also for usefulness among the Indians is even better than we anticipated. They are have enlarged their gardens very much this year and they now look very well. They are now on the shore of the lake fishing. They will return here immediately after payment. While they were here, the pagan Indians attended our meetings on the Sabbath better than I have ever seen them any time since I came into the country. We sometimes have a congregation of more than forty Indians. We hold all our meetings at our house as the school house is not yet built.

We have nothing particularly to trouble us here except mosquitoes; they are at present a somewhat serious annoyance. You cannot have an idea of their numbers here. They make a noise at night like a large swarm of bees; we cannot sleep at all without a mosquito net around the bed and then if we do not tuck it very tight around the bed, they will find us.

You have probably heard before this that Mr + Mrs Sproat have left the mission. His case has been a very painful one; his crime is of such a nature that I cannot write you about it. Before he left, we saw some sign of repentance. Mrs. S left us with an undiminished confidence and love of the mission. She is a poor broken-hearted woman. She was a good woman and I miss her very much.

Mr. W's health has not been very good for some weeks past. He has been very much troubled with biles. He is somewhat better now. The children are very well + enjoy their new home very much. I find it much easier to train them here than it was at L P. I do not fear the influence of the *wild Indian even* as much as I do of the French + half breed.

Lenny talks a great deal about his Grandpa. This morning he wanted me to tell him that he was going to see him. When he brings in any wood for me he wants to know if I won't write a letter to Granpapa and tell him that Lenny brings in his Mama's wood for her. Julia is quite a playmate of L. She runs about every where, tries to say everything she hears said, and do everything she sees done. She is a little sunbeam + a perfect little pet for every one. Mr. W and H [Hannah] join me in much love to all. Please write as soon as you receive this.

The letter Harriet's father writes to her from Lowell on September 20, 1846, suggests that he, too, finds life sad, difficult, and lonesome, partly because he misses his children. Indeed, the grim letters Harriet receives from her parents make hers seem miraculously cheerful, especially considering the challenges daily life presents her.

I now sit down to tell you that we are all comfortable, well enough. It has been very hot in Lowell this summer and is now but not so sickly as it has been. The dysentery was the first sickness that has abated + now the Typhus Fever is very prevalent. The amount of Death has been over twenty five. Newell boards to home with us as yet + we have had six boarders from New York boarding with us for one fortnight till Mr. North moved out of my house. Mr. Whitney is Pay Master to the locks + canal, so they appear to be Christian + they have been busy. They tell us that Fanny is going to be married to a Minister that is going out west; he may possibly be out by you.

I suppose you will want to know how we get along in the Churches. I am afraid there are more hearers than doers. The Churches here are very bad although we have got one of the most faithful Preachers that I ever heard. It shows us that man can only lead to the car, but God can speak to the heart.

I often when I come home from the store in the evening look up Northwest and think of my Dear Children + long to see you. Write me every opportunity you have; I hope to receive a good long letter from my son *Wheeler* + *tell* me *how you get* along + O, my Dear children remember me daily in your Prayers. I ask not your Prayers for to be riches or honor, but that we may all be born of the Spirit + that we may lay up our treasure in heaven. Give my love to all the Brethren & Sisters so I remain your affectionate

Father S Wood

On February 1, 1847, Harriet writes from Bad River to announce the birth of William, her first child following the move, but depression and ill health continue to haunt her.

I do not know but that you will infer from my long silence that I have buried my pen at Bad River; but if you have received my husband's last letter you will be able to account for it. I am gaining strength fast, am able to take care of my babe and be about with the family.

Mr. W gave you some of the particulars regarding my confinement; but I feel that I too must bear testimony to the kindness and faithfulness of our Heavenly Father. He has indeed been a very present help to us, in our time of need. I had suffered during the summer and fall from an *uncontrollable depression* of *spirits*.

Such seasons are I believe always seasons of anxiety to a woman, but to one situated as I am they are peculiarly so. I knew that when the hour of trial + suffering came, I had nothing to expect from human aid; my only hope must be in God. And I can truly say that it is good to trust in the Lord at all times and for all things. I had been quite unwell two days previous to the birth of our little boy, and had I been at home should probably have called a physician.

New Year's night, I put my little ones to bed as usual; but when I left them, I felt that before another sun should rise, they might be left motherless in this dark land. As soon as necessary arrangement could be made, we had a little season of prayer. There was no one present but Mrs. J [Johnson] and my husband. It was a very precious season to me. The remembrance of that hour will go with me to my grave. I felt that I could commit myself, soul and body into the hands of my compassionate Savior, that he could and would do all things well for me. I felt perfectly calm. All that fear, and terror which I had frequently felt when anticipating that hour, was now entirely taken from me. I was very sick about three hours, but was safely carried through. Surely it is better to trust in the Lord than to put confidence in man.

Our little boy is a large healthy child. He was sick the second and third days, but has been very well since. During my sickness I had everything that was necessary for my comfort. My room by taking up blankets around, was very comfortable although the weather was unusually severe. The soda crackers, tea, sugar, + cocoa which you and brother sent me were very useful, and I enjoyed them much more from the fact that they were provided for me by my own dear father, and brother. I seldom used them without thinking of you, and often wept at the remembrance of all your kindness.

Have you heard any thing from Mary of late? [Harriet's sister Mary has joined a Shaker community.] Hannah is well and is making very good progress in her studies. Mr W. in his last said something about her returning home next summer. The reason of his doing so, was because H has always said that it was expected she should return in three years from the time she left. She has received a letter from a young gentleman expressing his attachment to her, requesting to know if it was reciprocated. He is from Michigan, largely engaged in the mining speculation. As he is somewhat a stranger to us, and as he is destitute of Christian principle, we felt that we could not consent to any particular intimacy. H has written him a negative answer.

I suppose that before this you have received a letter containing our list. I have been afraid since we sent it that purchasing the articles might be too much tax upon mother's strength. Perhaps some black Alpaca would be suitable for Mr. W's coat, if you cannot find any thing better. The one he alluded to was made of a cheap calico. I have thought that perhaps you might get some remnants of woolen cloths cheap at the Lawrence's for Lenny's clothes

―――――――――

Harriet's letter also suggests that her friends in Lowell have lost some interest in supporting her mission work over the years. Still, she hopes that they might like to help the Indians acquire "civilized" dress.

We have thought that perhaps you might feel some delicacy about mentioning our winter needs to friends in L. If so, please purchase the articles we have sent for + Mr Greene will pay for them. We certainly are very much indebted to the friends in L for what they have done for us, + we shall ever retain a grateful remembrance of their many kindnesses. We know they have many calls. New and important objects are constantly urging their claims, and as we have been gone so long, we are probably personally strangers to a majority of the members of the churches. If there are any who would like to contribute to our aid, it will certainly be very gratefully received. I have thought of one way in which they might give essential aid. I think I have told you that the men wear calico shirts, and the women short gowns. It takes three or three and a half yards of calico to make one of these articles. In the course of the year we are obliged to hire some labor + they more frequently want 3 yards of calico for their pay than anything else. If there are a number of persons who would individually contribute calico enough for a shirt or short gown they would not only aid us, but would also confer a favor upon the poor Indians. Perhaps it will not be best to mention this. Please do as you think proper about it. You know the state of feeling at home much better than we do.

———————

And she asks for wallpaper and tea equipment, presumably so she can have tea parties in a properly decorated parlor.

*T*here were a few other articles which were forgotten when we sent our list. We shall be obliged to have some more paper for our house. We want enough to paper our front room. I think it will take twelve rolls. I think the glazed paper would be stronger. It might probably be bought for 15 cts a roll; I would like a buff or Lilac ground. We also need a black tin teapot, a good sized tin coffee pot, one Doz plated tea spoons (please do not purchase german silver), two tablespoons, a few yds of cheap edgings from two to six cts a yd.

My little babe will also need two or three yards of some woolen material for winter wear and some woolen hose, and shoes. I think some little kid shoes would be preferable to socks as the socks do not wear well.

Parents, for various reasons this letter is designed for your eyes alone. Give my love to all the family. Mr. W., Hannah, Lenny and Julia send their love to all.

Your Affectionate Daughter

Harriet Wheeler

———————

Harriet does not write to her parents about how the mission work proceeds at Bad River, presumably because protecting the health and welfare of her own family consumes her energy and attention, but her husband's letters to his father make clear that he thinks of little else. His reports when they first settle in Bad River suggest that, along with her other difficulties, Harriet must comfort a disappointed husband who writes a discouraged account of how things are going to his father on July 8, 1847. Any positive traits he notes in the Indians, he attributes to missionary influence.

You ask what trials we have. Some of them are peculiar to living among an uncivilized heathen people like our Indians. Insofar as our trials of a temporal nature are concerned, I might say the difficulty of commencing a new missionary station in such a community as this is considered by us all as something of a trial. If we conform to the habits of the natives we should want then a birch bark lodge which an old woman could put up in a couple of hours—an axe—gun—spear—fishnet, two or three knives and forks, as many pans dishes and kettles, together with a bark canoe, and we should consider ourselves comfortably fixed. But if we wish to keep up our habits of civilized life, we are not so easily made comfortable. We want a house, though it be a log one. We want cultivated land to some extent. We want a few domestic animals and consequently we want pasture-meadow-land and a barn. Now to have things which we are all accustomed to regard as almost indispensible to civilized life, requires time and expense. And *here* work is accomplished with no little difficulty as you can easily conceive. But little American labor can be hired because but few of this class of people are in the country. Most of the laborers to be employed are French, half breeds or Indians, the latter of which are no better than so many boys. Some among the other classes are much more skillful, but like the Indians are unstable as water. Solomon's description of an unfaithful man is strikingly applicable to them all. They attach but little sacredness to a promise and have little energy and perseverance to accomplish what they begin. They will perhaps begin a job of work and leave it half done or if they promise to begin a piece of work at a given time, they will perhaps come a week after or not at all. You can see that to deal with such is not a little perplexing to say the least.

I have been obliged to twist myself into as many shapes as the genius of ordinary men will admit, being farmer, carpenter, mason, physician, teacher, besides sustaining meetings in Indian and English upon the Sabbath.

One of our greatest trials is the trial of laboring to promote the highest good of a people who do not extensively appreciate our motives or seem to be savingly benefitted by our instruction. The Indians like all the heathen have no idea of gospel. It is difficult for them to see how others may be prompted by feelings of pure benevolence to care and labor among them for their good. They think they lay us under considerable obligation if they permit their children to attend school. They do not appreciate at all the advantages of school education. After listening to our preaching, they expect us to pay them for attending upon our instruction. They are often the most religiously inclined when they have the least to eat. Only fill their mouths with bread and they will give little evidence of hungering for the bread of life. Could we see the people giving evidence of being really born again, truly converted to God, our cup of joy would be full.

Our trials in this respect are not peculiar. They are more or less common to all ministers of the gospel everywhere who labor to convert the heathen to God. I have been surprised sometimes in reading the journals of our missionary brothers in other parts of the heathen world, to see how almost exactly their experience in this aspect corresponded with our own. There they find the same darkness of mind, the same corrupt affections, the same selfishness to contend with, till the light break in from above and the Spirit of God be passed out to give power to the truth.

You ask finally, "Do you think you are doing any good there? Are the Indians benefitted by your going among them?" If our usefulness is to be judged by the number of converts since we came among them, perhaps our friends would conclude that we could be more useful elsewhere than here. Candid observers would probably say our influence for good here could not well be spared. Our Indians have been gradually improving for a good many years. They are also generally well-dressed and have enough to eat. We do not mean by this that the Indians are very neat or tidy in their appearance, or that they set a very good table, but when compared with what they have been and compared with the Inland Indians generally, they are comfortably off. They are doing more towards cultivating the soil than formerly and are much more industrious. They have more than doubled the size of their farms here in four years. Till within three years past they have depended upon the traders for nearly all they had to eat except fish and potatoes. When they started for their sugar camps in the spring, they would go and take credit of the traders to be paid in sugar. When done, it would take nearly all their sugar to pay their credit. Last spring when they went to the sugar camps, very few of them had taken any credits. They made over twenty tons of sugar to sell to buy themselves clothing and to consume in their families. They are beginning to appreciate, in some good degree, the blessings of civilization.

Yet they manifest yet little interest in our school. Though there are something like a hundred children here of a suitable age to attend school—yet not more than 10 or 12 of them have been anything like regular scholars though more than sixty scholars have been into school during the last quarter. The parents have but little control over their children and when the latter choose to play rather than to go to school, they do so; yet the parents acknowledge that the superiority of the whites over them is owing chiefly to the fact that they know the book and many of them express a desire that their children may understand the book also.

In regard to their moral or religious improvement, there has been a great change wrought among them, as is acknowledged generally by those who have been acquainted with them for several years. Much of the natural fierceness of their character has been laid aside. They are now one of the most quiet peaceable bands in the nation—less disposed to commit depredations upon property. But still they love their superstitions and will not come to Christ that they may have life. They have received so much instruction, that they sin against great light many of them. The excuses they offer for not embracing the gospel plainly show that they do violence to their own consciousness to be continuing in sin. In regard to our future prospects of usefulness among them, I shall be obliged to defer that subject to another letter. In the meantime permit me to subscribe myself, your

Affectionate son,

Leonard

On January 30, 1848, Harriet's younger sister Hannah writes her parents in Lowell of her loneliness at Bad River.

*A*s Mr. Wheeler is to Fond du Lac and it is the Sabbath day and having no services I have a little time to spend in writing you a few lines. We are all well with the exception of little Willie who today is troubled with bowel complaints. He was one year old the first of this month, walks all about and has a mouthful of teeth. Sister Harriet has just weaned him. He was a very good boy about it; he tries to talk, but his language is very unintelligible. Leonard and Julia are grown very much. They often talk about Grand papa and Grand mama and have already learned that you "are way off to Lowell."

Since writing you I have been at La Pointe. Whilst there, they had a Temperance meeting. Mr. W. delivered an address; there is a great deal of interest manifested in the cause and most all of the civilized community have signed the pledge and joined the Association. There seems to be very little or no interest on the subject of religions. The church have prayed and continue to pray for a revival.

In my last letter home I told you we had a *little* community here this winter—and also that I was in school, a quite pleasant one now but will not be long when the wild Indians come in; however, I will not indulge myself to look upon the dark side. Sister H has said considerable of going home with Abby next summer. Mr. W tells her she may go and while she is at home, he will go to Red Lake (as he has long wished to do) and I would stay here and go on with my school. But as they are only air castles; they will most probably fall and break. I wish we might expect to see some of you here next summer, but I suppose you will say that it is impossible. I need not tell you that we would be *very, very* happy to see you here, for this you doubtless know.

Feb 1st This day has been very stormy. I have thought much of Mr. Wheeler who was intending to start for home this morning. You probably wonder at his going off so in the winter but a good opportunity presented itself and he had been wishing to go to that place to spend the Sabbath. He put on Indian leggings and an Indian cap, took his blanket and went. It is the first long tramp that he has ever taken. I do not think you have any reason to be anxious about me as long as I am with such a brother. He does all he can for my good and *brings me up* as I think Father would like. He is very kind *indeed* and seems more like a Father than a brother in law—but still there is a feeling in me that I cannot go to him as one. I cannot tell any one here my feelings as I could to you if I could but see you—but enough of this—

FEB 8TH. Yesterday Mr. W came home and was met with cordial reception from us. Although he had an unusually hard time, he enjoyed his visit very much. He found considerable interest manifested in the subject of religion. There is a little here, not so much as we could wish. I can assure you his return home was still *more* pleasant, if it could be so, when I found he had two letters—one from you, my dear parents. We were glad to hear of your health being better and to hear from *all* the family. It makes me feel sad to think of Mary. It hardly seems possible that she could come home so. [Since Mary Wood had joined a Shaker community, presumably she came home wearing Shaker garb.] Poor Julia; her pride was greatly wounded. I began to think the same pride that made Sister Mary go in and out the back door is what keeps her from writing her missionary sister. It was the last news I could wish to hear from Mary that she has become of the meek and lowly Jesus. I would love to write a long letter to her, but on account of other duties shall not be able to do so at present. Please give a great deal of love to her from me.

A few nights ago I dreamt that as I was at La Pointe I met Aunt Palmer Mercy and little Hans; it was of course an unexpected meeting. As I was going to inquire about you, I awoke and was very much disappointed to find it a dream.

I think you would love Julia very much; she calls herself and we call her Sissy. A few mornings ago, she was sitting very thoughtfully at the table; she said, "Sissy would love to go to Lowell and see her dear mama and dear papa *very* much." As she sleeps with me, she shares some of my "sad hours." She looks up in my face and wants to know if her "dear papa and dear mama love me"; she then throws her arms round my neck and says, "I love you too, Auntie." It is impossible to get her to sleep with any one else. I do love her very much. Leonard is too much as the Hall boys were for me to love him *as well*.

Harriet sends much love to you; she would have written you this mail but Rev. W wished her to write to friends in Vermont.

Once when Newell wrote to Harriet he said he was going to write me soon but I have never received the least lines from him. Well, I ought not expect to be remembered always. Give a great deal of love to sister Laura [Newell's wife]. Please kiss any little nephews at home. Although I write in great haste, I remain

Your aff daughter

Hannah

Love to all enquiring friends.

———

Even Susan Wetherbee seems lonely back in Lowell when she writes on April 29, 1848, but her account of her life makes clear its contrast with Harriet's. While Harriet gratefully chews on soda crackers sent her from Lowell as she awaits the birth of her third child, alone, Susan helps make red damask pillows for the church. But Susan tends to emphasize the sadness in her life, perhaps because she fears that describing joyous events might discourage her friend, for the letter also reveals that despite the differences in their situations, Susan understands and empathizes easily with Harriet, accurately guessing that she feels lonely and that the mission work proceeds slowly; then Susan immediately attempts to console the friend she has not seen for seven years, even suggesting that her home in the wilderness places Harriet closer to God than she could get in Lowell.

nother year has come, again it has been said, "A box is going to Harriet," and again I seat myself to write to one of my dearest friends. In looking at your last, I am surprised to find it dated Mar 46. How steadily Time moves on; and how many cares, trials, and changes mark the pathway of His might. We are none of us exempt from trials and each one knows the particular ingredients of his own cup. Could we always say, "God proffers it, take it from his hand," its bitterness, would be greatly mitigated, but some wrongdoing of our own, adds poignancy often to our sorrows. But perhaps you will say, "This is yours" and so perhaps it is, but anything is welcome from an old friend.

I learned from one of your letters home that the Sickness here last season was cause for great anxiety. It was indeed Dreadful to be in the midst of it, although none of our family suffered at all from it. Your friends, too, were kindly spared. May they be for years to come, if it is best. I suppose, although you are so far away, the idea that your friends still live, is a delightful one, and, although should a friend die you would not miss them in your daily paths, still your heart would bleed.

You had some idea it seems of visiting home this season; I need not say with what feelings your old friends would have welcomed you. O H, the happy days and hours, we have shared are gone, burst of tears they may awaken, as we retrace the intervening days and then look back up upon an Oasis in our pathway.

When you wrote last you were leaving La Pointe for a new station. That now has become your home. Is it preferable to the old one? How pleasant it must be for you having H [Hannah] with you, but while her mind was so unsettled did you not suffer exceedingly with her? Do you think as she did that she never was converted before or had she backslidden? I rejoice to learn of her happy change, and that she has such an interest in the Mission. I don't see how you could part with her, yet without a strong interest in the work, we could not expect her always to remain.

"Oh, had I the wings of a Dove" I would spread them and light down upon your dwelling some day when you little thought of it, and put you to crying though in one of your most cheerful moods, I reckon. John Street people are very busy now; those who take interest enough to assist in furnishing the Pews with Cushions, and covering them as many as they can with red damask. But there is not sufficient interest to complete it this Spring if at all, for it does not appeal so powerfully to the sympathy of the Benevolent, as some other calls do. Mrs. Southwick is interested and has worked very hard with us in picking the Moss and making the Cushion. This Moss is an article used in the place of hair; it grows on trees, at the South. We have assisted a good deal, and it is pretty hard work.

As it regards the state of Religions in our society, there are been some cases of conversion this spring and there are still some inquirers. How is it with you? Are your family encouraged and your hearts cheered by indications of good among your people? If not, you need not despair; the work is the Lord's; he regards the purpose of heart of his servants—not the accomplishment of his desires.

It seems to me I should not so much care about social matters as I used to, but perhaps I should. I think I never shall again. Amanda has led a gay life in New York; I hope she will one day consider.

I have made a Sack apron for your little boy as they are worn here and I think them very pretty. It buttons at the side in front, as you may see. I hope it will fit him. If he will step over and let me see what alteration it needs, tell him I will make it for him. Sister Margaret + Mary both sewed on the little apron so you can think of them. But is it not very painful to receive presents from home; would you not almost as soon dispense with them?

I yesterday returned from a Visit in Dracutt of a day or two with Mrs. D. Richardson whom you remember, although early in the season, 'tis pleasant to get out from the busy city to see the tiny brook pursue its happy unfettered course through the pasture land, to gather the Moss from the rock, and listen to the gentle Music of Nature. There is much in the City to Stifle Voice of Conscience, to exclude the Almighty from the work he has.

How I should love to see Mr. Wheeler. How is his health now; is he worn down and changed by labor and toil in that distant field? May he be strengthened and blessed, and dear H may you be doubly blessed in spirit and at last an abundant entrance be administered unto you into the kingdom of Christ.

Sister Mary was solicited a few Months since to go as a Foreign Missionary by a Gentleman from Andover who I presume would have been in every way worthy of her confidence, but she decided in the negative. If his life is prolonged, he will be very useful.

And now my dear H, I hope you will soon write me; if only a few lines, I would gladly receive it. Our family all send much love to you, Mr. W + Hannah. Kiss all the little ones for me. I remain as ever Yours, Aff Susan We.

The letter Harriet's stepmother writes to her on May 7, 1848, shows the extent of the Wheelers' dependence on supplies sent from Lowell as well as the depth of the religious faith that motivates Harriet's parents to help her even though their financial difficulties have apparently forced them to rent out part of their house and her stepmother raises extra money by taking in sewing. Despite their intense religiosity, the Woods refuse to visit Harriet's sister Mary at the Canterbury Shaker community, presumably because she has stepped outside the bounds of traditional religion.

he box is ready and I will try to explain some things to you which perhaps you would not understand. You will see that I have bought Hannah a cloak; I could not pattern the other. And I have bought her a dress. The alpaca comes with every variety & shade, no two pieces alike and our friends advised me to get a new one; it was only fifty-eight cents a yard.

If you will see the miniatures, it is thought by our friends that they are very natural. I told your Father I thought it would be a present as acceptable as anything he could give you.

You will see the shawls are not what you sent for, but I could not find any in the city. You sent for a heavy winter shawl and I think when you get the one I have sent, you will think it is large enough. I have had your dresses cut and basted; I wish you would let me know how they fit. There has not been much change in the fashion of dresses. They trim with fringes and buttons, but I suppose you would not like to have money spent for it. I made the skirts as far as I was able. I shall send the lining for Mr. W and dickies. I have not time to make them. I could not find a large white handkerchief in the city and shall send you the material to make one of. Mr E. D. Sweet sends the caps. Elvira sends the little trucks for Willy.

You have often inquired about Mary. I have sent you some of her writings and you can judge for yourself the state of her mind. We heard nothing from her since last fall. She was very anxious to have us visit her, but we do not intend to do so.

We are all in pretty good health with the exception of bad colds and I am so stupid from this cause that I can scarcely tell what I am doing; so much by way of apology for my bad writing.

We have let the back part of our house and occupy the front; we have five rooms. The cellar kitchen has been finished and we make use of it; we have the parlor and all the chambers in the front house. We receive seventy dollars a year from what we let. My own health has been better than the last year. I have taken in some fifteen dollars worth of sewing and shall continue to do so. I think your Father has been better for the last two or three months than for nearly two years; he seems as cheerful and happy as I ever knew him to be. He seemed somewhat disturbed about giving up his bedroom downstairs but we have the sitting room in our chamber and I have kept a fire so that he comes home and enjoys it as well as he did before. I keep the bedroom for a spare chamber and we occupy the front.

Julia is in school when her eyes will permit; they trouble her much. I look forward with some anxiety in reference to her. She has a great flow of spirits peculiarly susceptible to impressions from the influences around her and her companions are most of them thoughtless and, indeed, we see very little consistent piety even among those who profess to be Christians. I hope you will write to her and pray for her. I feel that nothing but the spirit of God can keep any of us from that spirit of fashionable worldliness which prevails all around us. I often think if Paul were here, his spirit would be ruined within him as it was when visiting at Athens to see the city wholly given to idolatry.

I have felt somewhat disappointed in not seeing you home this summer, but I hope the Lord will be with you there and enable you to be faithful. Your Father often says, "You do not know how happy I am when I think of my children at the west." Sometimes I ask him if he does not wish they were here and he will say, "*I want to see them* but if they are engaged in the course of Christ they are safe whether living or dying" and I have nothing to say. I think he seems happier in his own mind than I ever knew him.

The box is being mailed and I must stop. The apple was sent by Grandmother Kendell; she is with us visiting.

from your affectionate Mother
J M Wood

Harriet reports the arrival of the box in a letter written in La Pointe dated August 1848.

I hasten to write you a line although I must write in bed as I am unable to sit up. I met with an accident which obliges me to keep pretty quiet for a few days; I am much better today + think I shall be up again soon.

You have probably ere this received Mr. Wheeler's letter informing you of the arrival of our box from Lowell. We were very glad to receive it, but most of all the miniatures. I thank you a thousand times for it + wish it was in my power to send you anything that would give you half as much comfort or pleasure. We received H's [Hannah's] letter which informed us that the miniatures were in the box about three hours before we could get the box from the vessel. I can assure you we waited not a little impatiently till it came ashore. When we got the box opened, those were the first objects of our search; still, when I held it in my hand, I was almost afraid to open it. I expected that busy time had wrought as sad changes in your features as in mine but when I saw dear father sitting there just as I left him almost eight years ago, it did seem as if time has deemed him untouchable. Dear Mother seemed a little more changed to me, although hers is very natural but sister Julia has entirely outgrown all her childhood looks; I could hardly realize that it was possible it could be the little sister I left. My little ones were delighted to see it. Lenny said, "I wish they could jump right out of the picture; then we would kiss them very hard." Little Julia's first words were, "Mama, may I kiss them?" They very often at night before they go to bed bid you all good night.

The things in the box all came very well + we were very much pleased with all the articles. My dresses were too large, yet it is no work at all to alter them compared with what it would be to cut and fit them myself. It is work I dislike to do very much. I thank you *very much* for cutting them out for me + also Leonard's clothes. They were about two inches too short + about as much too big round, but they will do very well for him this summer. He is a tall slender boy.

The articles from the Young Ladies Society were very gratefully received. I plan on writing them as soon as possible. To whom shall I direct the letter? I fear, dear Mother, you do more for us in the line of sewing than you were supposed to do; I can only thank you for it + hope and wish you will be rewarded.

We are all of us now at La Pointe excepting my husband. He is at Bad River attending to some work there. We were driven from home by the heat and the Mosquitoes + as the Indians were to attend the payment, he thought we could be more useful here at present. We came here about three weeks since + shall probably remain till the first of September. It is now a very exciting time here. We have a new agent. He has a large and pleasant family. The payment this year is a much larger one than has been made for some years. Traders are consequently flocking in all eager for the spoils. We anticipate some trouble from whiskey but the Agent says he shall not pay out a single dollar while there is any whiskey on the island. There is a strong organization against it + we shall see this year whether law can stop it. Traders have come with a vile licentious look + exposed them publicly for sale. The law upon this subject has been posted + if they still persist, they will be prosecuted and sent out of the country. Gambling will also be noticed. So you see that if missions do nothing more, they do purify public sentiment. In fact, I feel that this place would be a perfect Saloon were it not for Missionary influence. If you hear Missions abused + slandered, you must not be surprised, for the wicked see their gains endangered +, of course, will cry out against us.

In a letter which we received from you about a fortnight since you said that Mr. and Mrs. Brooks[3] were traveling for her health and that possibly we might see them here. We have been looking for them every vessel, but as it is getting late in the season, we very much fear we shall not see them. I cannot help feeling disappointed; I do think if they knew the medicinal virtues of this climate, particularly for debilitated constitutions, they would certainly come. Invalids frequently come here for their health and I never knew a single case but there was benefit. The time is not probably far distant when Lake Superior will be a fashionable resort for invalids as Saratoga now is.

The children send much love + many kisses to you.

Very Affec

Your Daughter

Harriet

Harriet's letter of October 10, 1848, continues her account of the family's difficulties.

After payment we returned to Bad River. In about a fortnight after we returned, our sweet little Emma [Harriet's fourth child born living, whose formal name is Emily] was taken sick + for six long weary weeks lay balancing between life + death. She had a severe attack of cholera infantum attended with a disease of the kidney and bladder; about three weeks since, she passed a perfectly formed stone from the bladder about as large as half a pea. Since then she has been convalescent and for the last week has improved rapidly. I think I never saw a child suffer so much. There have been hours when I have felt that it would be a comfort to see her at rest even though it were in the arms of Death. For three days + three nights I do not think she was quiet one half hour. During all the time husband + I took care of her with the exception of two nights. Oh, you know not the trial of sickness at Bad River; we are so isolated + alone. Yet this Lord has wonderfully sustained + preserved me. I feel that his promise has been verified in my case "as to the day is so thy strength shall be." I trust I do feel some gratitude to him for preserving mercies; surely it is better to trust in the Lord than to put confidence in man.

By this time you will probably wish to know how it happens that we are at La P, so I must tell you. Both of our stations have suffered much for the want of help + it was thought best that while the Indians as a body were absent from our station, we should concentrate our efforts here. Mr. W commenced school last Monday. The new teachers will take it soon. This will leave Mr. W at liberty to make a route inland which he has long been anxious to do. Should the health of our family persist, he will probably leave us about new year's to visit the different mission stations in the country + the principal bands of Indians. This will be a journey of about two thousand miles on snow shoes; it will be a trial to me to have him go + I should feel exceedingly anxious about him; yet, it seems desirable that he should make the tour so I ought to cheerfully to acquiesce in it.

The Indians are now scattered about on the shore of the Lake doing their fall fishing. A few families will be settled at Bad River during the winter. We shall probably return there about the first of March.

Please give much love to friends in L, particularly S Wetherbee. I would write her by the vessel but I do not think it would be prudent for me to attempt it. Do write as soon as you can. Mr W. + the children send much love; little Julia said last Sabbath morning when I put on her woolen dress, "I wish I could see dear mama; I would thank her very much for making my clothes for me so nicely." I do not know what would have become of my poor children if you had not made them.

Very Affec, Your Daughter

Harriet

Although the Wheelers urge temperance on the Indians, Harriet's father's letter of April 22, 1849, suggests that they themselves drink. Samuel Wood, once again, warns Harriet and Leonard against indulging their children.

I have sat down to write a few lines to send in the box. I shall send in the box if I can send it safe 1 qt of Brandy + 2 qt of Mr. Marshall's wine for you when you are sick. I was very glad that we did not get the account of your sickness till we have the second letter informing us of your getting better. It makes me feel very sad that I can't see you or send you some things for your comfort. I was myself quite sick last Monday night. I come home from store; before coming, I called upon Doct Huntington; he gave me a blue pill which relieved me soon. I was part of the next day at home, but quite weak. I am very much tied to my store and have no one with me which confines me very much.

I see my Dear Children, that you are getting quite a large family of Children. There is one word I want to say to you. If you want to have your Children love you, make them obedient when young; don't wait till they get to be four or five years old, but do it when small if you want them to be Christian. My experience shows me when Children have their own way, there is very few of them converted + if they be, they make Crooked Christians. I don't know but my advice is needless; I hope it is.

Our Sabbath School is filling up fast. I have a Class; about twenty belong to it; we have had a very pleasant hour this noon time. I have been in the sabbath school for fifteen years + my health has been such that I have not been absent ten Sundays + I hope that I shall never leave the Sabbath schools as long as I can.

Kiss all my grandchildren + tell them that grandpa Say: they should be obedient to their Parents + if they be, I shall love them *very very* much. Give my Love to all the Mission Family.

Your Affectionate

Father Samel Wood

On July 10, 1849, Harriet writes her parents from La Pointe, where the family has once more fled the mosquitoes. She breaks the news of Hannah's wedding to her parents; Hannah, like Harriet, settled in Wisconsin.

We are now, at La P. where we have been driven by the Mosquitoes. They are always bad enough at Bad River this season of the year, but this year they are much worse than usual; my babe has been badly poisoned by them. We will probably remain here till after payment.

Before this reaches you, you will have welcomed Hannah to her home again. You will, I fear, be disappointed to find that she is married + so soon to return to the West as her permanent home. We regret that she could not return to you as she left. We both advised her to defer all matrimonial engagements until she had been at home six months. Her husband[4] is a worthy man, and I trust will make her a good husband; but he is somewhat older. I regret that you will not have an opportunity to see him longer as he improves upon an acquaintance. We felt somewhat lonesome at Bad River after we returned. Poor little J [Julia] began to cry when we came to our landing place; and said "Mama, I want Aunty; won't she never come to see us again?" I feel anxious about her as we learn that the Cholera is raging in the states. We have just learned that there have been cases in Boston; I shall feel exceedingly anxious about you all, "but I know you are in the hands of one who is able to cover you from the pestilence that walks at noonday." I wish it was practicable for you all to come and spend the summer with us.

H [Hannah] will inform you that we received the box before she left. We were very glad to see it. We feel very grateful to you for all the care and labor you have had in preparing it for us; and especially for getting so many articles made for us. Julia's dresses are a little large; but they can be easily altered. She laughs when she puts on the long sleeved apron you made her, and says why her "mama thought that her little Julia was a very *big girl.*" She was very much pleased to find some shoes in the box for little Emily. She had been quite anxious about her sister's feet for fear they would be cold. Please present our thanks to the kind friends who assisted in making the articles for us. Tell them that if they knew how gratifying these tokens of their remembrance were to us, they would, I trust, feel in a measure repaid for their labor of love.

You will learn by H our decision about visiting home this summer. You say in your last that Miss Spooner thinks my life depends upon my return. I have felt so myself until recently. When we came to consult the mission about the expediency of our returning, it seemed to me impossible to live another year with such a load of care + labor pressing upon me as I now have; but my health has improved the last weeks. It was a much greater trial for me to give up the idea of visiting you than I supposed it would be. Before we consulted the mission, I thought I had no will of my own about it; but when I found that they were going to decide in the negative, the tears would come in spite of me. I lost one night's rest and a day's disquiet. Since I have felt happy in their decision + have no wish to change it. If the Lord has anything for me to do, he can take care of me here as well as at home. There has been no time since we came that our absence would apparently be so disastrous to the interests of the mission as at present. We very much need reinforcing at Bad River; Husband has written the Board upon the subject. We hope to have help before long.

I have *much much* more that I wish to say but I fear if I sit up any longer, I shall have a visit from my old friend nervous headache tomorrow. Please remember me affectionately to old friends and write as soon as you receive this. Cannot some one of you write once a fortnight during the sickly season?

From Your Affectionate Daughter

Harriet Wheeler

On August 12, 1849, Harriet's father reports on Hannah's visit home.

I have had the Pleasure of seeing Hannah a few days but she has gone. My wife was very much disappointed of Hannah not coming home to stay, but as for myself I did not feel so. I was afraid if Hannah came home, she would be led into the wound for our Lowell has become, in my view, like vanity fair + if H was like Faithful she would suffer the same fate. She + her Husband came to my home the sixth day of July; we was very glad to receive them + H appeared well. Her friends were all glad to see her. They had a very Pleasant time. H wrote Mary that she was at home. Mary wrote back to me that she wanted to come but she had been sick. She wanted me to see if Newell + grandmamma won't send her money enough to come + see Hannah. I felt bad to have to go asking + I knew that N would not do anything. I waited about a week + I wrote her if the Shakers would pay her fare to + back from the cars, I would pay her passage on the cars down + the next day she come.

Hannah + Mr. Smith was gone to Dea Wetherbee's, but they came home + when Hannah saw Mary, she did not know her; her dress + cap altered her so. But they had a very Cordial Meeting. I find that Mary has not lost her affection for her friends. She told me Friday morn when I gave her the money to pay her fare, she felt very bad after she had written home. She was a great help to us. She appears the same as she used to be + would read with us + sing + be with us always in prayers. I hope Dear Harriet you will write her: Canterbury W/76 shaker village Square Shaker. N gave her a piece of sheeting; Mother gave her 2 table cloths + grandmother told uncle Jon to send her a piece of linen sheeting.

I suppose you will want to know if I like my son in law? I will tell you he appeared thin + then friends that saw him was pleased with him. He appears to be thoughtful.

So you will want to know the health of the city: it has been very good; it is now more sickly then has been. My paper tells me I must quit. Doct Hunting + wife was much pleased their present. Mrs. Hunting said the sugar was the nicest she ever saw + all the friends were pleased. And now dear children, you must write me often. It gives me great pleasure to hear from you + I hope if we should live till another summer that we shall have the pleasure of seeing you to Lowell. Remember us in your Prayers. Kiss all the dear grandchildren + tell them that grandpa + grandma want to see them *very much*.

From your Father S Wood

Dear Children you must excuse my bad spelling + writing. Remember I am an old man.

On January 8, 1850, Julia Wood brings Harriet up to date on events in Lowell. Her belated and almost casual mention of Harriet's nephew's death makes it clear that in mid-nineteenth-century America, suffering was common in the city as well as in the woods.

Our family are all in comfortable health. Newell and his wife are well. Their children have all been sick. I suppose you did not know that they have had another little son. He was six weeks old last Tuesday. He was a very healthy baby until about ten days since when he was taken with a long fever which terminated in death last Friday. Laura [Newell's wife] was in this afternoon; she says she does not know what to do with herself. She loved her baby *very much*, but she is very submissive. She feels that her little one has gone safely home and she would not call him back to this cold world again.

We received a letter from Hannah a few days since. She was well and in good spirits. She was anxious to have us come on there another summer, but I hardly think she will ever see us there. We have not the means to carry us there and if we had, I do not know that we should have the courage to start so long a journey.

Mr. and Mrs. Brooks have been called to see their oldest daughter. She had everything done for her which money and devoted parents could do for her, but all could not save her. I wish you could write to them. They are always so much interested in preparing your box; I feel that you are under some obligation to them.

The Wetherbees are all well. They're all at home. They always send their love.

Harriet, do you remember the Waught family? Ann, I believe, eloped and was married before you went away. Archibald was married three months before his parents knew it. About two months since, Nancy, the second daughter, went off unbeknownst to her parents with a man from Boston. It is said a bad man. She left a note on the table saying, "Dear Mother, I am away to be married." Since that time the youngest, only fifteen years old, went to Nashua with a young man seventeen and was married. They came back to Lowell and staid a few days. He went to some of his father's debtors and collected one hundred dollars, then they took the cars for Albany. His father went after them and found they had gone to New Orleans. By the way, his father is editor of the *Lowell Journal*. What must be those parents' feelings?

And now, Harriet, I think you will not need to take another *newspaper*.

We had a letter from Mary a few weeks since. Her health is not very good, says she is taking up a full cross and has constant pain. Poor child, we believe she is blinded. She wishes to be remembered to you and says if you come home, you must come and see her. She came home to see Hannah, but will not be able to come again. I do not think she is happy, but she thinks in this way to save her soul.

Tell the little ones that grandmother would like to see them very much and tell them all about their little cousins here. I would tell about that little one whose dear form I dressed for the grave a few days since. Little Sissy goes to the bed and says, "Baby gone; Baby gone." I would tell them how his father and mother and grandmother watched him all night expecting he would die every moment and many other things I would like to say to them, but I must close. Kiss them all for me. Ever your affect mother

J. H. Wood

Harriet's letter to her parents from La Pointe in February 1850 reveals that the woman whose Massachusetts minister worried about her docility has acquired the ability to gently assert herself with her parents, but she still longs for home and wants to be well dressed when she returns. The letter also reveals that the government's attempt to remove the Ojibwe has begun.

I trust I need not offer any apology for not writing oftener, longer or better letters. The mother of five children, the two youngest not able to go alone, surely has but little time for letter writing.

Husband has informed you of the recent communications our Agent has received from the Department at Washington. How soon or how materially they will affect our operations here we know not. Should the Indians be removed + the Board think it best to continue their Missions among them; we shall probably follow them; but the future is all dark + uncertain before us. You may perhaps suppose that the money expended at our station will be all lost; but we think we shall have no difficulty in disposing of our place. It is a fine location for a farm, the mining interest is rising rapidly and produce is very high in the country. Were our only object to make money we would never leave Bad River.

We shall probably visit home before we commen[ce] another station as we both feel the need of a little rest and change. We may possibly come next fall. I dare not think or say much about it, but oh, my dear parents, you do not know how much I want to see you.

Should we return next fall, what would be suitable for me in traveling dress + what for Julia and Emma? Would not calico be as suitable as anything? If there are any new patterns for sheet capes or little boys' aprons, please send them. If there is any clothing made, it should be large as our children are growing very fast and are large for their age. Will you add to our list three beech combs with tops?

The children send much love to Grandpapa + Grand mama. They talk a great deal about visiting you. Some time ago I told Lenny that if he would learn to read in the testament, I would ask his Grandpapa to buy him a nice little testament + have him write his own name + Lenny's in it. He has now learned to read so that he reads with us in the morning at worship + if you would buy him a testament, it would please him very much; I should like to have you expend two dollars for books suitable for children the ages of mine. Love to Susan Wetherbee + all the dear friends who take pains to inquire for us. *Do write as soon as you receive this.* Your Affec Daugh

H Wheeler

Apparently, Harriet has informed her stepmother that she has once again given birth. In her letter of April 30, 1850, Julia Wood promises to help make Harriet's "sickness dress," but also urges her stepdaughter to stop having children so frequently.

Private We received a letter from you two weeks since. We were very glad to hear of your returning health. I should think with your family, aside from all other cares, you would need *health, strength* and *wisdom*. I think it is very hard for you to have children so fast; it almost makes my head run round to think of it. A lady said to me this afternoon, "I think it is wrong for her and I think her Husband might prevent it, if he was disposed to do so." This has often been said to me before; I hope you will pardon me for writing what I have but I have written it for your benefit. You do not wish to part with any of the children you have, but I know you cannot desire to have the number increased. I pity you; I know you must have more care and anxiety than with your feeble health you are able to endure. I have tried to aid you as much as possible by making with some assistance your clothing. I have not carried anything into the society this year as they have been engaged with other things.

MAY 16. Monday, I went out and bought you the materials for your sickness dress. A lady came in after I had cut the sack and said she would make it. I got a dressmaker to work one day and a half on the dress; another one cut your Gingham, but I have not had time to finish the gingham + intended to send you a pattern but shall not be able to go out to get one for your children. Small figured calico or gingham are very pretty; everything in the shape of sack is worn here. You may make them with very little work; the one I have made for you will be warm as I have lined it. Ladies wear them very much for traveling as it makes a whole suit.

Your Father has written about Julia's [Harriet's stepsister's] health; she is better now than she was when he wrote. My own feelings in reference to the subject is *the will of the Lord be done*. It is true we should be very lonely without her as she is the only one left but to feel that she was *safely lodged* in the arms of her saviour would mitigate the pain of separation. With so frail a constitution, she must suffer much in such a world as this and she can never be very useful to others unless some change takes place.

Give my regards to all the friends there. Kiss the little ones for grandmother; tell them she has thought a great deal about them since she has been making their clothes and hopes they are very good obedient children and now I must say good by.

From your affect Mother

J A Wood

While Harriet stays home with their new child, Leonard Wheeler travels to the area in Minnesota where the government wants to move the Ojibwe, relishing the chance to explore new territory.

St. Louis River Sabbath Evening June 9, 1850

*D*ear Harriet,
    Last night we pitched our tents at this place to spend the Sabbath. It is at low end of Knife portage, one of the most wild + romantic spots you ever saw. In the middle of the stream before us is a huge mass of rock or rather island piled up some sixty or eighty feet high, the top of which is covered with a few scattering trees. On each side of this rock, the foaming water is tumbling in restless conversation. The portage takes us to the more navigable waters above. The distance across is some mile and a half through a fast path which is very comfortable walking. The geological structure of the country here is an upheaval of slate perpendicular, so that the stones stand up edge ways, hence the name *knife portage*. The slate sticks up through the soil in all quarters. Yesterday we made nine miles portage from Fond du Lac; this portage leading over the mountain as it did gave us a beautiful view of the farming below in several spots. The road through the portage was mostly good, with the exception of our sharp pitches. I think you would travel it without difficulty, + I almost thought we had better take our little family this way.

When he arrives in Minnesota, Leonard Wheeler meets other missionaries who have settled there and continues to enjoy the fresh landscapes.

Belle Prairie June 20, 1850

*D*ear Harriet
    We came here from Sandy Lake last week Saturday. I visited Gull Lake in company with brother [Frederick] Ayer[5] day before yesterday and returned last night, found Mr. [William] Warren's[6] family well. There are three lakes near each other, separated only by a narrow neck of land, and there are several beautiful sites for building. The Indians have made more extensive

improvements than I expected to find. The lakes are not sufficiently large to be very grand, but are truly beautiful. The good land though not very abundant, is sufficient for all their purposes. The timber is of the most excellent quality as is found in any quantity for building. Brother Ayer has given me an invitation to come + settle by him + engage with him in his school enterprise, but it would be premature to decide now what is our course of duty.

Crow Wing River

I never before saw a western Prairie. The Prairie may be said to begin here at Crow Wing + extends on indefinitely down the River, varying in width from two to five acres wide of good land. Some of it destitute of trees, + some of it covered with a scattered growth of small Oak, called the Oak Openings. These from their size and scattered position resemble an orchard; + the whole ground covered with a rich carpet of grass, fringed with flowers of every hue + of varieties entirely new to me, gives the prospect a fine appearance. The Season here is somewhat earlier than with us; crops look well, though the land is not as rich as the more southern prairies. Brother A has a beautiful building spot, + a chance for any quantity of land a man may need. Now I must bid you good bye, or perhaps you will not hear from us again till we come home. We have thus far been prospered in our journey. I shall have a long story to tell you when I get home. Tell the children to be good and obey mama. Love to all. From your husband.

L. H. Wheeler.

The Wheelers returned to Lowell in 1851. In this letter, Leonard writes to Mary Warren,[7] the daughter of Mary (Marie) Cadotte,[8] who was three-fourths Ojibwe, and Lyman Warren,[9] a Yankee trader. After both of her parents died, the Wheelers informally adopted Mary Warren, as her father had asked, but they left her behind in Bad River when they traveled east. A note at the top of this letter in Leonard Wheeler's handwriting says, "read with much pleasure February 2nd, 1872," indicating that twenty days before his death on February 22, 1872, Leonard still treasured his relationship with Mary Warren.

Lowell, March 6, 1851

*M*y Daughter Mary,

We have been happy to hear from Mr. Hall + Pulsifer[10] that you are doing well and making progress in your studies. I hope you will try and improve your time, in being useful in Mr. Hall's family, and also in making progress in your studies. Your future happiness and usefulness depend much upon the manner in which you spend the few years that are now immediately before you. We were glad to hear that your cousin George, and your relatives at La Pointe seem to appreciate the advantages that you enjoy. We wish you to remain in the mission till we return. We are expecting to return to Bad River, and hope then to be in a condition to bestow more attention upon the education of all our children, and give more efficiency to our school and all our operations among the Indians. I wish you would tell Moie and Anwin's wife, I wish they would both of them save me a mukluk or two of sugar, and I shall probably have something to give them in exchange, which they will like.

I will now tell you something about the children. Little Eddy is quite a smart little boy; he began to run along last November. He is a very busy, strong active child like Willy, but not as strong as Emmy. He very rarely cries, unless he is hungry or gets hurt. Emmy is all honesty and vinegar, and the transitions from one to the other are very sudden, but she is quite a favorite and is not in want of friends. Willy is at Bedford about a dozen miles from here, as wild, I expect, as ever. He often speaks of Mary at Bad River. I think Emily remembers you. A young lady came in the other day, and Emily says, "That's Mary." Leonard and Julia are living nearby us and send much love to Mary. They will have a good many new tunes to sing, I expect, when they come back to Indian country. Mrs. Wheeler, Leonard, Julia, the baby and I went down to Middleboro to see Mrs.

Sproat and we had a very pleasant visit. The children had a fine play together. We read several letters from California from Mr. Sproat. His description of his voyage around Cape Horn was very interesting. Lucy was considerably taller than Elvira. They both go to school and Mrs. Sproat is very comfortably off. She has a sister living with her who is a portrait painter. Middleboro is a very old town. I saw an old house there which was said to be built before King Philip's war; it looked very old. People tell a great many stories about the Indians that once lived in the place, but the Red men here have all been dead and gone a good many years.

We visited Boston which is a very large city. From the State House or some elevated place, you can see the vessels in the harbour, the masts looking like a great forest of dry trees. Other vessels you see coming into the harbor. They have many of them been on a long voyage across the ocean. In almost any other direction you can see the steam and smoke of the locomotives coming in from all parts of the country.

Mrs. Sproat sends much love to you and a valuable present also. I have often wished you were here; you would see many new and interesting things in this city of Spindles. They make all sorts of cotton cloth, calico and woolen goods. The cotton is all spun, and wove, and folded by machinery. The looms are so fixed that if a single thread breaks, they will stop. After it is woven, there is a machine which measures it in folds of just a yard in length, and then it is packed in boxes and sent off.

There is a quite a difference between the climate here and in Lake Superior. It is quite cold and there was a great deal of snow about New Year, but now the snow is nearly all gone and have been off for several weeks; the sleighs are all laid aside and the frost is most all out of the ground. The Indians and most of the inhabitants of La Pointe are now I suppose in the sugar camps. The weather is now as cold there or colder than it has been here this winter. We have had a good deal of rain here this winter and the changes of weather are quite sudden. In this respect, I like Lake Superior the best, for I have had a cold for more than a month past. I have now got me some good Indian rubber overshoes, and hope to be better soon.

Now I must bid you goodbye till we see you. Unless we hear something from Washington or from the Indian Country that shall decide us otherwise, you may expect us by the first of June. Mrs. Wheeler + the children send love.

Your friend and foster father

L. H. Wheeler

Harriet Wheeler adds this note:

Dear Mary,

I have been wanting to write you for a long time but really find no time to write letters. We have a great deal of company and I have a great many visits to make. I often wish you were here to enjoy the winter with us, but I hope you are making good progress in your studies and are also useful to Mrs. Hall. I expect to bring someone back to assist us in our family. So I hope we shall not be obliged to work as hard as we did last summer. I have purchased your dresses and think you will be very much pleased with them. Give my love to your Aunt also to Mr. Hall + Pulsifer families. Affec Yours H Wheeler

---

When the Wheelers return to Wisconsin, they leave Harriet's lonely father behind.

Lowell April 24, 1851

Dear Children,

Harriet, I never wanted to see you more + your family than I do now. I do want to see that Dear boy Edward that I had such a tussle with. I never shall forget that night, for I think I was wrong in trying to conquer him. I never shall forget the morning I carried you to the cars, how the little boy would pat

86

me on the shoulder + then look me in the face + laugh. Kiss the dear boy for me and all the dear children.

I remain your Affectionate Father

Sam L Wood

Harriet's stepmother, on the other hand, seems easily distracted from grief by social events.

Fall 51

Dear Children,
It is not two months since you left us and I suppose you are settled in your wilderness home. I was intending to give you a description of some weddings we have had here since you left as they are persons you know something of. Soon after you left, Mary A. Eyor was married to the Hon. Judge Prentice of Romeo, Michigan; Charlotte Cale to Mr. Smith of Syracuse, N Y. She had an expensive wardrobe: everything was made in Boston; but this affair was soon thrown into shade by the wedding of Miss Mariette Pead, daughter of Peansom Pead about twenty, to a Mr. Stevens, the keeper of the Revere house in Boston aged fifty-five. She was married at her father's on Taylor Street at ten in the morning, received her friends from eleven until two. Her Husband presented her with two thousand dollars worth of jewelry; she had a box of diamonds. She was in NY some weeks before getting ready; dresses were bought and made there. He has a daughter at home older than herself.

Within a few days we have heard of the death of Henry's wife [Henry is Harriet's brother]. She has left a little babe two months old. Hannah was there three weeks and left only four days before her death; she thought she was better. H [Hannah] says it was consumption. We feel very sad for H [Henry]; I cannot think what he will do with those two little children off there among strangers. He did not say anything about what he intended to do and we have received a letter from Hannah; she said he said nothing to her about what he intended to do. I do hope and pray that this sad event may be sanctified to him and to us all. We have heard from Mary two or three times since you left. She is very anxious we should visit her this summer.

I want to see the little ones very much. I want to kiss that little Eddy. Give my love to all. And kiss all the children for me and write soon.

Affc Mother Wood

If I had the time and patience I should like to give you a description of a costume which has been adopted by some of the females in this city and some other Places. They sew no skirts, but pants like gents only they are large and gather in the bottom; the upper garment comes a little below the knees. They wear a broad brimmed hat. A married lady passes here every day with one on. She has a little boy 9 years old. It has produced quite excitement. They first began to come out in the first part of the evening and the street was crowded with men and boys. The fourth of July comes next week and there is to be a large portion of bloomers & a Gent remarked to me the other day that his wife wanted to have one but if she did, she would not have his company on the street. There is to be a large company from Boston here on the fourth on purpose to see them but I have said enough and now dear H [Harriet]. If you have the patience to read what I have written, I shall be glad for it has been written in a room so dark that I can hardly read it myself.

Desperate for news of the Wheelers, Julia Wood suggests that her grandchildren Leonard and Julia are old enough to write, and Julia responds. The contrast between her cheerful note and the anguished letter from her mother that follows shows how well the Wheelers protect their children from their difficulties. Also, Julia's delight in the environment her mother frequently describes as mosquito infested is typical of a pioneer daughter. While the women born in the West tended to savor this new world, their mothers usually yearned for the place they had left.

Bad River Sept 21 1852

*D*ear Grandmother,

I cannot write very well but I think I will not wait any longer before I try to write you a letter. I go to school and study geography and arithmetic and spelling besides reading and writing. I know almost all the multiplication table. We have got some new geography and reading books.

A few weeks ago father and mother and all of us took a trip to Montreal River about fifteen miles from here. There is a beautiful waterfall there; we went among the rocks and hills. Eddy and I were very much afraid, but Emma laughed and wanted to have the water poured on her head. We picked a great many pretty agates on the shore. I send Aunt Julia this pretty flower that I picked there on a high mountain rock. Mother fell down in the water. Mr. Pulsifer lost his wife but he hunted around and found her again. Emma says, "Tell Grandmother I will send her some figs and candy." Eddy says, "Tell Grandmother she must come here." Willy can read very well and spell. Give my love to all my uncles and aunts and to Grandpapa and to all my cousins and to Mrs. Wetherbee and her family. Father and mother and aunt Abby send their love to all.

From your affectionate granddaughter

Julia M. Wheeler

Bad River Sept 27 1852

*D*ear Parents,

I fear you will think my long silence unaccountable; but could you know all my reasons for not writing I think you would pardon it. I was called to La Pointe to see a very sick women. When I returned, our darling little Eddy met me at the landing. He followed me into the house. I stepped to the table to lay down some articles I had in my hand when I heard him scream and felt him clinging to my dress. As I put my hand down to take him up, I found his dress was hot. The truth immediately flashed upon my mind. I sprung to the door and put him into a barrel of water, but the poor child was dreadfully scalded. His father gave him a large dose of paregoric, yet it was some minutes before we could hold him still enough to dress his burn. We wrapped him up in flour as well as we could and he soon went to sleep. I often wished during his sickness that you could see him. Mr. W often remarked that he did not think there was one in the family that could bear it with the patience and fortitude he did. His efforts to keep from crying were truly affecting. The night after the accident the bandage on one of his limbs slipped down. As I went to replace it, he began to cry. I said to him, "Now Eddy, don't cry. Be mama's brave boy." He looked up to me with a sweet smile and said, "Ma, I won't cry now." And although the limb was raw and it must have been very painful, yet he lay still and quiet until I had put the bandage on again. We were conscious about him for a few days but it healed kindly and he is now running around as well as ever. He is the general comforter and peace maker in the family and a pet with everyone. Mrs P [Pulsifer] tells me some time she fears we are making an idol of him and he will be . . .

———————

Harriet's part of the letter ends here, in midsentence. Apparently concerned about the anguish it causes his wife to describe Eddy's accident and its aftermath, Leonard Wheeler tells her to stop writing and brings the letter to a close for her.

*H*arriet is not very well tonight and though she was expecting to write you a long story, I told her to stop right here, and I would finish for her. Some of the friends shall hear from us again before long.

L. H. Wheeler

4.

Standing with the Ojibwe against Removal and Smallpox

In 1842, the Ojibwe of northern Wisconsin signed a treaty with the U.S. government selling their land but reserving the right to occupy it. No problems were anticipated with this agreement since the whites wanted only to mine the territory. But around 1850, the government claimed complete ownership of the property, telling the Ojibwe that they must remove to Minnesota to receive their annuities. Some Ojibwe did go to Sandy Lake, Minnesota, where they initially found only unhealthy food. After many died, the Ojibwe received payments they considered inadequate and returned home. Those who survived the journey refused to leave again, even though that meant they would receive no government payments.

When Leonard Wheeler traveled east during the winter of 1851, he went to Washington, D.C., where he and Rev. S. B. Treat of the American Board of Commissioners for Foreign Missions attempted to impress upon the commissioner of Indian Affairs, Luke Lea,¹ the importance of allowing the Ojibwe to remain on the southern shore of Lake Superior. When Leonard Wheeler returned to Bad River, he told the Ojibwe that adopting white customs and dress could save them from removal, so the Ojibwe followed his suggestion.

Both the Wheelers and the Ojibwe endured much anguish until the government deeded the Ojibwe the reservations at Bad River, Lac Courte Oreilles, Red Cliff, and Lac du Flambeau on September 30, 1854. On July 11, 1853, Harriet Wheeler writes her parents about their difficulties.

he little ones are in bed. Husband has gone to Bad River, and I have seated myself to commune with you for a few minutes. Do not attribute my long silence to forgetfulness, or ingratitude. Could you know how often every day and I might almost say every hour in the day my thoughts are with you, you would not think me chargeable with either; but the truth is whenever I think of writing a letter, there are so many things demanding immediate attention that writing is deferred to a more convenient season.

So many important events have transpired since I last wrote you I know not where to commence. The last winter was one of the most dreary, lonely, and trying ones we have ever spent in the country. Many things combined to make it such.

The breaking up of the Mission here, and the confused state of Indian affairs threw a gloom over the future. Often did I flee into my bedroom to hide the tears I could not control; through it all, our children were as happy and joyous as ever. They knew nothing of the crushing weight of care, anxiety and perplexity upon their parents. We often spoke of this as a cause for thankfulness.

The heat and burden of the day press heavily upon dear Husband. He has grown old fast since we returned from the East, and I sometimes look anxiously forward to the future. He is obliged to attend to all the secular affairs of our station, and has charge of the property of the Board here—oversees all our own and the Indians farming + the Dr for both places—Chairman of the Board of county commissioners, beside numberless other things too small to mention perhaps, but nevertheless break in upon his time and divert his mind from his more appropriate work. The truth is there is work enough here for three good men. Husband said to me Saturday night as he came from his study, "There is so much to be done here and the work is so great that somehow I feel like shrinking from it."

To human appearance, our people were never in better condition to profit by the preaching of the gospel and direct Missionary work than at present. We think there is hardly a possibility of removing them. Not a single family have gone yet from the Lake and they are fully determined not to go. They have lived two years without their payments and find they do not starve nor freeze.

Indeed, I doubt very much whether there is a band of Chipeways beyond the Mississippi with all their annuities that are as well fed and clothed as ours are. I must confess I was somewhat surprised to learn that Dr Boutwell had advocated the removal at last.

I can let you behind the curtain a little. When Gov Ramsey[2] first made the attempt to remove these Indians, knowing that Dr. B had great influence with the Indians, he went to him to get him to assent in the effort and first he positively refused to have anything to do with it. He told him he did not approve of an indiscriminate removal: he did not think it was just or right to remove civilized Indians who had built houses, and were living comfortably in them. Gov R assured him that *that* was not the intention of Government. And after much coaxing and pleading and the promise of four dollars a day, Mr. B consented to be engaged in it. Now, if the country west of the Mississippi is so much better for the Indians, and if there they are free from that bane of the red man whiskey, why not remove all? Surely it is no benevolence to the civilized ones to leave them where they "cannot live" and where they must inevitably fall before whiskey.

I was conversing a few days since with a gentleman who has just returned from the agency west of the Mississippi. He has been living in that vicinity for the last year and has been in the employment of the Government. He says he saw just before he left drunken Indians about the Agency, and about the farm house and said he they can get a barrel of whiskey there as easy as they can get a bottle here. They have only to cross the Mississippi or go down about twenty miles and they can get all they want. We have had but very little drinking here the past season. Just after our Indians came from the sugar bush one of them took some sugar and went to the Ontonagon + exchanged it for whiskey. He brought a keg to the gardens and commenced selling it to the Indians. Mr. W [Wheeler] prosecuted him.

A Steamer is in sight + I must hasten to close this. Tell Julia I commenced a letter to her three months ago but was obliged to put it aside to take care of Simon one of our native Christians who was brought down from the sugar bush to die with us. He was a lovely Christian + his last end was peace. You will probably see some notice of him in the *Herald*.

Mr W has just returned from B.R. He and the children join me in much love to all.

Very Affec
Your Daughter
Harriet

———————

While Harriet simply calls Simon a "lovely Christian," Leonard Wheeler's account of Simon's life and death for the Missionary Herald *emphasizes Simon's conversion not only from heathenism but also from Catholicism, although Leonard somehow manages to fuse these two commitments. Leonard undoubtedly has a more acute sense of doctrinal distinction than his wife because he must report to the board on his conversions in order to secure its support for his work.*

From *the Missionary Herald*[3]

Mr. Wheeler has given a brief sketch of a pious Indian, who died a few months ago, which will be read with pleasure.

When Simon came under the influence of the mission, he was a Roman Catholic; but his mind was in the darkness of heathenism, in all that relates to spiritual religion. But when he came to a knowledge of the truth, he forsook the errors of the Romish church, and embraced the gospel. His Catholic friends tried in vain to dissuade him from attending our meetings. The truth took deep root in his heart; and he was ready to forsake all and follow Christ. He united with the church in the fall of 1850; and since that time he has always maintained a consistent Christian walk, so far as we know. Indeed, we may say that he has been a convert of more than ordinary integrity and decision.

Simon loved his Bible. He always greeted us with a smile, when we visited him for the purpose of religious instruction. He was constant in his attendance upon our meetings. Though most of the time a cripple, he could often be seen hobbling through the deep snow that his soul might be fed with the bread of life, when many Christians, more enlightened, would have felt themselves fully justified in staying at home.

The fruit of his piety was seen in his determination to forsake every vestige of heathenism. The white man's religion, the white man's medicine, and the white man's civilization, were what he wanted. We were never pained to hear of his attending an Indian feast, and rarely was he present, as a spectator even, at any heathen ceremonies.

That his last end should be peace, was what we might have expected. He had been a suffering invalid for years, from a white swelling in the knee-joint. When he went into the sugar camps last spring, he took cold, and was thrown into a fever. We had not seen him for a little time, when one day we met him coming down the river in his canoe, to see if we could not do something for him. He needed medical aid; he needed a wholesome diet; he needed every attention which we can suppose a sick man to need in an Indian lodge, at this cold season of the year, destitute of food, with no comfortable clothing, and nobody to take care of him, save an infirm widowed mother. What he himself wanted most, was the privilege of being with us when he died. He felt he should not recover, as he was in the last stages of typhus fever. We did what we could to make him comfortable, and felt that it was a privilege to stand by and witness such an illustration of the sustaining power of the gospel.

When asked if he did not wish to recover, he said, "When I was well, I gave my body and all I have to the Lord, to do with me just as he should think best." At another time he said, "I am tired of waiting; I long to depart." He was fond of singing, and had his favorite hymns, which were a great comfort to him when he was sick; one in particular, which I sang to him just before he died, "Jesus, my all, to heaven has gone," or, as it is in his language, "Jesus in whom I trust, has gone above; I see the way he has gone, and I shall follow him." Though his tongue was palsied in death, his lips moved to the words as they were sung, and the tear of joy beamed in his eye. This was his last conscious act. What a transformation! To pass from the sorrows, pains and sins of these ignorant and degraded sons of the forest, to the presence of the Savior!

Although the Wheelers obviously have a positive impact on the religious commitments of others, in her letter of July 17, 1853, Harriet's stepmother doubts that the children Harriet persists in having can acquire an adequate religious education in the woods. She also fears Harriet's patience with her children's religious development does not acknowledge the reality that they could perish, unsaved, at any moment.

I often think of you on the Sabbath and wonder how you can make it profitable and interesting to your children. Here we have the Bible class, the Sabbath school, the minister to preach, Sabbath school concerts and a great variety of exercises to interest our children. There you must be preacher and teacher and instructor. It is true he has said, "My grace is sufficient for thee" and it must require *grace* and *wisdom* to instruct your children on that subject on which most of all they should be instructed without making it an old story.

Our minister in speaking of the early conversion of children not long since reminded me of what I heard you say when you were here: you hardly dared urge your children to immediate submission fearing they would think they had done so when they had not and rest upon a false hope. Mr. Foster says death does not *wait* for them nor for us; they may be taken from us and we from them and then how happy shall we be if we have done our whole duty in urging them to that saviour who said suffer the *little ones* to come to me. Perhaps you will think it is ill-timed and out of place for me who have been *so deficient* in the discharge of my duty to say a word to others who are more faithful, but there is one thing I do desire that all our children and grandchildren may be so instructed and may so live that they may all be admitted through the gates into the city. When we think of the temptations, trials and conflicts and continual warfare which all must pass through, well may we exclaim, "Who is sufficient for these things but he who save all that will put their trust in him."

Perhaps Julia Wood's anxiety about salvation results from fears that she shares responsibility for Mary Wood becoming a Shaker. In any case, she and her husband

finally visit Mary at the Shaker community at Harvard, Massachusetts, where Mary
has moved from the community in Canterbury, New Hampshire. According to an
earlier letter, Stephen Goodhue, a former resident of Lowell whom the Woods also
encounter at Harvard, used to be a Millerite. Perhaps he moved on to the Shakers
when he did not ascend to heaven on October 23, 1844, as the Millerites believed they
would. Julia Wood's warning to Goodhue against dancing is probably inspired by the
fact that Shakers dance and sing at their religious services.

JULY 25. Since writing the above I have been to Harvard to see Mary. Your Father, and myself went up in the morning and came back at night. We saw Mr. Goodhue, Mrs. Hedge and they seemed very happy to see us. Mr. G said he should not try to make Shakers of us; he knew us too well; said he should let the Lord do that. I told him I thought the Lord would have done it if it ever were to be done. I asked him if he danced any because he was obliged to be careful about it; he would burn, but he could sing for them. Mrs. Hedge and Mary are the cooks; they have forty in the family. She seemed very happy. I had but little time to see her as there was other company there. The Elder said I must have a book and gave me one lately published. I have been looking at it a little and it is astonishing how any person who has had any religious instruction can be so blinded, but it shows us our weakness when left to ourselves.

Our family are in usual health. They were out to church yesterday. We had a converted Catholic to preach for us all day; we like him very much. He was educated at Cork; he thinks we are in great danger from the Catholics: the place that is laid for our destruction in the old world is deep and broad and it depends upon the American church whether that plan should be carried out. He urged of Christians to pray for his poor deluded countrymen.

But I am drawing near the end of my paper and I have not said one word to the little ones. Are they all well *good* and *happy*? Do they all love one another and try to make each other happy? Do they love to study? I suppose Leonard and Julia have received our letters before this. When will they answer them? We have not heard from you for a long time. Shall we not have a letter soon? I suppose you are very busy but do write a little.

97

Kiss all the children for me and accept this from
Your Affectionate Mother
J. M. Wood

———————

In In Unnamed Wisconsin, *J. N. Davidson cites the following letter, which the Wheeler's oldest child, Leonard, wrote at La Pointe on August 31, 1853, as perhaps the last evidence of cannibalism among the Ojibwe.* [4] *The account of a ten-year-old boy seems a slender basis for such a charge, especially since the part of his note suggesting that an Ojibwe enjoyed eating a Frenchman lacks the lyricism of the earlier, more benign, report. In other words, the language describing cannibalism seems more appropriate to a ten-old-boy than to an Ojibwe funeral orator.*

ear Grandfather,
   I have often wished to see you and sometimes dream of being at home with you and then I wake and find myself in my own little bed and it makes me disappointed all day. Aunt Abby thinks Julia and I understand our arithmetic very well. I expect I shall be able to keep your accounts by and by.

I was going to tell you about an Indian funeral. Julia has written some to Aunt Julia about it, but she did not tell what the Indians said in their speeches to the dead child. I understood them, so I will tell you some as near as I can remember. Old Buffalo, the first chief, made his speech first and told the child it would take him two days to get to the spirit land and before he got there, his friends would come to meet him and that the fishes would jump into the canoe and would be his food and when he got to the mouth of Bad River, he would hear the roar of the guns of the spirit land and his friends would come and meet him and would be his playmates. One of them said, "Once I shot a Frenchman + blowed his brains out. Then I cut a piece of his flesh and ate it and it was very good and you may have the same for your food on your journey."

This is all I have to say.
Please give my love to all.

From your own grand son
Leonard H. Wheeler Jr

On October 20, 1853, Harriet reports to her parents from La Pointe that the government has broken down and resumed paying annuities to the Ojibwe in northern Wisconsin.

I have now time only to tell you that we are all alive and well and will you believe me when I tell you that we are just in the midst of the bustle and excitement of *Payment*. How often have I wished you were here. The last few days America does not contain a happier company than is congregated on this island tonight I have been out this eve to some of the lodges to rejoice with those that do rejoice. The payment has thus far been one of the best that had ever been made They have a great many more goods than usual. This Payment took us all by surprise. We knew nothing about it until the Agent came to make the payment. Some of our people were so happy and so excited that they could not sleep at all the first night.

Leonard adds a note on October 27, 1853.

*O*ur Indians are made very happy in receiving their annuities, paid once more at La Pointe. It is now almost certain that no further attempts will be made to remove these Indians. There is but little doubt that the old order of things will be restored. That the farmers, carpenters, Blacksmiths will be given back to them, & missionaries be encouraged to go on with their labors as formerly. The late efforts to remove the Indians has not only proved a failure, but are now clearly seen by the Department at Washington to have originated with a few designing men who wanted the Indians removed that they might get their money. As astonishing amount of fraud has been discovered and the former agent[5] is now under arrest by the U.S. Govt to answer for some of his villainous conduct. The Lord reigns. We hope for brighter days ahead. Pray for us, Our Indians were never in a more hopeful condition to be operated upon religiously + we need much wisdom + grace to discharge the duties that will devolve upon us. Good bye for the present with love to all the friends.

But as Harriet first reports to her parents on February 11, 1854, the Wheelers and the Ojibwe must deal with a smallpox epidemic the following winter.

You will learn by Julia's letter that the Small Pox is here. Two have died with it and there are a number of others sick at La Pointe. There were people exposed before the nature of the disease was known. As soon as it was ascertained to be the Small Pox, they sent for Mr. W [Wheeler]. He happened to have some vaccine matter that was sent to the Mission in 52. He used one scab here and took the other to La Pointe. The one here proved a failure but the other was good. Four days ago a woman came here from L.P. bringing a little girl who had a fine arm & just in the right state to vaccinate from. Mr. W immediately vaccinated most of the people here who had not been vaccinated before. As soon as he can get the materials, he will vaccinate everybody in this vicinity. We have disbanded our schools and shall have no meeting for the present. Mr. W has sent word to L.P. to have no one come here from there unless sent by the Board of Health and has told our people not to gather. He advised them not to visit from house to house but to remain quietly at home.

It has seemed very lonely here to day no one moving about. The people acquiesce very cheerfully in any regulation Mr. W proposes. One man told me yesterday that the Indians here had given their bodies to Mr. W. They trusted in him and anything he told them to do they should do. This disease is a fearful one anywhere but much more so here in this isolated place where there are no physicians—but little medicine, and where the habits of the people are so peculiarly favorable for the spreading and retaining of any contagious disease.

Our family are well now if we except the three youngest children who are having the whooping cough. They have however had it there comparatively light. Quite a number of children have it here; some very hard. Two have died with it.

Our meetings have been unusually solemn and interesting of late. We think there are some here who feel the importance of religions and are anxious to know what they shall do to be served. Last Saturday eve we have a very interesting female prayer meeting. We regret very much the necessity of giving up our meetings just now; but we would be still and see what the Lord will do. We know it is safe to trust in Him.

I have felt for some time past exceedingly anxious about our children. Oh, it is a fearful thing to see them exposed every day & every hour to death and yet without hope. I have no doubt my dear parents but that you pray for them, but I have felt for some time past that it would be exceedingly gratifying to unite with you in a concert of prayer for them. I have thought probably that the hour from eight to nine Sabbath eve would be as convenient to you as any. Please inform me in your next what you think of it. Allow me here to express my thanks for all the interest you have manifested in their spiritual welfare. The advice and warnings you have given us have been fully appreciated & we do sincerely thank you for it. Husband united with me much love to you *all*.

Very Affect

Your Daughter

Dear Grandparents,

We are all well and hope you are the same. Mother would write you if she had time to do so. She has to work very hard and sits up at night to sew. The small pox is at L P and yesterday father vaccinated the Indians till he was faint and then mother vaccinated a while. One of the first chiefs is dead. He was the chief orator in the place. I am afraid that little Fredy will get the small pox. He loves me very much and when I come home from school he comes running to me and laughs and then he calls, "Aunty, Aunty." I will send you a lock of his hair.

FEB. 10 yesterday we heard that an old woman was dead. She died of the small pox. A good many people are sick with it. We are going to have a pest house. Our school is broken up and Father has vaccinated Fredy. Freddy's looks well this morning. I send much love to you and all my little cousins and Aunts and Uncles. Good bye

From your affectionate

Julia Maria Wheeler

Mishkig River March 6, 54

*D*ear Parents,

I had intended to write you and several other Lowell friends long letters by this mail, but the past fortnight has been one of peculiar trial and anxiety with us. We have passed through all the horrors of the Small Pox. A fortnight ago, a company of Indians came here from across the Lake in a state of the greatest excitement and alarm. Three or four of their number had been taken down with the Small Pox. These they had left behind. Mr. Wheeler immediately vaccinated all of them, but the next day two were taken down. Mr. W fitted up a house and put them into it and hired a Frenchman and his wife who had had the disease to take care of them. The next day there were three others brought down. One of them had the most virulent kind, the confluent Small Pox, and died in about a week after he was taken. The others are all rapidly recovering, and we think will be able to be out this week. We have all been much exposed, particularly Mr. W as he visited the patients almost every day. We have used every preventative in our power; I smoked Mr. W most thoroughly I can assure you every time after coming from the Hospital. We were all vaccinated again; all took well excepting Willie. Mr. W's arm and mine were very lame. The families that have been exposed have been kept entirely separate from the others; the disease is arrested. We are all in the hands of our Heavenly Father, and here we feel we are safe. We do find it good to trust in the Lord.

We think our Indians are making progress. Six families are now getting lumber for houses this spring. Every step they take in civilization adds to our labor. Mr. W must see that their lumber is hewed right—that their underpinnings are put down right—and watch at every step. They are like so many ignorant children who must be taught every thing. How we are to get through this spring is more than I can tell. I often fear Mr. Wheeler will break down under his accumulating labors but I try to remember that sufficient unto the day is the evil thereof.

You will with this receive our List. With regard to the bonnets I should like to have you select some such as you think suitable, not very expensive. Mary thought that perhaps green with white trimming would be as becoming as anything. She wishes to consult your taste, however; she has black hair and eyes, complexion brunette. Mr. W. has put down something for each of the children because they think so much of finding something in the box for them. If not too much trouble, I would like to have Julia's cloak cut, a pattern sent. For Freddy's whistle, perhaps something more useful had better be substituted. Will sister Julia please purchase three or four little dolls such as she had in her cottage, one of them a little larger so that will answer for mother and her family? In purchasing the remnants I would like to have six yds of it cherry for a quilt.

I must now close as we wish to send our mail to La Pointe this afternoon. I must apologize for my short & disjointed letter; my hand trembles so it is almost impossible to write. We received a letter from you last week for which we must sincerely thank you. Give much love to all—from all of us.

Your Affec Daughter
Harriet Wheeler

The letter Julia Wheeler writes her grandmother on November 18, 1854, suggests that the Wheelers now enjoy a lively social life at Bad River.

*D*ear Grandmother,

We are all well except Mother; she took a trip on the lake a few days ago and they had a cold time and it made her almost sick. Henry Blatchford[6] and his family have come back from Crow Wing and I am very glad for now I can play with Hatty and Maggy. Mr. Pulsifer and his wife and Mr. Welton[7] and his wife and Edwin Hall[8] and Pony the horse have come. We are very glad that they have come. We went to La Pointe last summer and while we were there, Mr. Gilbert[9] and his wife and two children, their names were Lucy and Grace—sometimes they came to our house and we had very good times together. Mrs. Watrous, the wife of the former Indian agent and her daughter Madaline came to La Pointe last summer. They visited at our house four or five times. While they were going home, the steam boat they were on burnt up and they were lost. Little Madaline's body was found and sent home to be buried. We felt very sad to hear about it. The Mother's body was not found.

There is a settlement began somewhere on the lake. Mr. Whittlesey[10] his wife and child who have been here several months live there now. Mrs. Whittlesley, father and mother and there family have come to live with them. A few days ago Mother, father and Leonard went to see them. The boys got acquainted in a minute and mother says she got acquainted with Mrs. very quick.

Yesterday I told Fred that grandmother had gone way off and then he kept saying, "Go upstairs kiss grandmother; I go upstairs kiss grandmother." Father, mother, Miss Spooner and all the children and myself send their love to you and the rest. Good bye

From your affectionate

Julia M. Wheeler

Harriet Wheeler's continuation of Julia's letter indicates that La Pointe, too, has plenty of social activity. She seems relieved to have it behind her when she returns to Bad River, but she takes unambiguous pleasure in the treaty the government signed with the Ojibwe, deeding them the reservations at Bad River, Lac Courte Oreilles,

*Red Cliff, and Lac du Flambeau. But as the Ojibwe's difficulties abate, the Wheelers'
health difficulties escalate.*

We have had a very busy summer. Our house at La Pointe was thronged
with company most of the time. We have seen all we want of fashionable society. We have met with some most excellent people. We have received
all the attention and kindness which was probably best for us to receive, and
have had some valuable presents.

This summer has been an eventful one to our people. They have made
a treaty with the Gov. selling most of their lands east of the Mississippi. The
Gov. here made reservations for the Indians where they desired it. Bad River is
one of those reservations. To think if the President ratifies the treaty, which he
undoubtedly will, our people have a permanent home. This treaty has more
than realized our most sanguine hopes. We shall write you more fully about it
as soon as we are able.

I have been hoping to write you a long letter ever since our return from L.P.
but have not been able to. I came very near being killed instantly on our way
from L.P. here. We came each in the night in order to avoid the high winds which
prevail during the day at this season of the year. Mr Pulsifer was steering the boat.
The rest of the men were towing on the beach a large tree of flood wood that had
floated on into the Lake. When the men left the boat, threw their oars directly
across it. As we came to the tree, the oars hit it, an oar pin just back of them
acted as a fulcrum. They bounced up, and fell directly across the top of my head.
They were very large heavy oars. Mr. W [Wheeler] seeing what had happened,
sprang into the boat and threw some cold water into my face + on my head. I
was very cold, faint and sick at my stomach with a distracting pain in my head.
We reached home about two o'clock in the morning. I suffered much for a week
from a severe pain in my head and almost constant nausea. My head was cupped
and kept wet constantly with cold water. In about a week, I had a discharge of
clotted blood from my head which relieved it very much + it is now usually well.

Mr. Wheeler had a dreadful fall yesterday afternoon. He fell from a building
fourteen feet onto the hard frozen ground. He struck on to his hip and lower

part of his back. He suffered dreadfully yesterday afternoon + the first part of
the night, but was very much relieved before morning. He has but little fever
and seems decidedly better this morning. I should not have written you about
it until he was well, but we have an opportunity to send to L.P. now and may
not have again for two or three weeks as our river is just freezing. Mr. W intends
writing you and the John St. Church as soon as he is able to. I feel very anxious
about him, but hope he has seen the worst of it.

Newell and Laura are indeed afflicted. I cannot yet realize that dear Little
Laura is gone, but oh, how comforting the thought that she is safely housed in
those blessed mansions where sin and sorrow never come. Do give much love
to them and tell them we most deeply sympathize with them in this trial. We
loved the sweet child while living + shall now love to think of her as an angel
in heaven. May we all meet there, not one be found missing.

Give much love to all who inquire, for I hope to write you more particularly
about the children before long. They are all well + send much love. I fear you
will not be able to read this as my hand trembles as I find it almost impossible
to write. Do write soon.

Very Affec
Your Daughter
Harriet

Bad River March 31/55

Dear Parents
I remarked to Mrs. P [Pulsifer] yesterday that I was almost ashamed
to send my list home, it was so long since I had written. She replied she did not
think my mother would wonder at my silence if she knew how much sickness
our families had had this winter. We are now all of us well, but it is the first
time we have been so since we returned from LaPointe last fall. I have had a fit
sickness which confined me to my room some days and I am now just recovering from the effects of two Whitlows" one on each thumb which completely
disabled me for about three weeks. They were the most painful things I ever

endured. Leonard's health has been very miserable this winter. He has been able to attend school but very little for the year past. He suffers from chronic inflammation of the mucous membrane of the stomach.

Julia has suffered much from the effects of her burn. It seemed to produce entire prostration of the nervous system. She is better and will escape with but one permanent scar and that a high neck dress will cover. Mr. W's back is much better. Yet it is by no means well. If he works hard or walks far he suffers from lameness. Our people are now all at their sugar camps and Mr W. and Leony have gone up to the sugar bush to attend meetings with the people tomorrow.

You have probably heard before this that the treaty is ratified at Washington and our people now have a permanent home. We can hardly realize that it is so. You can scarcely conceive what a change the past year has made in our condition and prospects, yet our past experience has been such that we would not trust in man, we would not trust in the Government, but we will trust in the Lord God of Israel. Oh my dear parents, *it is good* to trust in Him at all times. He can and does bring light out of darkness.

There have been dark days since we returned to this country and I have often exclaimed to myself, "Oh, why did we ever come back here?" But it is all clear to me now. Probably during no four years of his life has Mr W. been able to accomplish so much for the real good of the people as he has done during the storm through which we have just passed. The Gov. are now pursuing precisely the policy with these Indians that Mr. Treat and Wheeler urged when they were at Washington.

You have probably before this seen the letter Mr. W wrote the John St church.[12] In that you will learn the spiritual condition of our people. At one last communion season, one Indian woman was received into the church and there are others who seem to be inquiring what they shall do to be saved. Julia felt considerable interest in the subject of religion during her sickness, but I feel it is wearing off now. Lenny feels deeply at times. He told me a short time since that he often wished he had died when he was an infant, for he felt as if he could never be a Christian. I feel exceedingly anxious about them. But is it not our privilege to leave our impenitent children into the hands of our Heavenly Father? Is it not one of the *all cares* he permits us to cast upon him?

We received your letter recently dated Nov. We were sorry to hear that mother's health was so poor. I have tried hard to make up my mind to send all our list to Boston this year. Bur we feel as if we could hardly get along without *expecting* and *receiving* a box from Lowell. Abba often asks, "What would you do, Harriet, without your mother." God grant I may be spared the bitter experience of knowing. If your health is no better, please give the list to Dea Thompson and if Julia, Laura or Susan Wetherbee would look after a few things, he could furnish the articles. Please get a dressmaker to fit my dresses and make it as easy for yourself as possible. Will someone please send a street cape pattern for myself and Julia?

The Wheelers have accepted the philosophy of their time that children who do not pay their own way make undisciplined adults. So, the Wheeler children farm along with the Ojibwe and their parents to raise the money for their educations. By current standards this may seem harsh, but given the vicissitudes of life in the late nineteenth century, preparing children to take responsibility for their own lives may have been prudent. It certainly served the Wheeler children well when their parents became ill.

The children send five dollars which you will please accept as a present from them. It is some of the avails of their gardening. They have now 150 bushels of potatoes in the cellar for sale which will bring them a dollar a bushel. I have just had an order to day for 50 bushels at that price. When they sell their potatoes they will have two hundred dollars. This we call their education fund. We do not send you this money to pay you for your trouble, for we know it will not. It is the first five dollars they have ever sent you, but we hope it will not be the last. They certainly owe you a debt of gratitude they can never repay.

Please remember us affectionately to all our friends. Abba + all send love
Affect Yours Harriet

On May 26, 1855, Susan Wetherbee writes Harriet, rejoicing in the progress the missionary family has made.

y Dearest Early Friend, My own Harriet,

This quiet morning hour shall waft me to thee in thy distant missionary home. Oh, might I but seat myself for one short hour by thy side and look into that "soul lit face," which it was my privilege so often to view in days, "Lang sine"—but it may not be, and so my Pen must compensate as best it may the want of nearer communion. Your Sister Julia yesterday read me your letter home. I gave it a tearful welcome—And your way, it seems, is bright now, and you feel that your place of labor is there. I was struck with the fact that you have had cause for regretting your return there; and still I think you consider the last few years as the most useful of your Wisconsin missionary labor. "The darkest wave has bright foam near it," but tis not always discernable to the struggling tempest tost voyager. But dear H [Harriet], the Saviour knows, and he will not forget your devotion to that benighted people. And I suppose I should congratulate you that your way is made plain there, fitter as you both are with a knowledge of the language of the Indians and from long experience have become acquainted with their prejudices, & predilections, and manner of life; you have indeed a reserve fund, if so I may express it, and one that is not exactly transferable either, and so "God speed you," dear friends, and impart unto you both needed wisdom and grace for your work.

"The Cross is heavy; but the Crown; the Crown"! I sympathize with you in your desires for the spiritual good of your own family. May those dear Children, Leonard & Julia, early give their hearts to the Saviour. Poor Julia suffered much, did she not, from her burn but it may prove good for her that she has suffered affliction even at this early age. I know the anxiety and care which sickness brings into a family, and would express my sympathy dear H for you. "Oh for the wings of a Dove" I would land me some quiet Evening 'er the season of Snow returns again, at your dwelling, and greet you with one sweet kiss, maybe I should be no respecter of persons, but husband, Children and all would have to take it, but as I am likely to soar aloft at present, only in imagination.

Harriet you remember Mrs. Vana Richardson of Dracutt. Shall I tell you she died some months since of Small Pox! Dear woman she was amoung my *choice friends* and many, many pleasant hours and days I have spent in her rural home. I could go out any time in *their milkwagon* and return the next morning, or prolong my visit as I chose. She has left a fine family of Children, smart and energetic, possessing traits of character which would fit them better to stem the tide of life without a tender Mother's care, than any I know of. Did Mr. Ephraim Kendall who married my Cousin Susan, attend our Sewing Circle when you lived here? He has recently died at his residence in Andover; his *death was most triumphant.* Oh, what does so exhibit the worth of the blessed Gospel, as the calm and joyful meeting of this grim messenger?

Do not you remember one Sabbath noon our walking toward your home? The neighborhood of South St awakens many recollections of the past, in my mind. It puts in motion, if so I may say, a mental kaleidoscope, and past scenes appear to my eye with almost paralyzing force. Yes: precious past has wandered there, that never more will walk on earth.

Susan W.

But if past remembrances stir my heart within me, how must it be with you, my friend, when recalling the past in that far off home. A short time since Cousin Park Newell wrote me "I think if we can get to heaven we will try and get into the same neighborhood"—I was struck with that expression. Ever Yours Susan M. Wetherbee

---

Harriet's handwriting in the letter she writes from Bad River on August 3, 1855, certifies that despite her joy over the situation at the mission, she suffers. It is barely legible. To give a sense of how her writing has deteriorated, brackets indicate the portions of the letter one must fill in to make it comprehensible.

*D*ear Parents

　　When I last wrote you, I fully intended to write all my brothers and sisters in Lowell by the next mail, but the effort of making out our list and writin[g] you was altogether too much f[or] my head and it was a long ti[me] before I got over the effects of it. [M]y head still troubles me much. I h[ave] been very unwell the last month. [I']m not able now to sit up.

　　This is my excuse [for not] writ[ing] before. I am suffering general debility and loss of app[etite]. We miss the bracing lake breezes [we] were accu[s]tomed to at Lapointe. Our boxes have all [arrived] safely. Every thing was in g[ood] order and just what we wanted. [I like] my dress very much and very [glad] you have one like it. Please tell N we thank him very much for the crackers he sent us; they keep me from starving nowadays. We feel very grateful to you, my dear parents for the pains you [have] taken in selecting the articles for us I have very much I want to say to you about our prospects here but dare not. My head warns me that I must close. Pay[ment] is just at hand. Most of our Indians have left here for a few weeks. They will be back again after payment. Husband [prea]ches at Lapointe every Sabbath in Engl[ish] [and] Indian.

　　Please [give] [m]uch love to Susan W and tell her if [she] knew how much good her letter did m[e] [s]he would feel paid for writing it. I sha[ll] [an]swer it as soon as I feel able. Mr W, Miss Spooner join me in much lov[e] [to] all, Do Excuse these few lines it [is] all I feel able to write. Very Affec Your Daughter Harriet Wheeler

Please write as soon as you receive this

5.

Struggling against Sickness

As Harriet's health deteriorates, her children's early training in responsibility serves the family well. Julia, for instance, helps out with Harriet's correspondence. In April 1856, Julia's report to her mother's family in Lowell reveals that Odanah and La Pointe have become lively places and that things go well at the mission.

Dear Grandfather,

Our family are all well except mother. She has been very sick, but is better now. She walks the house and has been out to ride a few times.

We have got another little brother he has got a good deal of long black hair and mother says that I must send some of it to you because it looks so much like yours. There are several houses in Odanah now. David Green has got a very pretty one whitewashed inside and out. We intend to have a boarding school here sometime and Mr. Stoddard has received orders from Government to put up a large warehouse to put the payment goods in. The Indians are now in their sugar bushes. I wish I could send you some of the nice sugar that they are making but there are no boxes going to Lowell. Little Freddy talks a great deal about his grandpa and often asks where Grandpa lives. If the children do anything naughty he says, "Well, grandfather won't love you." Some times he looks up in to the clouds and says, "I see grandpa."

Mother says she would like to write you very much but she is not able to. We all want to visit Lowell very much and perhaps we shall in the course of a year or two. We shall have to go to school soon. Mother promised us that when we had got five hundred dollars, we might go and when we have sold our potatoes we shall just about have five hundred dollars, but mother thinks that we shall have to wait a year or two for father cannot leave the station just now. From your affectionate granddaughter

Julia Wheeler

Odanah April 1856

*D*ear Aunt Julia,

I wish you would come out here next summer. We do not think you would be lonesome here for we probably will have a great deal of company for the payment is to be made here and if you want to go home next fall, there will be plenty of gentlemen to escort you home as far as Cleveland.

There were a great many strangers at La Pointe last summer. Five hundred came up on one boat. Mr. Gilbert, the Indian agent was among them and so was Senator [Lewis] Cass[1] and there were four other senators. Grace Greenwood,[2] a cousin of Mr. Gilbert, was up here. She is rather odd; she has got a beautiful full eye and a nose almost as large as mother. She was writing a new work last summer called, I believe, *The Indian.* We had two pleasure boats that came up here; among them was the commissioner Senator Stevens.[3] Senator Robley and his wife wanted to come but she said "she had mercy on mother"; she had so much company she was afraid it would make her sick.

Can you send me a few flower seeds? I should like some annual climbing vine. Can you send the crimson Cyprus vine and the white and buff Hibernian? You can put them right in an envelope and direct the letter to father and it will go free of postage for he is postmaster. All letters must hereafter be directed to Odanah Lapoint Co. Wisconsin. Mother and all the children including myself send their love to you.

From your affec niece
Julia Wheeler

Finally, Harriet puts her latest baby to bed and writes her parents in May 1856.

It is now almost half past ten at night. I have just finished the labors of the day and laid my dear little Jean in his cradle for the night. I am too tired to write a long letter, but I thought I could not let the boat leave tomorrow without taking a few lines to you to let you know that you have a daughter in this wilderness that still loves you dearly, and thinks of you often. My health is improving although I have not regained my strength yet.

Baby is suffering for the want of suitable nourishment. He is a poor puny little babe and I sometimes fear he will not live through the summer. We all love him dearly and Grandpa & Grandmother must find a spare corner in their hearts for dear little Jean.

We have recently received Julia's letter and were rejoiced to learn that there was a possibility that she and perhaps you all would make us a visit. Oh, how I wish we were rich for a little while; want of funds would not stand in the way of your coming. I assure you our children would like to pay something towards repaying the expenses of the journey. I think they can afford and would love to give twenty dollars. I do not say much to the children and *I try not to think much* about it myself for fear of being disappointed. And *do, do come* if you can. We shall all wait very impatiently for your next letter.

We have tried to send as short a list as possible this spring and perhaps we ought not have sent any considering your poor health. Please tell Susan W [Wetherbee] I intended to write her this evening, but I am so tired, Oh *so very* tired, I cannot do it; but tell her not to punish me by letting me search the box in vain for a letter from her. Give much love to her.

Write soon

Very Affectionately
Your Daughter
Harriet

It seems ironic that in the same letter where Susan Wetherbee gently reprimands Harriet for not writing, she romanticizes the environment that has silenced her friend. If Susan Wetherbee had to endure the circumstances Harriet does, not only would her view of the forest as a fairyland disintegrate, she probably would lack the energy to muse on friendship.

Lowell June 10, 56

*M*y Ever dear Harriet,

This pleasant evening I would commune a while with thee, my Friend, my *long loved early Friend!* Time rolls along and brings its changes but to our hearts no change comes, and if we meet again e'er long; as I trust we may, should the education of your little ones lure you from missionary labor to revisit our home once more, I feel that nothing will have chilled your warm loving heart; no, although added little ones claim a share of affection, the fountain still is full.

How I would love to visit you in your own home to greet all the Lambs of the fold; and meet your dear husband too, and feasting eyes on beautiful scenery of your Lake Superior home. This is one advantage you have over your friend whose home is in the city; the charms of the country which are themselves balm to the spirit, and implant an enduring love of Nature. Yet I must say for our own City, she is becoming more country like year by year as her trees, which are numerous, increase in size. The front view from our own dwelling is somewhat forest like—perhaps Leonard will be tempted to smile at that expression and think there is nothing so near my home much resembling a Forest. Well, tell him I would love to ramble with him and his Sister Julia in their own native forest, and beside their beautiful water and cull their lovely wild flowers and crown some of the little ones for a fairy queen. Give much love to them from Susan and kiss all the little ones for me.

My dear H although a *few lines only* from yourself, would be such a source of pleasure for me & *even a little* note. Still, I do not feel to blame you at all, or think you negligent, or with all your domestic cares and duties I think it very excusable in you to allow them to monopolize your time. Mary says, "I think her very excusable for not writing; I have not written since I had a Baby to take care of. Tell her I sympathize with her in her domestic cares." Yes, Harriet the care of two with what assistance she has requires all her time and strength.

My Harriet,—"Oh I remember long ago, so long ago tis but a dream"—the pleasant hours of intercourse we shared, "make dear remembrances." Then life was in its freshness, friendship was indeed a reality; Harriet, friends between whom so much congeniality of spirit exists "grow not on every bough." Perhaps we would find more of those who should somewhat resemble the dearest, did we confidingly open our own hearts to others; but I had no idea of writing an essay on friendship when I commenced.—We read the folds of the heart. Writing to you H, brought to light some hidden fold, opens some little package which might have not, just then seen the light.

If Julia will write me I will be happy to answer it. She may be quite a useful little correspondent for her Mama. Tell her I wish she would come in here some day and we will go in and see Mr Hanks' little son a month or two old which his father says is an abolitionist. Present affairs at Congress may make everybody an abolitionist.[4]

Lowell June 13, 1856

ear Harriet,
    I now set down to inform you that I have got your goods together & shall send them to Boston tomorrow. I have sent 6 Books to my Dear Grandchildren. You must divide them as you think best. The two Instruments are for Edward & Frederick. I do want to see you all very much, more so than

ever before & if you will come on, I have room enough so that you all could live together.

I often think of that winter that you was here with deep regret that I could not do better by you than I did, but I could do better by you now. You will find wheels for a carriage in the box given by Mr. Weaver, the box of soda Crackers by your Brother Newell. Your Sister Laura is very Miserable; her lung troubles her much & she has a cough. I don't think that she will live many years; your Brother Newell is fixing over his Home and don't let any of it. His health is very good; he works very hard. I heard from Henry a few days ago; he was then in Vera Cruz, but was going up to the city of Mexico soon.

Our Mr. Foster,[5] his forenoon discourse was to the young. His text: "Remember thy creator in the days of thy youth" & he preached an excellent sermon. He had a full house. He preached on the outrage upon Mr. [Senator Charles] Sumner Sabbath before last. He felt so that he wept & I did not know that he would hardly be through but he did. There was many that wept that afternoon. We do all love him, for he is a Holy man. I never did believe in perfection, but I think he is as near Perfection as any I ever saw.

I see Harriet that you have one more added to your number. Mr. Wheeler says he has as many children as Father Wood. I hope he will be directed to train them up aright which if you do, they will be a Blessing to you & to our Country. I often look back with regret on how I have trained my children: many times I have punished my Children with a wrong Spirit. I never regret making them obedient, but the Spirit I did it in. Oh, my dear Children you must look to God alone for wisdom to direct you. I do pray my Dear Grandchildren may become Christians while young that they may be some use to the world. If one becomes a Christian in old age, what is he good for? He has to work hard against old habits & it is as much as he do to keep his head out of water. Tell my Children to give their hearts to the Savior while young & then they will have peace in this world & joy forever in Heaven.

Kiss all the little ones for me. Give my love to all Inquiring friends.

Fr your Affectionate Father

Sam L Wood

On August 10, 1856, Harriet writes to Leonard, who has apparently gone to Detroit. The supplies she requests gives a sense of how little they have. The content of the list also suggests that Harriet's and Leonard's daughter Julia has been injured and must wear a shoulder brace.

Dear Husband

Where are you now, and what are you doing? We miss you much. The Indians are most of them gone and it seems very lonesome here. Emma counts the Sabbaths very anxiously: I told her you would be gone four Sabbaths.

Our Boxes from Boston and Lowell came the day you left. The things were in good order—unusually so. We have a beautiful set of Crockery and but two cups and one dish broken. The preserve plates are wanting; could you not get a Doz of them in Detroit? They should be white stone china. A good many things we sent for have not come, and as we cannot find the invoice, we know not but that one box is lost. I have been obliged to borrow Indian Meal from Mr Van Tossel; will you see that it is replaced? Could not some of the good people in Ohio or Michigan make us a donation of some Indian Meal or corn? Don't forget the socks, yarn and dried fruit.

I will here give you a list of some articles that did not come on in the box which we must have

6 yds of Nankeen
3 Doz Metal coat Buttons
6 sticks of White Serpentine braid
3 pr of Shoes for Julia
" " " " " Emily
6 Tin Cups—1 pr of Shoulder Braces Julia
1 Gross of black pants buttons
1 *Air Tight* Stove
1 bll of Pork for Henry. His is so bad he cannot eat it.

If we whitewash our house we shall need some more Whiting and Glue. Please get our Flour for winter use of new wheat so as to avoid the grown wheat of last year.

Harriet's letter to her parents on July 13, 1857, suggests that her health has recovered enough for her to make a trip home to Lowell, where she can get better care than she does at Odanah. The letter also reveals that during her sixteen years in Wisconsin, she has lost a significant amount of hair.

I have hesitated considerably about coming home on account of mother's poor health, but I think if we find it is too much for her, Father can perhaps let us have two or three rooms and we can keep house.

Leonard and Julia must go below this fall[6] and I must either send them off alone not knowing what hands they will fall into or leave my husband alone here; either of these alternatives are trying ones to me. We have decided to leave here the first of Sept or the first of Oct. The time of leaving will depend upon the time of payment here.

The weather here is very warm and the mosquitoes intolerable. I am now doing my work alone with the exception of native help which is little better than none. My head troubles me very much this summer and I sometimes feel that my life depends upon my fleeing for a short time from my cares and labors here.

Do you hear anything from Henry of late? Should he come on before I do, tell him to be sure to come here and make us a visit. It will not be burden for such a traveler as he is.

We feel that our people are really making progress. Our chiefs have recently had a counsel and have unanimously resolved to renounce paganism and nominally embrace the white man's religions. They wish to sign a paper to this effect. They have had but one dance here this year here and that was quite a distance from the Mission for fear it would make Mr. W feel bad to see it

With regard to our list, we have tried to make it as short as possible. I regret,

Dear Mother, to be obliged to trouble you with it at all, although I know you do it cheerfully. Cannot Julia attend to it? The dress might be made of velvet ribbon or any thing you think best. The morning cap I want to put on on board the Boat or at the hotel when I have not time to dress my hair. It should be simple. I have not as much hair as I used to have.

The traveling dress I would like to have made long Basque, the sleeves gathered into and ending at the wrist and a cuff of the same. Do as you think best about the traveling wrap or cloak. I leave for you to decide the size for Jean's dresses. He is a large child for his age. These things we would like to have purchased and sent on as soon as possible as I want to leave in season to avoid the fall winds. Please give much love to all and tell Susan Wetherbee, Newell, and Julia that they will find my letter to them in the third of John 13 and 14 verses.[7]

The children all send love.

Your Affec—Daughter

Harriet Wheeler

Harriet's oldest child, Leonard, seems anxious to comfort his mother when he writes from school at Tallmadge, Ohio, on March 19, 1858.[8] Undoubtedly, his report that he may be experiencing grace pleased her.

hope, dear mother, you will not worry yourself about us. We are doing well enough. I know that Julia has wrote you some pretty sad letters. Never mind, she is doing just as well as can be expected to be. Sure, she has to walk a mile and a half to school but what is that in good weather? She stays in stormy weather with the teacher. She has not done as she ought to and I must confess I have not either, but I hope you will forgive me. Mother, the prayers and the tears you have offered up in my behalf, I think have been answered; for, mother, I am just as happy and contented here as I can be knowing that it is best for me to be here. Julia has not that feeling on the subject of religion I wish she had, though I think she has some. Has Tommy any feelings on this subject since the death of his dear sister? Tell him I mean to write him a good long letter in regard to the change in my feelings. Tell him he must write me often or he must not be afraid; I will not show his letters to any one if he does not wish me to. I hope he will think more of his downward career toward death.

———————

Harriet's letter to her parents on July 23, 1858, indicates that her health deteriorated so much that she could not travel to Lowell, but feels that she needs to travel there in the future to preserve it.

*J*t is with no ordinary emotion I sit down to write you once more. Since I last wrote I have felt many times that you had probably received your last letter from me. How many changes have taken place since then. My dear brother Henry has left us.[9] When thinking of visiting the East last fall, I had anticipated much pleasure in meeting him there, but alas, we shall meet no more until we meet at the face of God. I have thought much about him during my last sickness. When tossing about with a burning fever I have thought of those *dreadful three days*; what days of agony they must have been to him, with no friend or relative to bathe his burning throbbing brow, or to perform those thousand little attentions so grateful to the sick. Oh my dear parents, it seems as if no one in our family could realize his trial and suffering as I can.

My health during the past year has been very miserable. Some of the time I have been very sick and have felt that it was very doubtful about my recovery. Last summer I had two severe attacks of Cholera Morbus, which left me very weak. Indeed I was not able to sit up half of the time for six weeks. Last fall and winter I have two attacks of congestion of the Lungs, and I have not yet fully recovered from the effects of that. I was *very much disappointed* in not being able to visit home last fall; but my health was such that it was impossible for me to get there. You have doubtless thought it very strange that I did not write you, but I am sure could you see how I am situated, you would feel that I was excusable. I find enough to do to consume three times the amount of time or strength I have, and I am obliged to leave undone many things which seem absolutely necessary to be done.

My children suffered much last fall for the want of suitable clothing. Mrs. T [Trousdells] used to say she was really afraid Fred would freeze before I could get his winter clothing made and when I was able to work, I worked day and night. Twelve + sometimes one o'clock at night still found me plying my needle. The best month of the time I worked in this way I had more or less fever every day. About the middle of Feb, I took a severe cold which settled upon my lungs and for three weeks I could not speak a loud word and for as many more only with the greatest difficulty.

I have now a little babe three months old. She was born the 8th of March. My health has been such I have not been able to nurse her and she has consequently been feeble and puny. For the last three weeks, she seems to be improving. We call her Harriet Martha.

Physicians still tell me that if I wish to live, *I must leave here*. The Prudential Committee at Boston have given me leave to visit the states. We have accordingly concluded if my health and the babes will admit, to leave here the first of Sept; attend the annual meeting of the Board at Detroit the 9th, call at Cleveland for Leonard and Julia + shall probably be in Lowell about the middle of the month. Mr. Wheeler will go with me as far as Cleveland, and then return to this place. If he can leave the people, he will come on in Feb. or March.

We are now just in the care labor and anxiety of erecting buildings for our Boarding School operation. Our Schoolhouse is most finished and the boarding house will be commenced in a few days. This is a great addition to Mr. W's cares and labors and I sometimes fear he will sink under it. He grows old fast. Some of our people remarked last Sabbath that he looked like a person just getting up from a protracted fit of sickness. Under these circumstances, it is very trying for me to leave him here alone. Pray much for us my dear Parents that we may be guided by infinite wisdom; and that as our day is, so our strength may be.

In this contemplated visit, we wish to make you just as little trouble as possible. We know you are willing to do all in your power for us, but I shall have eight children with me and we think this is altogether too large an addition for your family. We therefore think it will be best to commence housekeeping at once as soon as we get there. Could you rent us one of your tenements? I want to get as near to you as possible.

I received a letter from Julia day before yesterday. They are both well. You know not how trying this separation has been to me this winter, but if L is truly a Christian I feel amply repaid for it all. Do pray much for them my dear parents. The children all send much love to all + are impatient to have the time come when they will start for L. Husband joins me in much love to all.

Your Affect Harriet.

After Harriet arrives in Lowell with her eight children, she reports on September 24, 1858, to Leonard on their journey and on her longing for him. She also questions whether she can handle her increased responsibilities.

The children are all gone to bed and I hasten to improve a few moments of quiet to write you a few lines. I suppose tonight you reach La Pointe and perhaps Odanah. In imagination, I have followed you all the way back to *our home*; for I can call no place home where you are not. How does it seem at Odanah without us? Oh, it frightens me to think you are so far from us. It seems as if we should never get together again.

We had a sad dreary ride after you left us at Albany, but the children behaved very well. One lady on the cars remarked that "they were very sweet mannered children." She had been observing them and she thought them "remarkably considerate." Hattie seemed quite sick through the day and cried considerably. When we reached the Worcester station it was raining very hard + the cars were just on the point of leaving, but we succeeded in getting on board. We reached father's about seven o'clock and I can assure you I was glad to get to my journey's end. Susan + M. Wetherbee were there in a few moments. Saturday night we took our first meal in our hired house. N [Newell] rents the house and he had it all newly papered and painted. Mother cooked up quite a quantity of food and sent it to us. They have also furnished us with our crockery and bedsteads.

Mr. Mack rents us two stoves for five dollars. Father bought us a doz of chairs + 1 table; these can be sold back again in the spring for nearly as much as they cost us. Provisions are high here: butter 22 cts a lb.

The children are a little homesick and it will take us all a little time to get the "hang" of city life. They are all with the exception of L [Leonard] & J [Julia] attending school now, and seem to be doing very well. The baby has been very sick but seemed decidedly better today. Father and Mother have been quite anxious about her. Father says he is afraid she will take wings and fly away from us one of these days. Dr. Huntington attends her. He has ordered a change in her diet. We give her now gelatin and arrow root with a little milk.

Sab Eve Dear Husband,

Although it is against my principles to write on the Sabbath, I thought I would add a few lines to this as I am anxious you should get it by the next trip of the Star. I attended church for the first time today at the John St. I saw but few familiar faces there and they have grown old about as fast as you and I have. It seemed sad to see a stranger occupying Mrs. Hanks place. She seemed, however, a very pleasant woman. She remarked tonight that she felt acquainted with us; she had so often heard Mr. Hanks speak of us. I have not seen him yet; but his wife says they shall call as soon as he returns. I have seen the Brooks family, Dea [Deacon] Wetherbee + Mr. Richardson, Mrs. Fox, Margaret, Mrs. Southwick + Mrs. Prout. Our children all attend the Sabbath school and like it very much. L is in Mr. Brooks class.

You have now, I suppose, closed the labor of the day and are sitting in the big rocking chair all alone in the dining room. Oh how gladly, would I take my seat at your side; but this cannot be. Still, we have one blessed privilege left: think of meeting at the mercy seat. I know my dear Husband you will remember us daily here. I feel that a fearful responsibility is resting upon me this winter. Pray much that I may have grace given me to faithfully discharge all my duties to our children. They all send much love to dear father. They often speak about you—sometimes feel quite sad when they think how far you are from us. So write us often. I want to hear about everybody + everything at Odanah. Be careful when they raise the boarding house + *please don't go onto the building yourself.* Give much love to all. Our little Hattie is very much better + is a great pet of Grandpa's.

Affectionately Yours

Harriet

On October 1, 1858, Emily reports to her father that she and her siblings long for him and home.

I want to see you very much. I go to Miss Gates' school. The boys think they cannot move without getting in somebody's way and it makes us lonesome here. If I had the Wings of a dove how quick would I fly to Odanah. We have a very nice house and a carpet on the parlor floor. The ladies have given us a bureau, a center table and a couple of stands, but the clock has struck eight so good night.

From your daughter

Emily A Wheeler

Oct 9 1858

*D*ear Husband,

The children have all gone to sing and I thought I would improve the quiet this gives me to write you a line. I have been waiting for a few days hoping to have something more favorable to write you about our little Hattie. She does not improve as far as we hoped she would when we wrote you last; her diarrhea still continues very bad. She looks sunken and thin and I sometimes fear she will never be any better. I am now getting milk for her from Cousin Caroline in Dracutt. It seems to be very good and I expected much from the change, but her diarrhea is worse today than usual.

Last week Jean had an attack of vomiting and diarrhea and he been quite unwell since. He has had just fever enough to quicken his memory and he has talked about his birdies + his turkeys + tiger. He frequently says "Mama, I want papa."

Leonard was quite unwell last week, but is better now and is attending school. Willie is doing very well in school. His teacher told Willie Wood a few days since that although his cousin had not attended school as much as he had, yet he was ahead of him and if he continued to do as well as he had done since he came there, he would make an extra smart man one of these days. He studies morning noon + night. His eyes are troubling him some and if I can leave the babe this week, I shall take him to Boston to see Dr Williams a celebrated oculist.

Odanah, Wis. Nov 22, 1858

My Dear Harriet,

I hope you will get Willy's eyes straightened + get relief for your throat. I hope you succeeded in getting you a good girl. I fear that unless you get a good girl to help you, you will not get as much rest as you ought to have. I hope you will not let the consideration of expense hinder you from keeping a good girl if you can find one for all winter. I hope the children will learn all they can. The winter will soon pass away.

Our school is now prospering better. Quite a number of children now attend school. Two weeks ago, we commenced our Sabbath school having it take the place of the Indian service in the Afternoon. We had forty-five the first Sabbath and about the same numbers last Sabbath. Mr. Stedman, Franklin + Blake have classes in English, and Henry [Blatchford] Mary [Warren], + I have each a class in Indian. We think when the people return from the fishing ground we shall have a full school.

Joseph Green thinks he has become a Christian. He is very punctual at meeting + appears better than I ever knew him. Our River froze up a week ago Saturday. There has been but little snow since + the boys + young man have had a fine time skating. We have just caught Bill + got him in the barn. He had got so wild that nobody could get next him but me. I succeeded—with a good deal of coaxing—by carrying along before him some oats in getting him into the barn. Our turkeys are doing well.

Dec 3

*D*ear Harriet,

A week ago last Monday I had occasion to spend the day + part of the day following in the cellar of the Boarding House, fixing it up to prevent the things in it from freezing. It was damp + I suppose I took cold. By Friday was confined to the house with general aches + pain in my teeth. Saturday + Sunday + Monday I was really more unwell than I have been before for several years. Mr. Welton bathed me—I took also some pills, ate but little + remained in the house till Tuesday. I am now quite smart again. Friends were kind, but I missed you much. I think I shall not let you go again for so long unless I go, too.

We have got our family arrangements fixed for the winter. George + wife occupy the dining room + our bedroom + I occupy the front room for my study is bedroom + Mary at present occupies the front chamber—Mrs. Trousdells' folks cannot furnish her a room at their house now. They both board here. This room I now occupy is convenient for me. I can go to + from my meals without disturbing my neighbors, + they have no passage through my room. Henry + the Indians too can visit me without passing through the other part of the house. Tell brother Hanks, if you see him, that I am living now more like an Andover Student than at any time before since I left the Seminary in so far as a room is concerned. I have Mr. Welton for a Chum. He came here a week ago last Tuesday + will stay several days at longest.

Leonard submits his accounting of the mission's expenses to Harriet for approval, demonstrating his confidence in her abilities.

I send by this mail our estimates of expenses for the year 1859, aside from the Boarding School interest. Please write me what you think of it. I hope you will write often. I know your responsibilities are great; I would gladly share them with you, but the Lord has said, "If any of your lack wisdom, let him ask of God. Look to him—casting all your care upon him, for he careth for you." Let us meet at the throne of God, and pray that we may each in our places serve our Master faithfully + we shall be permitted to meet together again as a family. With much love to all the children.

The letter Harriet writes to Leonard on Thanksgiving 1858 shows that she has begun to make decisions on her own.

*D*ear Husband,

I shall send you the boys' cards + you can see for yourself what their recital and deportment have been. Leonard has been absent a great deal on account of ill health. Willie's teacher told me that he was a very exemplary boy + brilliant scholar. There are five cousins in his class. He is the youngest of them all + he's advanced considerably further in arithmetic than any of them. I have hired a piano + Julia is taking lessons in instrumental and vocal music of Mr. Willy. I suspect Eddy will go into the grammar school next term. I have made arrangements to send Leonard to Philips Academy[10] next term. I can not now tell you all the reasons that have induced me to take this course, but I am confident you would think it best if you were here. I talked with Mr. Treat about it and he advised me to. I found Mr. T a very pleasant man and he says he will do all he can for L. I have engaged him a room. He will board in a club. The expense of board per week is about 1.75 cts per week. I will send you a catalogue so you see what the terms are. L has not wholly given up his tobacco yet but uses it occasionally. I hope you will write him about it. Mr. Taylor told me that it was not allowed at all in the school. Can you collect any of the children's money to bring on with you? If it is among the possibilities, I wish you would. I think we ought to pay L's expenses out of the children's money. It is Thanksgiving tomorrow. We will go to Father's. How I wish you could be with us. The children send their love to dear father.

Affect your Harriet.

Odanah Wis. Dec. 23, 1858

Dear Harriet,

I was glad to hear that the family are all so well when you wrote. With so much sickness in the family, your strength has been not a little taxed. You say that our separation is unnatural in that death will separate us soon enough. I was writing in the same sentiment when your letter came. I will quote a letter: "Friends are kind, but the joy of my household is not here—my wife + little ones are away."

It is better for you to be where you are. I feel that we have special cause for thankfulness that our separation is not the reach of death which has cut so many tender ties in the circle of dear friends + relations. Through all our sickness + dangers—we have both been spared so our family is as yet unbroken. I can hardly realize that we have got along so far in life's journey—but when I count the numbers on the milestones of life, I see that we have passed many of them.

I feel that some of my passing cares are beginning to ease up a little. I will be glad when our Boarding House is done—furnished + its working machinery is in. Our Sabbath school is increasingly interesting + our meetings and day school are very well attended. The young men are about to commence an evening school. Our Friday Evening meeting is attended in the East wing of our new school house. We had a good meeting last week. I hope to have one tomorrow evening. Our people need a good deal of careful instruction. Thus I feel an increased spirit of prayer + I hope we shall see some tokens of the Divine presence before the Indians go into their sugar Camps. There are several who think they have become Christians, but whether it is best to receive them to the church now or wait till March, I am not certain. I wish to give my individual attention to the spiritual goal of the people, especially while they are now so accessible + quiet. When I see what God is doing abroad in the Churches, I ask myself—Is not the Lord ready to bless us also?—Is it not our privilege to pray + labor + expect that He will bless our people? Pray for us that God will, according to the riches of his grace in Jesus Christ, shed down his Spirit in mighty power upon us.

Our Indian women say it makes them sad to come here now for their *donqua* is gone. I tell them you will probably be back in the Spring. How many of the children do you intend to leave East + when do you get homes for them? You probably judged wisely in sending Lenny to Andover. I hope there will be some *permanency* in his stay there + that he will make some proficiency in his studies + that he will show that he has some stability of character.

How do you suppose I am going to find time to come after you + when shall I come? I would like to come so as to spend a little time in visiting among friends, but should I leave home in March I shall reach Lowell about the first or middle of April. I could spend no more than a week + then if we should start the first of May, we might reach home by the middle of the month or first of June. Or I might leave home the first of June—go down in the Steam-Boat + return with the family + teacher so as to reach here the first of July. But let us look a little carefully at the facts in the case + see what interests we have to see to + what we can best sacrifice if any.

Lowell Jan 1859

*D*ear Husband

We received your letter a few days since and I can assure you never was a letter more welcome. It found me very unwell and under the Dr's care. I told him a few nights before it came that a letter from you would do more good than any thing he could do for me. I supposed you was sick and was feeling exceedingly anxious about you. If you wish me to get well, you must write oftener. We are all, with the exception of Leonard and Julia, suffering from colds. Emma has not been able to go to school for a fortnight. She has a severe cold + cough. The weather has been very changeable of late. Last Monday was very cold. L [Leonard] walked most of the way to Andover in the morning and came very near freezing. He had no drawers on nor overcoat. His Grandfather lent him his shawl. He became very sleepy before he reached there and it was with great difficulty he could keep awake. The stupor continued till the next morning. He comes home every Saturday. He seems to be doing very well there. Little Hattie is growing finely. She has six teeth and I have just weaned her from the bottle. She is a very sweet babe. I think I told about the children singing an Indian hymn in the sabbath school concert. Mr. Richardson wants them to sing in Dr Blanchard's next concert. Last Thursday eve, I took all the children except the youngest to the sewing circle. Three of the Indians were present and we all sang a hymn in Indian together. Susan W [Wetherbee] thought my bonnet was not quite good enough, so she spoke to Mrs. Hanks about it. In a few minutes she had money enough collected to get me a new one.

The people here are very kind to us. I have had a surprise party and in a few days the ladies are coming to sew for me. They bring their own supper. I like this very much: it saves one all the fatigue of cooking and I have nothing to do but to enjoy it. You do not know what a warm kind friend I have in Susan W. She and the family are out here very often. The ladies in Mr. Jenkins' church, formerly Mr. Child's, are going to furnish a room in our boarding house. They have commenced making the bedding.

I want a copy of the plan of the Boarding House. The children all send love.

Jan 26 1859

Dear Husband,

Since writing the first sheet I have been quite sick. When I wrote you last I was much better and hoped it would be permanent but the day after my lung difficulties all returned and I have been quite unwell most of the time since. I am better now and have been out today. The Dr. says that if these symptoms had occurred in earlier life, he should have been more alarmed. He thinks the swelling in my throat is scrofulous and is giving me iodine and sarsaparilla. I am now using an oil externally on my chest and he wants me to keep up an irritation there for some time. You say in your last that when you think of the privileges I enjoy here you feel that it is best for me to be here. I sometimes feel that as far as that is concerned, I might as well be at Odanah as here. I have not been able to go to church but half a day on the Sabbath and I have been to but three or four evening meetings. I have not attended a scientific lecture yet + have not returned the first calls made on me. I have missed you much very much this winter, I miss you in the family and since I have felt sick and miserable, I have missed you more than ever. I am waiting impatiently for the first of March for then I think you will start for Lowell. How I shall count the days and the hours after that; I shall be with you all your journey home.

I have received quite a number of calls recently from old friends. Dea Bancroft + wife were here a few evenings since. He is out of business and is very poor. They sent much love to you. The same evening Dea Thompson called. He is here on a visit from the West. He has been selling a lamp. He left one here for you. He wishes you to receive it as a present from him. It is for your study table. It gives a beautiful light. He sends much love to you, took your address and says he shall try and write you. He likes the West much.

I find it very expensive living here. Flour is eight dollars a barrel; butter twenty five cts + meat from eight to fifteen cts per pound . I have drawn on the Board three hundred and seventy five dollars since I came here and I fear I shall be seventy five dollars in debt when you come.

The letter Leonard writes Harriet on February 4, 1859, reveals that both Wheelers have lost their teeth at Odanah. His casual mention of this fact gives a sense of how brutal the Wheelers' sojourn in Wisconsin has been for them.

Christmas must have been a very happy day to you all. The uncles + Aunts + Cousins the Christmas tree—presents must have made such a Christmas as the children never enjoyed before. Emily's description of the

Sabbath school concert was good. Your Indian singing must have been quite edifying; I am glad the children seem to enjoy themselves so well,—find so many kind friends,—enjoy such good health + are doing so well in their studies.

The Lake is all open a little ways from the mouth of Bad River. Henry says I ought to start early. If I do not, I will find the snow soft + the traveling hard towards Chippewa River. But I have a great many things to see to before I can start. I shall try to be on my way by at least the first of March, + perhaps before; I would like at least to have a solid month to visit among friends in + about Lowell besides as much more time to visit Friends in Vt. The distance from here to Chippewa Falls is some 170 miles—which will be all I shall want to do in one week. I don't know how my back will stand it. I may go with my horse to Mr. Sibley's + from there to Lac Courte Oreilles is but two days + one night more will bring me to the first shanty. But we shall see.

I wish now to tell you a little about the children's funds. I have succeeded much better than I expected at Bayfield. What Mr. Coke owed me $68.17. Mr N. [Nourse?] will give me a draft for $105.08 which you see will make $173.29. This will be the children's. The produce of their garden last summer above expenses will be some 79.00 dollars, which will be better than I expected. Now then, what about teachers? Mr. Morse[11] can be got if his services should be wanted for 229 dollars per year + his board—but only to teach—he does not think he will be competent to act as superintendent. Dr. Ellis[12] could perhaps be got who would make an excellent superintendent + teacher.

I am very glad to hear you say at your last letter that your health had improved. You say nothing about your teeth; have you got a set yet? I must stay East long enough to get me some. We have had a mild, pleasant winter, but to tell you the truth, I have been more lonesome than I expected to be. Neither business nor books—nor kind neighbors can dispel the images of my dear wife + children from my mind. They constantly float before my mental vision. I cannot say I feel anxious about you, for I know you are well cared for, but I somehow feel a stranger in my own house. Our white people have had have a more quiet + pleasant start of things than we had last year. Our English meetings are better attended and we have also interesting Indian meetings. The members of the church seem to be in a better condition spiritually than they were last fall. Joseph Yellow Thunder appears quite decided. Several of his consider themselves as converts + inquirers. I hope they are Christians—but they need more instruction + a longer probation before they are received to the church. Sometimes things look dark + forbidding. But Jesus, the great captain of our salvation, has infinite resources at his command. There is no intellect so dark that he cannot enlighten Faith, earnest prayer, confidence in God, faithful endeavors to bring men to a knowledge of truth—with perseverance therein is what is wanted. I cannot but feel that the Lord has a great blessing in store for us. "Lord increase our Faith." Pray for me that I may have a prosperous journey by the will of God. With much love to the children + all enquiring friends I am your Affectionate Husband

---

Harriet's letter to her husband on February 17, 1859, shows that she not only takes full responsibility for the children, she has now become a full partner in handling the mission. Indeed, she delivers instructions to Leonard.

I have had a visit today from Mr. Treat and I have fully laid upon him those subjects you wished me to in your letter.

With regard to teachers, he thinks that you will be more likely to find them at the west. He says you know what is wanted better than he does. You can give them a better idea of what will be expected of them there. He says he has made inquiries here, but can hear of no one that will go. He thinks it's important that we get the right kind of a man to start with. If we do not, a great deal of care and anxiety will devolve on you.

He wishes you to go to Oberlin on your way here and see who you can find there. He proposes if you find any one that will go that you should stay with him two or three days. See all you can of him yourself; and learn all you can from others. With regard to a salary, he remarked that if they would go as we do, it would perhaps be best; but if they wished, the Board would pay them a reasonable salary. He is *very* anxious that the school should be kept small the first year. He thinks that success depends very much upon this. No more than ten or twelve should be taken. If we have not more than this number, could we not get along with out a superintendent the first year? I do not think it will be possible to get a teacher here. Lowell is sadly changed since we knew it. Could you not find one in Oberlin?

I hope whoever comes, you will not fail to tell them of the trials and difficulties they will have to encounter. Give them the darkest side of the picture so that if they are disappointed, it will be happily. If they cannot look at trial and obstacles at a distance, what will they do when they come to the stern reality?

I regret much that you must do so much business before you can reach here, for I fear it will detain you several days and the days and weeks are growing very long to us now. It has been quite a task to my missionary spirit, I can assure you, to write this letter, but I try to say duty first and pleasure afterwards. The children are all well. They have a vacation this week and next. My own health is improving.

L [Leonard] is at Andover. He was at home on Saturday. Julia is still tending to her music. Willie is taking lessons in vocal music. His teacher says he will make a splendid alto singer. He says when he takes hold, he makes all gold again. Mr. Treat approved very much of Julia's taking lessons in music; he says it will make her independent. Do write us as soon as you receive this and let me know when I may expect you. Need I add, do hasten home as quick as possible.

Affect Yours
Harriet

Lowell March 9th/59

Dear Husband,
We have just received your letter containing the joyful intelligence that you were to leave soon for Lowell. I cannot tell you how rejoiced we are to hear this.

I have heard nothing more with regard to teachers. I hope you will find a suitable person at Oberlin. I feel, dear husband, that you need much wisdom to guide you. Mr. Treat thinks you will be more likely to succeed there than anywhere else because they are interested in and acquainted with Indian missions.

It would perhaps be well to see if you could find a suitable place there for Lenny. You may think it best for him to go there. It would be less expensive than at Andover. Philips Academy is a very large and popular school, but there are a great many wild boys there. I like Ohio much better than Mass. He is doing I should think well at A—Is getting quite a taste for reading. Our children are enjoying their vacation very much, but will be ready for school next week.

This is the season for concerts here. I went to one last eve with Newell. It was given by a German club from Boston. It was very fine. I only wished you were there to enjoy it with me. Mr. Willey's class gives one tomorrow eve. Julia sings with them. I was rejoiced to learn that our little church were in so good a state spiritually. I feel with you that the Lord has a rich blessing in store for us. Let us labor and pray and wait patiently and trustingly.

I must now close hoping that my next communication with you will be by word of mouth.

Apparently, Leonard made it to Lowell and then went to Washington, D.C., in an attempt to help the Ojibwe.

Washington City D.C. March 29, 1859

Dear Harriet,
Today has been a day of progress with me in Indian Matters. I have had a very fine talk with Mr. Mix[13] + he is disposed to look carefully into the affairs of our Indians + see that some of the promises made our people by different agents are fulfilled. But we could not finish our business today; he wishes me to call again tomorrow morning. I shall think the day well spent if we can make as much progress as we have to day—let us show patience there.

I went out to Georgetown for a walk just before night. Saw the Potomac + the Heights of Georgetown. Passed the President's house.

Your affectionate husband

L. H Wheeler

During this trip east, Leonard's lungs began to hemorrhage, making him the ill parent and giving Harriet responsibility for him, the mission, and their children. Leonard's earlier inclusion of Harriet in the mission's business provided good preparation for the decisions she later had to make herself. On June 24, 1859, she writes her parents from Odanah.

If you have received my last, you will be anxious to hear from us again. I am very happy to tell you that my dear husband still lives and his symptoms are more favorable. He has not bled any time since last Friday. He is still very weak, but sits up a little, coughs and raises some. The great danger now is that it will end in consumption. The Dr says he feels somewhat encouraged about him. The season of the year is favorable and nature seems to be doing all we could reasonably expect. He told me last week that he felt that he was standing on the verge of the Dark Valley, ready to go down into it or to return to life, just as the Great Master should see best.

I feel exceedingly anxious about him. It seems as if he could not be spared from his family now. And our poor people, what will they do without him? They express a great deal of sympathy and anxiety. Some of them say they can not sleep for they feel as if their father was going to be taken away from them. Others, as they take my hand, exclaim, "Oh, surely trouble has come to us now!" The Dr. sent word to them by a chief that they must not come to see him, but they frequently come to the kitchen to inquire for him. For a few days past I have admitted a few to see him and they almost invariably thank the Great Spirit for permitting them to see him again. Our white friends have also been kind. Some of them from Ashland + Bay City have been assisting in taking care of him; they have not allowed me to take care of him a single night. Were I in L [Lowell], I don't know as I could have more help then I have here.

Should Mr. W get able to travel, I think we shall go to Marquette to consult a physician there. The Dr. says if he should get better, it will be a long time before he is able to preach, if ever. Could you send me the book you was speaking to me about when I was in L? I think the title of it is *Consumption Is Cured by Inhalation*. I think you remarked that Mr. Dodge was cured by it. I enclose a dollar for it. Please send it immediately. With regard to the things I left, perhaps you had better pack them in a small box and send them to the Missionary rooms in Boston and request Mr. Waldo[14] to send them on to the care of the Boarding House as soon as possible. I would like to have the photographs put in; I hope I shall find yours there. If you find Miss Beecher's receipt book, please send that. Please give much love to all; Mr. W and the children join me in this. Write soon

Your Affect Daughter

Harriet

Abigail Spooner went to La Pointe with the Wheelers to teach school. Her few surviving letters, including this one written to Harriet on October 21, 1859, from Greenville, Michigan, suggest a warm, religious woman fascinated by, indeed, somewhat fixated on, children. She seems remarkably indifferent to Leonard and Harriet's struggles.

One week ago this evening I reached this place and surprised and delighted my friends by my arrival—I had a very fine journey. It seems as if my Heavenly Father put his arms around me and brought me safely here—How good he is—

I found my cousin's family in tolerable health and *much pleasanter* circumstances than when I was with them before—but they have passed through a sea of trial since that time. They have five interesting children one son & four daughters—They are rather feeble children—could not probably endure half that your children can—what a blessing is health—I expect to teach them, and a few other children perhaps, if I remain here the coming winter—which I think is probable. They seem to think I belong here and must stay—The children seem perfectly delighted to have me here—Mary Eliza says, "It seems too good to be true." Now do write me immediately and not you alone but anybody that can—Do tell me about the dear children—How does my dear Freddy do? And Eddie & Emma and *all all* of them—I want to hear from every one—Tell them I send them ever so much love and a hundred kisses—Tell them to kiss each other for Aunt Abby. Give my love to all and each one of the mission families. I hope you will have a good girl so that Mary can go into school. Give my love to all the indians—to members of the church and their families particularly—and to all enquiring friends. Tell Willy and Emma and Eddie to write me soon—very soon and tell me about Eugene and Freddy and all the folks.

Goodbye dear Sister—may the Lord bless and prosper you and yours and the mission.

Abbie

Odanah Feb 1860

Dear Parents

A longer time than usual has elapsed since writing you but the care of my eight children + sick husband and the many duties incident to a missionary's life leave me but little time or strength for letter writing. Many little items of business that Mr. W. formerly attended too now devolve upon me. I have spent most of the time for two days this week in getting our accounts ready for the Board. The business has passed through as many hands this summer that we find books and bills in confusion.

Mr. W has been more feeble for a month past. He seemed to be improving slowly but steadily until about a month since. He undertook to assist Dr. Spencer make a sled. He overworked and is now suffering the consequences. He coughs more than he has at any time since last summer and complains of feeling very weak and exhausted. This month and next will probably be a very trying time for him. He has had no return of the Hemorrhage since last summer. He was examined by five different physicians last summer and all agreed that the great danger in his case was the extreme exhaustion of his whole system. The first part of winter he preached a number of times, but I think it was an injury to him. This difficulty has been coming on for more than a year. He was unwell when he left here for the East last spring and he did not see a well day while he was there. He was suffering from congestion of the lungs most of the time and I wonder he did not bleed while there.

The children are now all at home. The three older boys have drawn and sawed and split our year's supply of wood besides taking care of the stock this winter. They will all be taken out of school to work on the farm this summer. Julia is teaching with Mr. Miner[15] and gets along much better than I expected.

Our boarding school is prospering finely. We have now thirteen boarding scholars all contented and happy. We shall probably be obliged to limit the number to fifteen this year.

Our darling Hattie is learning to talk very fast. Thursday afternoon, she went to the drawer that contained the photographs and tried to open it and said, "Gan ma Gan ma" and she would not be quiet until I got her Gan ma to see + kiss. I one day took out the Daguerreotype and showed it to her. She laughed as soon as she saw it and stretched out her little hands to take it and kiss it. She is a very affectionate child. Twice she came near dying from the effect of eating matches, once while I was absent from home. She had convulsions and we thought she could not live. We gave her the whites of eggs. We are obliged to keep matches entirely out of her reach or she will eat them.

Mr. W and the children join me in much love to all. I must close as it is getting very late and I find I cannot sit up at late as I used to sew without suffering for it.

From your affect

Daughter

Harriet

———

Harriet's letter to her Shaker sister, Mary, in April 1860 shows none of her parents' condemnation of Mary's choice. Instead, it suggests a strong bond that allows Harriet to write openly about her feelings; she even talks of enjoying a visit to the Shaker community at Harvard when she was in Massachusetts.

Your truly kind letter reached me some months since. It came to me when I most needed sympathy and I can assure you it was very gratefully received. Do not impute my long silence to ingratitude or forgetfulness. Did you know how I am situated and what a heart crushing sorrow I have had for the past year, you would not.

You have heard of my dear Husband's severe and protracted illness. He was not well a day while in Lowell last spring. Coming up the Lakes he seemed to improve and I fondly hoped that when we were settled at home, he would be well. When we reached home, we found our house very damp and he took a severe cold and soon after was taken bleeding at the lungs. For weeks, his life hung on a very slender thread. He told me at the time that he felt as if he was standing on the outer verge of the dark valley ready to go down into it or to return to life just as the Great Master should see best. As soon as he was able to travel, I went with him down the Lake about three hundred miles to Marquette to consult a physician there. We there found kind friends and a good physician. Soon after our arrival, his lungs were examined thoroughly with a stethoscope. The Dr. said there was no disease about them that would prove fatal, but the great danger in his case arose from the fact that his whole system was completely exhausted. It had been overtaxed and overworked so long that he could not assure me that it would ever rally again. He recommends traveling on the Lake on Steamboat during the Summer and a *very nutritious diet*. He told him he must be perfectly free from care and labor for a year and he did not think he would ever be able to preach again. He seemed to improve slowly but steadily during the summer and for part of winter. He preached a few times but it was probably an injury to him. About two months since, he overworked and has been suffering from a relapse ever since. He coughs some and appears very weak and debilitated. I feel exceeding anxious about him.

I have seen some sad hours since I parted with you, my dear sister. At times, I feel almost overwhelmed in view of the future, but at others, I feel as if I could calmly and cheerfully leave myself, my children and my dear husband in the hands of my heavenly Father knowing and feeling that he will do all things well. Our people have manifested much sympathy and kindness during all this bitter trial. When he was lying so low the Dr. told them that they must not come to the house, but I would frequently find them in the kitchen when I got up, waiting to learn how he was. They said they could not sleep, they were so anxious about him. One old chief as he met me took my hand and said, "Don't my friend feel that you alone are troubled. We are all in trouble now. We feel as if our father was going to be taken from us. Our hearts are very heavy." When they were first permitted to go into his room, they almost every one of them took his hand, thanked the Great Spirit for being permitted to see his face again. Our white neighbors were also very kind. One of them walked eighteen miles, some of them through a swamp that would be thought impassable East. Had I been in Lowell, I could not have had more sympathy or help.

Our Boarding School is now fairly commenced. We have thirteen boarding scholars and are expecting more soon. The children are bright and interesting and are learning fast. We hope much from them. Our day school and meetings have been well attended this winter and our people seem to be making substantial progress in civilization.

Our children are all at home now. Julia is teaching. Lenny + Willie will work on the farm this summer. They all with Mr. W join me in much love to Aunt Mary. Please remember me particularly to Mrs H [Hedge]. Tell them I shall not soon forget my pleasant visit at Harvard. Remember me affectionately to any who may inquire for me. I think of them with much interest. Please write soon. I not had but one letter from home since I left. From Your Affect Sister

Harriet Wheeler.

Leonard must travel east in search of medical care. He wrote this letter to Harriet on June 16, 1860, as he waited for a boat to take him from Bayfield, Wisconsin. His note reveals the broad array of responsibilities that have been passed on to Harriet.

ou see, I am not yet off. I am stopping at Mr Nourse's.[16] I have to look out for the evening air. It is much more chilly than with us. I feel anxious to hear from the little ones.

I send my account book—our mail. Two oranges + a lemon for you + the little ones. You see I got my pay of Mr. Drew.[17] We may get something of the government for the attendance of day scholars. See that the cabbage transplanted immediately. You had better employ a man for this purpose. The only other work about our place is the getting out of our manure to be put in a pile + making our garden fence. Do no more than is absolutely necessary for the Mission or Boarding school. If labor is hired to build a pasture fence, or any part of the work of putting it up by the Boarding House, let the expenses be charged to Boarding House. Don't employ four men to do what two will do just as well.

Marquette June 26, 1860

ear Harriet,

I have seen Dr. Hewitt[18] + told him my story. He said I looked a great deal better than I did last year + that I had improved as much as could be expected + was pursuing the right course now to recover: "air, diet + exercise" were the great remedies. The inhaling system he said he had no confidence in; it might afford temporary relief—but to build up the general health of the system was what I needed. A little good old whiskey might be beneficial to take especially after exercising + feeling a sensation of exhaustion. I am boarding at Judge Edwards.[19] Mrs. E. [Edwards] taken first rate care of me: I have fresh beef every day—bowels regular. Raise a little every morning + some during the day but not so much as when at home. I think I am gaining some strength. Our friends here all think I have improved much in appearance since last summer. I don't know what to think about going East.

Leonard writes about the possibility of Rhoda Spicer becoming part of the mission. Eventually, she not only joined the Wheelers at Bad River, she married their eldest son, Leonard.

I have made enquiry about Miss Spicer. They are well acquainted with her + say she is a fine girl—plays the mandolin but doubt about her being able to sing. Think there is not much singing in the family. Her parents are substantial farmers in good circumstances + Miss Spicer has good domestic training. Now the question is if she is ready to come, shall we accept her, if she cannot sing?

Despite his illness, Leonard Wheeler still takes his job seriously, even suggesting that he and Harriet entertain the Presbytery in a little over two months.

Now about the meeting of our Presbytery. The friends here are ready to come up to our place the first of Sept. if it is best. In that case, I should endeavor to be back myself, during the month of Aug. Please write what you think.

In regard to going East, I think perhaps I had better go. As yet the warm weather has been better for me than the cold. My plan rather is to go to Cleveland next week on the Star or perhaps then go on to Boston. If any Indians enquire for work down this way I have to say, that I know of more now.

JUNE 27. I had rather a poor day yesterday: the air was cold, I took a little cold but had a good night last night + feel better today. I would like much to see you + the little ones + the big ones too. I think little about home so far as the work is concerned. I think more about our people + more still about the family. How do you get along with the mosquitoes? I suppose little Hattie's face shows the marks. Jean, is he as imperative in his commands as he was when he was sick? I suppose Emily helps mother a good deal. And the boys, I suppose they relieve mother entirely of nearly all the care about the herd, pigs + cows + use their hoes some in the garden. Give a great deal of love to Henry + family + all the Boarding house folks. Mrs. E's [Edward's] + husband send much love. As to myself, could you be with me, I should enjoy myself much better. The thought of going East without you is not a little trying. I expect to feel lonely, but the Lord is our keeper + friend. I would much rather be at home did not a regard to health make it necessary for me to be absent. From your affectionate Husband

    L. H. Wheeler.

Lowell July 26, 1860

*D*ear Harriet,

    Give much love to all family + neighbors. I have a favorite walk up among Mr. Whipple's old powder mills. One day under a spell of romance I went up on the top of Fort Hill + saw the identical great rock where we sat down in the days of youthful love + the rock felt as though it had been warm ever since. Tell Jeanie + Hattie that papa thinks of them every day. I hope the older ones will try to make themselves useful + help mother all they can. Good bye from your affec husband

    L. H. W.

Bridgeport, Vt. Aug 18, 1860

*D*ear Harriet,

    I send a line to say that I am just recovering from a sudden + severe attack of fever. It will be impossible for me to be home the first of Sept. I hope to start from Cleveland Sept 6 if I can. I will write again when I have more strength.

Your affect Husband

L. H. W.

Odanah Nov 20/60

Dear Parents,

I have deferred writing for some time just hoping to find time to sit down and write you a long letter but I fear that time will never come. The summer has been an unusually busy one. The first fortnight after Mr. W's return, he was so sick as to require all my time. Since then we have had our annual payment and now cold weather is upon us and finds me wholly unprepared for it. I cannot work nights now as I used to.

You will probably be anxious to hear about Mr. Wheeler's health. You have learned before this that he took a severe cold at Detroit and was very sick all the way up the Lake. The weather was unusually rough and cold so that the Steamer was behind time three days. I left here at half past three o'clock Sabbath night expecting the boat would be at La Pointe early in the morning, but it did not come in until Thursday morning. I stopped at La Pointe expecting the Star would stop there first, but it passed in the night, and went to Bayfield. About daybreak it came over to La Pointe. I was one of the first on the wharf. The wind was blowing very fresh so that it was some time before the boat could get up to the wharf sufficiently near to land passengers, but the captain came out to the stern of the boat and said, "The Lady Elgin is lost with three hundred passengers on board."[20] You can imagine the sensation it produced as it was expected at La Pointe any moment. Indeed, we supposed when we first heard the whistle of the Star that it was the Elgin. Two prominent men here were supposed to be on board. A friend who was standing near me called to the Capt and asked him if Mr. Wheeler was on board. He said he was. He then went in and told Mr. W that there was a lady looking up a lost husband. Mr. W put on his overcoat + came down to the gangway so we could see him but oh, what a *looking man so frail, so ghostly.* I turned to our friend Dr. Ellis who was standing by me + exclaimed, "How pale + thin he is." He replied, "Oh no." I saw there were tears in his eyes, and I knew by his evasive answer what he thought. *I felt* that he had come home only to die with us. The first words he said to me when I got on board was, "Oh, Harriet I never was half as glad to see you before + have been fighting with the pleurisy all night." We took him to the house of a friend where he had all the care and attention needed. The wind continued to blow so that we would not get home until late Saturday night. There was joy in our household, I can assure you, when we got home, but with me there was a dreadful fear that he would soon go out to return no more to us. The next day was the Sabbath. Many of the Indians came to see him. They were sadly disappointed to see him look so. They expected he would come home well on Monday. He was taken with a severe diarrhea which lasted all the week.

Harriet Wood Wheeler.

Leonard Hemenway Wheeler.

La Pointe Harbor in 1842. The Wheelers arrived here by boat in the summer of 1841.

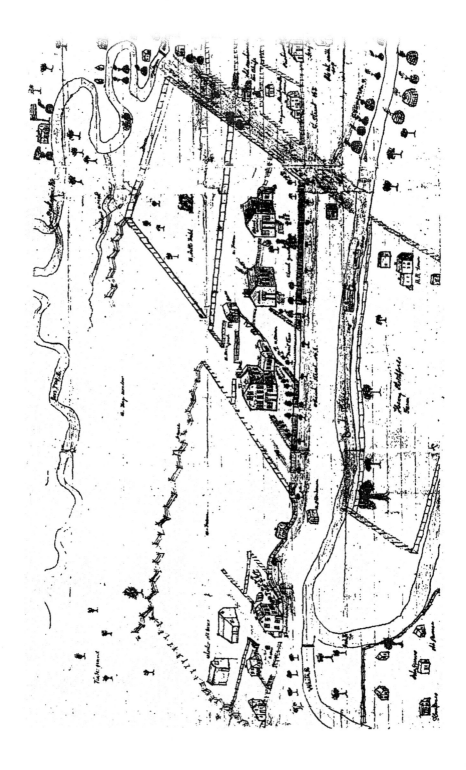

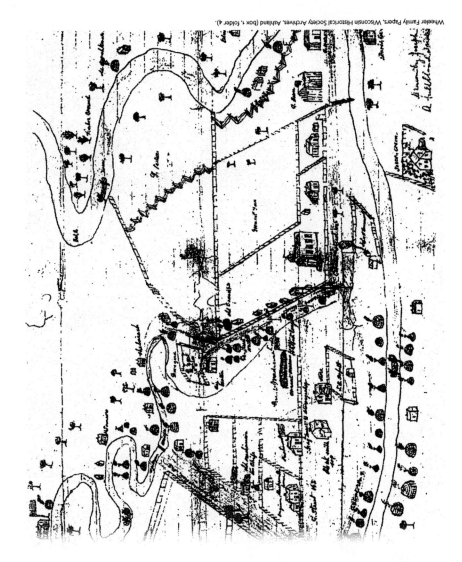

Map of Odanah drawn between 1859 and 1966 by Joseph Green, an Ojibwe. Previous page: left portion; this page: right portion.

The gorge on the Bad River, where the Wheelers established their mission in 1845, they named the community Odanah.

Ojibwe home in Odanah, Wisconsin.

Ojibwe burying ground in Odanah, Wisconsin.

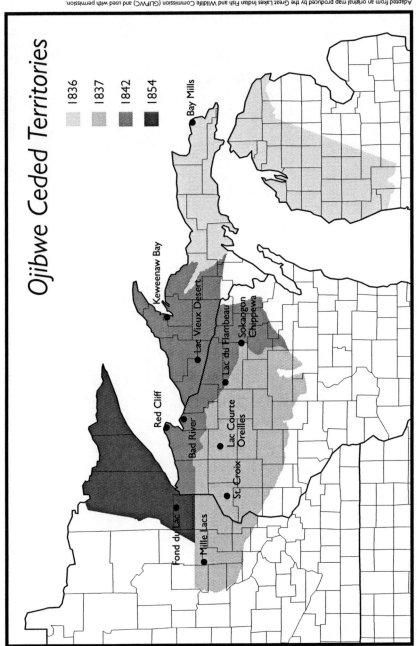

Ojibwe Ceded Territories

- 1836
- 1837
- 1842
- 1854

Bay Mills

Keweenaw Bay

Lac Vieux Desert

Lac du Flambeau

Sokaogon
Chippewa

Red Cliff

Bad River

Lac Courte
Oreilles

St. Croix

Fond du Lac

Mille Lacs

Abigail ("Abbie") Spooner.

Wheeler and Wood Families. Harriet ("Hattie") Wheeler (front row center, wearing white), Hannah Wood Hoagland (second row, behind Hattie, left) and Mary Warren English (directly behind Hattie). Hattie's dog rests at her feet.

William Wheeler.

Emily Wheeler.

Fred Wheeler.

E. P. Wheeler.

Walter Wheeler.

Charles Eugene Wheeler.

Harriet Wheeler's home in Beloit, Wisconsin.

Hattie, E. P., Eugene, and William Wheeler with the original model of the Eclipse Windmill. The bandages represent injuries suffered during the mill's creation.

6.

Harriet's Children

As Harriet's and Leonard's children move out into the world, their actions reveal the same courage and sense of social responsibility their parents possessed. By virtue of growing up with the Ojibwe in northern Wisconsin, they add to these qualities a delight in their natural environment and an ability to easily cross cultural lines. The prime example of these last two qualities is Mary Warren. At her father's request, the Wheelers informally adopted her after her parents' deaths, and when she writes her "sister" Julia Wheeler on June 30, 1861, from her teaching post in Long Prairie, Minnesota,[1] her note makes clear that she functions happily and fully in both the Indian and white worlds.

I received your letter a few days since, and as you may well imagine, was very happy to hear from my dear sister. And so you are teaching school at La Pointe; I know you are enjoying yourself very much indeed. I trust you will have good success. I am so glad they have such excellent teachers at the boarding school.

Oh dear Julia I wish you were here, if only for a little while. You would be perfectly charmed with Long Prairie, I know. It is the most lovely place. If it was only situated on the shores of Lake Superior, I would never ask for a better place to live. The Prairie is now covered with the most beautiful wild flowers, and the most charming clusters which remind me of orchids in Ohio. I have learned to ride horseback. Lizzie Wanblene and myself had great times galloping where and whenever we chose. The Major owns a large group of Red River pines;

there are three or four nice little Lakes two miles from here; we frequently go out there and have a good time.

I am having very good success with my school. The children are learning fast. How different from Indian children when one has to have the *patience* of *Job* to be within *decent bounds*.

My school is not large, but I have enough to keep me busy during school hours. I work with a good heart I assure you; it is so much more pleasant to be employed than to live in idleness, of which I am always guilty whenever I go to my sisters. They never let me do anything and there are not enough children there to have school. My sister Julia's husband has been sick all summer, and he is at present very feeble and his constitution is entirely shattered. I am fearful he will not live long. She has three little children. They have a very comfortable home. My brother in law, Mr Prince, has joined the Volunteer Co, of Minnesota[2] and my sister Charlotte is stopping at Fort Snelling.[3] How dreadful this civil war is; I only hope it will be the end of Slavery, and then, and only then, will the many lives that will be lost and the blood spilt, be richly paid.

Major Cam[4] has gone to St Paul. He will be appointed to command some of the troops. He is an excellent good man, a devoted Christian, and so cheerful and pleasant with all he has to do with, he has held commissions in the United States Army before. Well, I must tell you good bye. Write again and soon. Love to all at Odanah and to all enquiring friends at La Pointe, "God bless you."

Affectionately Yours,

Mary

P.S. If you should see my Aunt Shefault at La Pointe tell her I am well, and send her much love and to the rest of my relatives.

In the summer of 1863, Julia Wheeler moved to the mining town of Hancock, Michigan, to teach school. Her first letters show that she took her concern for the Ojibwe and the mission with her to Michigan. She seems particularly outraged that troops were sent

to northern Wisconsin because of the fear that the Ojibwe, like the Minnesota Sioux
in 1862, would attack whites. She finds the notion ludicrous.

My dear Parents,

I have at length reached my journey's end, and am now comfortably settled in my new home, feeling very happy in the consciousness that I have left *barbarism* and *Bayfield* so far behind me. I enjoyed the trip down the Lake very much. The weather was delightful, and I found so many kind friends on board the boat that I really hated to leave it—Cher Ward,[5] the owner, with his wife, children, stepfather-in-law and some Detroit friends were on board, and introduced themselves to me before I had been there half an hour. They are the best people I ever met. Mrs. Nichols (Mrs. Ward's mother) is very much interested in missions, and gives a great deal towards their support. Now I have some pleasant news to communicate. She will make you a valuable donation in the shape of a first-class melodeon for the mission Church. She told me you should have the *best* she could find, and that she should herself pay $100.00 towards it. She promises to send it *immediately*—so you may expect a very superior instrument. We talked all the time day and night.

They inquired very particularly about government matters—the sending of troops to Bayfield etc. I told them that it was an *outrageous imposition*. I never felt so *encouraged* about Indians affairs as I do now. I wish I could find time to tell you some things that the Ward family told me but I have not. You have warm friends in them, who will sustain any movement you may make in reference to your troubles with the Bayfield wretches—Sen. Rice[6] + Co. You will probably receive a visit from Mrs. Ward this summer. They are so very kind. I do wish I could see you long enough to tell you what they told me. It would do you good—and if altogether too rich for anything that is to pass through the Bayfield post office. Don't neglect to acknowledge the melodeon. You must thank Mrs. Nichols for that. She resides in St Clair Co. Mich. She is very wealthy and is busy in founding churches etc. She told me that your mission would receive attention thereafter, and that several influential people would visit it this summer. She will request some personal friends to do so. Oh, I cannot tell you anything—but don't give up the ship yet.

I have a very pleasant boarding place in the family of Mr. Cleaves, the Superintendent of the Smelting works, whose three sons are my pupils, and the best behaved boys I ever saw.[7] I have the best view from my windows, on Lake Superior. My room is in the second story + is very large + has three large windows in front—the floor is nicely carpeted and I can have a stove in it this winter.

Now about the piano. I have had several applications made already and can have all the pupils I shall find time to teach. I am very anxious to get started as soon as possible: it will take time to get started, and I have a reputation yet to make. I hope you will send it by the next boat without fail. As it belongs to the Board, I will pay them any reasonable rent for it. Send it the care of Perkins + co. *Franklin Dock*, Hancock. Portage Lake. Tell Leonard I want him to follow my directions exactly about packing it up. He knows where the old box is. In your trunk upstairs—you will find a large paper of long screws—which belong to it. I saw them the day I left home. Take the pedal off first and remove the pedal sticks. Lock the piano so the *lid will not move*: unscrew the legs. By examining the bottom of the piano you will see place for the screws—which are to go through the outside of the box (where you will find the places) into the instrument. This will prevent its moving round. I shall want the stool. There is room for it in the box if you unscrew the legs—and take off the top.

Hancock June 1863

*M*y Dear Mother:
I have just closed one letter to you but did not say half that I wanted to. I have a very pleasant home in the family of Mrs. Cleaves,[8] who, by the way is a Lowell lady. I had a very pleasant journey down the Lake, and made some new acquaintances that I shall never forget. Mrs. Nichols who makes you such a rich donation, says she will try and visit the mission this summer. Be sure and have a quantity of Graham flour—so that she can have Graham bread. She is a

warm-hearted, whole-souled woman, who is very much interested in missions, and has the convenient accompaniment of wealth and high position which is not to be *despised*.

My school is large and is increasing every day. The scholars have been accustomed to do about as they pleased and I am putting them through a course of more than military drill. It is taking the *fat* off from me already, but will be much easier by and by. In my last I told you about the piano. Don't fail to send it immediately. It is important that I commence at once.

I must have a few books; you can fit them in my trunk when you send it. I want both of my instruction books, Bassini's[9] and Richardson's[10]—all my sheet music—a copy of the Eclectic[11] which you will find in my room with my name on it—the book Dr Wood gave me + the chorus Glee Book,[12] Longfellow's poems, Whittier poems Vol 2nd (I have the 1st here),[13] Farquelle's French Lessons,[14] Arnold Latin Lessons,[15] Andrew + Stoddard's Latin Grammar, Andrew's Latin Reader.[16] If Eddie does not want to use Caesar's Commentaries, I wish he would lend me a copy; but I am not particular. Burritt's astronomy; the Atlas to go with the astronomy is on the top of my book case.[17] Send also my natural Philosophy[18] and Hitchcock's Geology.[19] Like of Charlotte Bronte, + Wilson's Treatise in Punctuation[20] which I shall use a great deal, Rand's Psychology and *The Imitation of Christ* by Thomas A Kempis.

I wish you would send me two pictures—the rabbits and the sick soldier. I want to finish and hang them over the piano in my music room. My portrait of the Virgin—you will pack very carefully so it will not be broken. I wish you would put it in the top of my work box, and fill the bottom with tamarack, and a few of the spruce cones from the trees in the flower garden. Tell Emma to put in a few of the best shell cones she can find in my boxes. Can you let me have linen enough for one or two collars? You will find the laces you gave me for them wrapped up in paper in my bureau drawer.

It does not take long for Julia's persistently weak lungs to make themselves felt.

Portage Lake August 8th 1863

*M*y dear mother:

You are doubtless surprised at the non-appearance of a letter from me. My school keeps me very busy and I am not very well. My old cough commenced before I had been here two weeks, and has continued to the present time, so that it is now somewhat troublesome. Do not be alarmed now and think or imagine that I am *sick*. No such thing. My left lung has not been *perfectly* sound for two years. During that time, there has been but few days that I have not suffered more or less from them, and they trouble me a little more than usual now. *That's all*. I often feel a dull, heavy pain through my left lung, when I am at all tired, especially after climbing these abominable hills. I do not try to study at all, and do not even read the newspapers half of the time. I am absolutely the laziest good-for-nothing girl breathing. I bathe all over every day, am careful about my food, and have used mustard poultices enough to cure or kill a dozen persons. So you see I am using all the remedies I can. My school term ends the 16th of Sept which will soon be here. I shall have a few days vacation then, and will spend it stopping a few days at Ontonagon.

I have commenced giving music lessons, but shall not attempt to take more than two or three pupils, until fall. Don't tell *anyone that I am sick. I am not.* I am very much pleased with my school, and do not intend to leave it until I am obliged to do so. Miss Livermore[21] and her brother in law Mr McIntyre, have called to see me. I would rather have half-a-dozen ugly fangs extracted from my jaws than return it, but suppose I shall *have* to. Mr Smith[22] is now at L'Anse. He learned from a pupil of mine that I was teaching school and sent me a message, that he would stop and see me, as he had a great many questions to ask, and a great deal to talk about. I sent him a note immediately and expect to see him soon. If he is not *enlightened* in regard to Indian Affairs in Wis, it will be not the fault of Julia Wheeler.

Do you know that I think the *morning* will soon dawn on the Indians. There is a healthy tone of sentiment in regard to this unfortunate people, in Michigan that I *like*.

I feel as exhausted when school closes, that I do not feel like writing, or anything else out of it. I hope to get over this soon. Kiss my baby Walter for sister Julia—also Eugene + Hattie. Tell Emma I will try + write her soon. Give my regards to the boarding house people + to Henry's family.

If I felt able to do what I want to, I would by all means go to Detroit during my vacation; but the thought of meeting so many strangers appalls me. I shall want to visit Ann Arbor, Kalamazoo and Monroe and of course St. Clair + Detroit. What glorious news we are having from the seat of war. I am expecting to hear that Charleston is laid in ashes before long.

Love to all,

Your daughter

Hancock August/ 63

My dear mother,

My school keeps me very busy—and numbers at present over seventy pupils—a mixed heterogeneous company, good, bad and different, French, Irish, German, Cornish, Welsh and American of various ages, from four to those who are older than I am. Having so many different grades, makes a great many different classes and I am busy hearing recitation from nine to twelve and from one to four through both recesses without any intermission. The School Board and the parents seem very much pleased with the school, and say their children never learned as far as at present. It will be much larger and very much harder this winter; but never mind, "Better wear out than pass out."

I have made a few very pleasant acquaintances here. Foremost among these is the family of Ann Brigham[23] who resides at Houghton. A few individuals who profess to be very literary have just organized a club, a literary association to meet once a week during the fall and winter. Original articles are to be read—music to form a large part of the entertainment and private theatricals are to be enacted occasionally to break up the monotony. This club is very *select* and exclusive: imagine my surprise at being *urged* to become one of the leading members. I felt quite inclined (over the left shoulder as the boys say) to hide my diminished cranium and say with Paul Fry—"Hope I shan't intrude."

I am very sorry that I sent for the piano as it will do no good. I am not able to practice myself at present, but have taken one pupil so that it will be no expense to me. I can have all the pupils I can possibly attend to, but cannot do anything out of school now. Perhaps I shall be stronger bye and bye; I receive no benefit from it whatever now as I am so tired after school that I cannot think of taking mere recreation of any kind. I never open it for my own improvement, but only to play for company when requested, and to give a lesson to a pupil twice a week. I will have it tuned and repaired here and if it will be of any use to Emma you had better have it at home. It is *possible* I may be able to teach music this winter, but this is very doubtful and I certainly cannot do this now. I am very sorry that I cannot do more. One is *obliged* to bear the many pangs and aches, the "thousand natural shocks that flesh is heir to—until they have shuffled off this instant evil" as I believe Shakespeare expresses it, and I have about concluded that the best way be to endure these aches is not to notice them at all, or rather by a strong determined will to endure at least to rise above and triumph over mere physical suffering.

My school closes in just five weeks and two days. By that time I think I shall be ready for a day or two of rest, ditto Cod Liver Oil and a Sea voyage which is sufficiently rough enough for all practical purposes. In plainer words, I shall be ready for two weeks vacation. Kiss the little ones for me. Your daughter Julia

———

At the same time, Julia writes her father a note warning him that people want his mission gone.

I have seen *Mr Smith* and had such a good long talk with him. There has been a stronger effort than you imagine made to break up the mission. Perhaps I have already said more than I ought, in a letter. Should this chance to meet your eyes-Gen Webb,²⁴ or those of your wretched minions, I hope you will enjoy its perusal. "Tell your father and mother," said Mr. Smith "to keep up good courage and never despair. The devil is not dead in the world yet." Dear good, honest Mr. Smith: You are one of the true heroes of earth, though for the noble stand you have taken against corruption and fraud, you will never receive a reward here; for the world knows not such as you.

———

After a while, Julia finds that Houghton's politics make her teaching job difficult. Articles in the Houghton Miner *validate Julia's complaints about the quality of the schools and also show that she was the highest paid teacher in Houghton. Julia's response to her dilemma suggests that she has some of her parents' courage—and righteousness.*

Houghton December 9th 1863

*M*y dear, dear mother,
I am now sitting at my desk in the school-room and as I have nothing particular to do just now as my pupils are having their morning's recess; I think that I can best improve the short interval in writing you. My pupils are making commendable progress in their studies, and the *Houghton High* School is in as flourishing a condition as can be expected under present circumstances. But Oh! I shall be so thankful when my term is out. My situation is *peculiarly* a trying one. I shall for no consideration retain it longer than next spring. There is a very large foreign element in the population consisting principally of Irish who have no affection for but rather a strong aversion for American institutions. They have a secret society in full force here, called the St. Patrick, the members of which encourage the strong party feeling by every means in their power, and march around the streets, wearing Irish national colors (green sashes with silver fringes) with a brass band playing national airs. We have here a population of ten thousand inhabitants, and of these a very large majority are *Irish*, who now constitute a very formidable class. They have been flattered by politicians, feel very important. Serious riots have several times been apprehended.

When the subject of having a high school first came up for consideration last summer, a public meeting was held as the law requires the subject to be decided by a vote. Many prominent citizens gathered at an early hour at the Court House, and when the doors were opened, in poured a crowd of Irish, half of them drunk and all very angry and excited, swearing that no change should be made in the old school system and that they were fully prepared to successfully resist every effort to organize such a system. The reason they gave for their insolent conduct was that such a system would *increase* their rate of taxes. The Americans present were perfectly thunderstruck. They were shrewd enough, however, to conceal their feelings, and assumed a careless, unconcerned appearance saying that they had better adjourn, and to let the matter rest. They then went around and enlisted every native born American they could find at a sudden meeting, and before the Irish had time to come, voted to appropriate to twenty thousand dollars for a building and organized a High School, appointing me teacher in the highest department. A board of Trustees were chosen consisting of the *meanest men* in the place, and who are *themselves divided into two opposite parties* which of course makes it very unpleasant.

The other teachers will consent to be imposed upon to an unlimited extent, and stand very much in fear of the trustees. I won't be imposed upon and I am not afraid of the trustees. But here's the *rub*. One of the most prominent members of the boards is an Hon (!!!) Member of the Legislature himself an *Irishman* who obtained his situation solely by Irish votes. Of course, he must favor the Irish and their demands, however *unreasonable* these may be. The Irish wished to have an Irish man for one of the assistant teachers, and brought forward one recently from the "ould country" named Patrick Sullivan. I was present at all the examination which took place at the Court House. Mr. Sullivan was an exceedingly ignorant man, and had such a strong Irish accent and brogue that it was almost possible to understand him. Another of the candidates was a Cornish girl (Miss Newcombe) who was no more competent to teach than our Hattie. To my great surprise, however, and indignation, they both received a *certificate*. The citizens laughed, but said they must *compromise*. The aristocracy all send their sons and daughters, those who are sufficiently advanced to enter it, to my room, and the younger ones go to the next room taught by a young lady from Ohio. So it made no difference to them who taught the other departments, and they like to please the *foreign* element by a wretched compromise.

The other teachers were indignant but did not dare open their mouths for fear of losing their own places. I never was so angry in my life. I met the Board of trustees. I told one of them (the Hon Mr. McKernan[25]) that I had no objection to his doing all he could for his political constituents but I had some pride for my reputation as a teacher and utterly refused to teach unless Mr. Pat Sullivan and Miss Newcombe were discharged. So Mr. Sullivan was removed, and Miss Newcombe attends my school as a *pupil*. The other teachers are much older than I am, most of my pupils are older than myself, the daughters and sons of the wealthy who think the almighty dollar will do everything for them.

People are very kind to me though I am *poor* (ain't it strange), but Oh mother you don't know what a hard time I have. Oh! This long, long winter! How can I ever endure it? They want a strong man in my place, one who can *fight* a great many hard battles. It is no place for me and I cannot endure it long. I have a large class in music, all that I can attend to. I work very hard I assure you. I have an excellent music room, which I have rented in the heart of Houghton. I would drop some of my music pupils if I could afford it, but I cannot in order to make any profit at all. My expenses are enormous. I pay $5.00 a week for board.

Much love to all enquiring friends.

Yours affect.

Julia

The school records published in the Portage Lake Miner Gazette *suggest that Julia taught very little in 1864, presumably because of illness. In the meantime, the Wheelers' son William dropped out of Beloit College in Wisconsin to fight in the Civil War. A letter from Martha Lathrop, the head of the household where he lived in Beloit, fills his mother in on the details.*

Beloit June 14th 1864

*M*y dear Mrs. Wheeler,

As William intended writing you soon after he left here nearly a month ago, you no doubt have learned before this that he has joined a company of hundred days men that went from this place. This regiment "the 40th Wisconsin" pushed through Clinton, a place a few miles from here, on their way to Washington, this forenoon. I cannot tell you how unhappy his going away had made me. It seemed to me that I *could not* have him go, and you may be sure that if any amount of persuasion or entreaty would have prevented it, he would never have gone. He has been a great comfort to me, and done very much towards making home cheerful and pleasant since he has been in the family, and we miss him dreadfully. And then to think of his being in the Army, but I do hope that this Regiment will not see active service, nor be prevailed upon to re-enlist when their term has expired.

His teachers are very much attached to him, and did everything they thought best to do to prevent his going, especially as he was obliged to go without obtaining the consent of his parents. But he argued that it would be impossible to consult them and that he was sure they would be willing. Do not *blame* him. I am sure he did not make up his mind to go from caprice or willfulness but pure patriotism, and trust he will be kept from all kinds of harm—and come back with new ambition to his studies in the fall.

Now you must not think because Willie started away from his home, and hadn't his mother to see him that he went uncared for. He is one that finds his way to everybody's heart. I did everything I could do to keep him at home. And when I found he must go, it was a relief and pleasure to me to do all I could think of for his comfort in going—He has promised to let me know if he is in want of anything that can be sent to him at any time, and Prof. Blaisdell,[26] his Chaplain, has agreed to send word if he is sick, and send him home if possible. I have loved to do for him all that I would have done if he had been one of my own family.

It is very lonely here without him. The children set the table for him every meal as usual with his napkin rolled up just as he left it the morning he left home, and his things lie about the house just as he left them. I will not have one of them moved. I feel so sorry for you. I know it must have been sad news to you.

The one hundred days began last Tuesday—We shall count the days in the family until they are gone. If he does not go home at the expiration of his term of service, cannot you meet him here? I shall be very glad to have you do so. I have had two letters from him while in Camp and he has promised that I shall hear from him often although he does not love to write letters. I shall be very glad to hear from you, and wish to know how you feel about his going—

Truly yours,

Martha H. Lathrop.

In the fall of 1864, Leonard Wheeler traveled to Houghton to get Julia, their piano, and himself home over a turbulent Lake Superior.

Portage Lake Sept 23, 1864

Dear Harriet,

You see I am still here. Returned to this place the next morning after you left Marquette and have been waiting for a boat. The piano is all boxed up + will be put on board the Traveler in the course of an hour, and then we shall be one our way home. I suppose you found Willy all right + ready to proceed again with his studies. I hope the weather will be better on the lake next month than it is now. I am glad you will have to travel only from Marquette home on the water. Much love to all the friends. We shall have occasion to be thankful if we can reach home again in safety.

Your affectionate husband,

L. H. Wheeler

P.S. I cannot help turning my thoughts homeward + thinking of the little ones.

Meanwhile, Harriet travels with their son William, who has returned from the war with serious eye injuries. But she also searches for a mission teacher on this journey.

Ripon Sept 27/64

_D_ear Husband

Willie and I reached the place at 12 o'clock last night—We are detained here until 3 this afternoon when we take the stage. On my way from Green Bay, I got track of a teacher at Ripon from Fond Du Lac, took the stage to Ripon and stopped there one night. I visited Mr. Merriman[27] and Mrs. Tracy.[28] Mr. M was not personally acquainted with the lady in question but Mrs. T had known her for some years. She said she would fill our bill with the exception of two things: she lacked health and energy. As these were two such important qualifications, I thought it best to do nothing more about it and come on directly to Beloit. I reached there about six o clock in the eve. Found Willie at Mrs. Lathrop's. Glad to see me, I assure you. The poor boy has been sick with fever and ague. He is taking Quinine + iron and I think his fever is broken up. He was in the hospital a week before he left Memphis—He looks thin and pale, but has a good appetite. I thought the trip here might do him good. His school commences Thursday.

Rockford Oct 2

_I_ want to start for home next week but it is uncertain; I am getting almost homesick. Oh I do want to see you all so much. Tell the boarding house girls I hope to hear they have all been good. Tell our children that Mother should have a great many stories to tell them about Willie when I get home. I am feeling quite anxious about this teaching matter. I really do not know where to look next—I shall talk with _Mr_ Fisk[29] and _Prof_ Emerson[30] about it. If we can do no other way, would Mary Warren answer for this winter? I wish I could consult you a few moments now. Take good care of darling Wallie [her son, Walter Wheeler]; you don't know how I want to see him. Do be careful husband and not get sick. Your Affect Wife

H W W

Having to leave Houghton does not daunt Julia Wheeler's courage, as the following article she wrote on the Sioux uprising shows.[31] *In it, she defends the Sioux, while admitting that they killed or injured 800 settlers. The essay appeared on the front page of the* Beloit Journal *on December 22, 1864.*

The Indians of the Northwest

The attention of the public was for a time directed to the condition of Indian affairs in the Northwest with more than an ordinary degree of interest, by the Sioux massacre of Minnesota. A momentary thrill of horror passed through the Nation, when in the Summer of 1862, the saddest and strangest ever known in the beautiful state of Minnesota, the first fearful war cry rang over the western prairies—a cry which was echoed from the shores of the Atlantic to the Pacific. Ah! What scenes of tragedy and pathos those summer suns witnessed; an infuriated, vindictive horde suddenly invaded the peaceful frontier settlements, and murdered the innocent inhabitants with every conceivable form of torture which savage ingenuity could devise, wrought up to a fearful pitch of madness by a knowledge of the wrongs which had been inflicted on them for years. Thriving villages which had sprung up like a dream of enchantment as the onward tide of population had neared the plains of Dacotah, were destroyed, and the homeless refugees, reduced to the most abject beggary filled every town in the State. For a time it seemed as if the Indians had by the barbarities they had committed placed themselves wholly beyond the pale of public sympathy. Yet a thoughtful observer who was acquainted with the policy Minnesota has ever pursued in dealing with her Indians could see in this outbreak, the avenging hand of the Almighty laid heavily upon the State. Though a fearful it was a just punishment. We reap as we sow; and in the Sioux massacre of 1862 Minnesota only reaped the legitimate fruits of those deadly seeds of distrust and iniquity her politicians had been assiduously sowing in the hearts of this unfortunate race for years, and which ripened in those days of reckoning for a fearful harvest of blood. Upon her innocent border settlers fell the punishment; upon her wicked statesmen must inevitably fall the disgrace when the causes which led to the massacre are fully known. "There is not a man in America," says that noble philanthropist, Bishop Whipple,[32] of the Minnesota "who ever gave an hour's calm reflection to this subject who does not know that our Indian system is an organized system of robbery, and has been for years a disgrace to the nation. It has left savage men without governmental control; it has looked on unconcerned at every crime against the law of God and man; it has fostered savage life by wasting thousands of dollars in the purchase of paint, beads, scalping knives and tomahawks; it has squandered the funds for civilization and schools; it has fostered a trade which robbed the thrifty and virtuous to pay the debts of the indolent and vicious; it has connived at theft; it has winked at murder; and at last, after dragging the savage down to a brutishness unknown to his fathers, it has brought a harvest of blood to our own door."

Under this wretched system the Sioux had been suffering for years. The treaty by which they disposed of their lands in the southern part of Minnesota,[33] was born in fraud, and left a deep feeling of injustice and hatred, which rankled in savage hearts for ten years. The dissatisfaction was increased in 1856 by a knowledge of the dishonesty and the gigantic frauds which accompanied the sale of eight hundred thousand acres of land, for which they never received a farthing as it was all absorbed in claims. This alone was sufficient to secure a massacre in time. The last cause of irritation which preceded the massacre, was in the summer of 1862, when they were kept waiting two months at the agency for their annuities, and then found that one half of their annuity money had been retained at Washington for traders' claims. Goaded to madness by the monstrous wrong, they resolve on savage vengeance. Then came the most fearful massacre in History which desolated the most beautiful part of the state and in which eight hundred peaceful citizens fell, murdered in cold blood—victims of that atrocious system which has brought us nothing but sorrow. After the battle of Wood Lake in which the Sioux were defeated by Gen. Sibley,[34] a large party of friendly Indians headed by Wabeshaw[35] and Toope,[36] came in under a flag of truce bringing with them two hundred captive white women and children, whom they had rescued at the peril of their own lives from Little Crow[37] and his hostile followers. By order of the President, Gen. Sibley held a Military Commission, by which all who were convicted of the slightest participation in the massacre were condemned to death. Thirty-seven were hung and by a subsequent order from the President the order for the execution of the remaining three hundred was changed to one of imprisonment for life. Those who were honorably acquitted and against whom not the slightest suspicion rests, were the friendly Sioux led by Wabeshaw and Toope to whom the country is indebted for the rescue and preservation of two hundred women and children. The nation owed these Indians a debt of gratitude for preserving their fealty under such trying circumstances. But how has their fidelity been rewarded? My heart sickens, and my cheek crimsons with shame when I think of the treatment to which they have been subjected. They were driven from their homes, and taken to a desert on the upper Missouri, where over one thousand have perished since their removal.

The soil is so poor as to be utterly incapable of cultivation. Rev. J. P. Williamson[38] a missionary of the A.B.C. F. M. reports that potatoes planted never came up. A few spears of corn came through the soil in August. Gen. Sully reports to the Department that they must all perish unless removed to a more favorable location. Rev. Mr. Hinman,[39] a devoted Dacotah missionary who accompanied his flock of Christian Indians to this region says their situation is awful, "a desert as to location, starvation as to condition." Government appropriated large sums of money for the removal and support of those Indians. I believe that the policy of our Government is intended to be humane; but the kind intentions are thwarted by swindling agents and government employees. Government pledged itself to furnish 4 lbs. of beef a week to each Sioux on the Missouri. Messrs Hubbell & Hawley[40] obtained a license to trade with the

Indians, and had the contract for supplying them with their weekly allowance of beef. These traders purchased beef on the old Winnebago Reservation in Minnesota, which was so badly damaged as to have been condemned two years previously as unfitted for sale. This was taken up the Missouri and doled out to the Indians. These same licensed traders are furnishing the Indians flour at the rate of *sixty dollars* per barrel, and with potatoes and onions at *five cents apiece*. It is due to the unfortunate red men, to remove them at the soonest possible moment to a more favorable location. Let not this dark stain of ingratitude be longer permitted to tarnish the fame and honor of our country. It is too late to undo all wrong. We can not bring back the dead; but it is our solemn duty to do justice to the living. Until this is done, it is but mockery to ask for the blessing of Almighty God upon our efforts to secure permanent peace and tranquility on our western border. Every feeling of Justice and Humanity demands a reform of this crying evil. By everything that is dear to us—for the honor of our country—by the memory of our eight hundred border friends who are now sleeping in their lone, nameless graves on our western prairies, to protect the border settlers from their fate, let the union lay blame of this great crime where it belongs, and where History will place it, at the door of our wicked Indian system, and demand its reform.

———————

Shortly after her article defending the Sioux appeared, Julia contacted Charles Sumner about Indian matters. He replied on January 18, 1865.

I hasten to acknowledge your letter of January 13th. The condition of our Indian tribes has always caused me solicitude. The difficulty seems to me to be not so much in the system as in the men who are employed to carry it out. The same spirit animating its agents, no system could have succeeded, and the problem is to find men who, coming from the West, and familiar with Indian character and habits, are at once honest, unprejudiced and willing to work for the small compensation which the government can offer. Even if such men could be found, it is not easy for the appointing power to discriminate between honest men and well recommended rogues; and once appointed, there are great difficulties in detecting fraud, especially as the feeling of the border population upon the subject of the Indians is far from just. I shall be glad of any suggestions you may have be able to give me. Accept my best wishes and believe me

    Faithfully yours,
    Charles Sumner

In her letter of September 15, 1865, Harriet writes from Odanah to inform her husband, who is in Chicago, that the American Board of Commissioners for Foreign Missions is withdrawing its support and offering the Wheelers, and their many children, land in Odanah as a retirement plan, even though living there has undermined the Wheelers' health. Still, Harriet reports their children all want to stay.

Willie brought home with him from Bayfield a letter from Mr. Treat which seems to me important. I infer from this letter that the Board have fully decided to abandon the mission. The reasons given are the great expense and so little fruit. Should the Board break up here, *when* will it be best for us to leave?

There are three reasons in favor of our leaving this fall. First your health. Secondly Willie's; I am really feeling quite anxious about him. He took cold when he went to Bayfield and his eyes have been very bad since his return. He is not able to do anything. He started the hay press but it required so much of his attention then he stopped it for a few days.

The Dr cupped Willie's eyes this morning and will repeat it tomorrow morning. The Dr says he would make some application to his eyes, but he is afraid of injuring them. Willie's general health is not good. He is getting very thin. Two years ago he weighed two hundred and forty eight lbs. Now he weighs one hundred and twenty eight. I fear it will be necessary for him to go to some eye infirmary. Would it not be well to inquire at Chicago the expense of sending him there? The poor boy is feeling quite discouraged about himself. He wants you to purchase for him a pair of London smoke Glasses with side glasses as soon as possible and send them by mail. Another reason for our leaving this fall is on Julia's account. She thinks she cannot spend the winter here. If we should go to Ripon or Fon du Lac,[41] I think she would go with us and go on with her own work. *On the other hand* I fear it will be more expensive for us to leave this fall.

Mr. Treat says in his letter, "You will need help. How would you like to take part of the property and how much?" This is a grave question for us to decide. Dr. Ellis thinks it is hardly safe for us to take the place expecting to support our family from it. Will not the Board let us have the refusal of it for a year? By that time we can judge what the effect of change of climate will have upon your health. And what we can do toward our own support then? In any case, you can assure Mr. Treat that it will be much more trying to us to call upon the Board for aid than it will be for the Board to grant it. The children do not like the idea of giving up the place.

One thing I hope you will confirm freely with Mr. Treat. That is the destitute condition we are in now. It surely is not just that we should leave the Board so. There has never been a time since we have been connected with it that we were so short for bedding, table linen and wearing apparel as now. Should the Boarding School break up, would there be an objection to our taking these things from there sufficient to make us comfortable?

In getting a place it seems very desirable that you should select one so located and of such dimensions that we would reasonably expect to obtain much of our support from it.

Would it not be well to secure the two hundred + fifty dollars now in possession of the Board belonging to us and have it put into Gov. bonds?

Leonard accepts the board's final decision with heartbreaking grace.

Chicago Oct 5, 1865

*D*ear Harriet,

We are now on the last day of the Board meeting. I saw Mr. Treat a few moments yesterday, and shall see him again for a full conference tomorrow. Mr. Treat I think is ready to have us bring matters to a close at Odanah, as soon as practicable, unless things assume a more hopeful appearance. I have arranged with a lady of Beloit who will go up if needed + help Mrs. Ellis or teach as needed She has a good education and of great force of character.

The Board will give us a land and a home if we wish to live in one, sell if we wish. Mr. Treat thinks we had better by all means take it. This is all he can do for us in getting a home. You may well suppose I am with a quandary to know just what to do, but we will see.

Your affectionate husband

L. H. Wheeler

We are having a blessed meeting—I wish you were all here to enjoy it.

When Julia writes her sister Emma[42] from Odanah on October 20, 1865, it is clear that her life there includes frequent and easy interactions with Indians. She claims that she wants to leave the mission for her mother's sake, but she also makes nostalgic tours of the area and preserves its leaves.

Oct 20th 1865

*M*y dear sister Emma!

Your very welcome letter was received this afternoon. It gave me much pleasure to hear from you, though I was sorry to learn of your home-sickness. I hope by this time you are feeling better. We are looking for father every hour. He wrote as if we might leave this fall if he could arrange matters satisfactorily there. I hope we shall be able to leave this fall. Mother is very anxious to leave Odanah as soon as possible.

Though the Inland Indians have been waiting here for six weeks, Mr. Webb has gone to Grand Portage to pay the Indians there and is not looked for here till next Monday. You ask me if mother is not afraid? No, she is not now. I do not think there's danger of an insurrection here. Me-shin-a-way[43] comes up to see me as often as ever. My dearly beloved Na-wa-ge-won[44] once. Hitche-a-ge-ma makes me an occasional call. Mary Warren has not come yet and we do not expect her. Her cousin George Warren[45] is here now.

We had a grand time singing when Leonard came down last and spoke of you many times. We should have enjoyed ourselves so much more if the dear absent ones could have been with us. But God willing, we will be all together again before many months.

I see from your letter that your time is very much occupied. You say that if you can find time, you propose doing washing for some of Eddie's friends. Mother wishes me to say that you must not think of doing any such thing. I must utter my protest too against such a course. You work quite as much as you ought to now. My dear sister it makes my heart ache to have you do as much as you are now doing. You must not attempt any more. Remember that it is very important for you to study now. You will soon be able to teach an excellent school.

I am getting along finely with my own work. If we do not leave the Lake this fall I have promised to teach the La Pointe school which has been offered me. I have made a very pleasant visit to La Pointe since you left and rambled over the old mission Home and went up to the little Protestant burying ground on the hill.

Mother is very busy as usual preparing for company. Little Walter often speaks of you. He came in one day from his play very tired and hungry crying for you to give him some milk. He said, "My darling Emma, give me milk." Oh Emma, you have no idea how beautiful the woods are now in all the glory and gorgeousness of their autumn coloring. I have pressed a great many of the forest leaves.

All send much love. Write as often as you can and I will pledge myself to do the same.

From your affectionate sister

Julia

By the time Julia writes her sister again in early November, she thinks it wrong to abandon the mission and feels certain that her father wants to stay.

Odanah Nov 1st 1865

*M*r Dear Emma:

I received a very interesting letter from you some time ago and wrote you in reply a lengthy epistle which with characteristic stupidity I neglected to put in the Post Office. A few days since, since having a general "cleaning up time," much to my sorrow I came across said letter in one of my bureau drawers. You know I do not disturb my drawers very often, my strict adherence to the precept of having a place for everything and every thing in its place. This accounts for my not finding your letter before. But it is not necessary for me to enlarge on my habits of order. You surely cannot have forgotten the Saturday evening lectures in which father while urging upon you younger ones the importance of doing up things *systematically*, always referred to me as an example for you poor sinners to copy. "Now here's Julia! If you would only do as she does" etc. etc.

I suppose Willy is now with you. Poor fellow!

I am now teaching school with the Doctor. Augusta attends regularly—so does Maggie and Virginia. The Boarding School was broken up some time ago.

We have received two very valuable donation boxes this week, and are now very plentifully supplied with underclothing. There is also a large quantity of nice shirts for father and the boys. Just the things for Willie and Eddie. I send you samples of the dress patterns. The brown delaine and calico are mothers. The purple is mine.

Mother is well and as busy as ever.

Walter is growing full and is very rugged. He speaks of you and Eddie very often.

Now about our leaving Odanah, I think just as you do about it. I do not believe Father would be contented away from the Indians, nor do I think it would be right to abandon this station. Things are much more encouraging now than when you left. The school is filling up, and more attend church than formerly. I do not think father wants to leave now if he can get funds from any board of Mission to carry on the missionary work here.

But I must close as it is about school time. Much love to Edie and yourself. It will give me much pleasure to hear from you often.

Julia W. Wheeler.

Despite the turmoil of their lives, when Emma writes asking for advice about school, her parents write thoughtful replies; Harriet Wheeler also offers her much love and compassion. Apparently, the Wheelers have no money to spare, since Emma's brother Leonard must pay for her music lessons. The letter begins in her father's handwriting.

Odanah Dec 2 1865

Dear Daughter Emily,

While we were seated at the dinner table, in came the mail and a letter from yourself and Eddy from Ripon and one from Willy from Fond du Lac. We are very glad indeed to hear from you all.

I will add a word about your coming home and break your studies. So far as expense is concerned, it would be better for you to remain where you are, as it will cost you $60 to come and return. And yet it may be best for you to do so. You will be wanted to teach here and to help your mother and to engage in some work. To help you, it would probably be better for your health. Should Eddy come home we could put him to work on the farm. But in regard to this whole subject, we think you had better have no particular plan at present. So many things may take place to change present plans between now and spring. But make the most of the *present* and we shall know better what to do a few months ahead than now.

As to what you ought to study, your teachers generally are the best judges on this point. Mr. Merriman thought that even if you studied but two terms in Latin it would help you much in understanding the general principles of English grammar. It would help you also in the study of Botany and chemistry and also to understand the denomination of many English words and yet I would like to have you study English Grammar too. I want to have you make thorough work of arithmetic, both of the common higher departments. I would like also to have you attend to music. Leonard says he will pay the expense of it. But would it be better for you to attend to that by and by when the warm weather of Spring returns? Have you time to attend to it now without sacrificing something else of perhaps more importance? You had better perhaps consult your teachers upon some of these points.

*M*y Dear Emma,

Father has left a little space for me but I have so many things to say I know not where to begin. I have felt very anxious about your health since you left. I feel sad when I think how hard you were obliged to work last summer. I fear you may feel the affects of it this winter. Be careful and not expose yourself. You know not how sorely mother misses you both. It seems so lonely here now. It seems as if I could not stay here another winter. Everything is very uncertain. I hope we shall be able to decide upon some ideas for the future before long. I think we had better keep this place, but perhaps we can rent it. With regard to your coming home next spring, we cannot tell now. I will wish to have you.

Your father has written about your studies. I think it is very desirable that you should attend the English grammar. Could you not attend to that and Latin, too, if you gave up reading and spelling? Do you overtax yourself? Be careful of your health. Remember you can do nothing without good health.

Julia is teaching with the Dr.[46] Mary Warren is teaching at La Pointe. They are both well. Let us hear from one of you at least once a week and keep your feet warm and dry. Should you or E have a sore throat, gargle it at the commencement with salt and water. The children all send much love.

Your Affec Mother

Abigail Spooner has returned home to Athol, Massachusetts, but took her intense interest in the Wheeler children with her, as shown by this letter she writes to Eddie and Emma on February 15, 1866.

My ever dear Emma and Eddie,

Do you think Aunt Abbie has forgotten you? If you do you are *exceedingly* mistaken—But am I mistaken in thinking my dear Emma & Eddie have forgotten Aunt Abbie? I hope you will convince me of the contrary before long—I have given you many warm hearted thoughts, and sent up many earnest prayers for you, since I heard you were away off at school, far from me, and far from home—and I have wished to write to you, but did not know how to direct a letter—yesterday my heart was gladdened by receiving letters from you folks—from *our* home—from your father, Leonard, Freddie and Mary Warren. O how glad and thankful I was—I had been *sadly* waiting for them for a long time. They seem to be getting along nicely. Mary Warren was there visiting and they had just been having a great time at *New Year's*—and *Christmas* together. Is it not a pretty hard case that we could not be there too! Such a number of those pleasant seasons have passed since I was permitted to meet with you all. I hope not so many more will pass, before I am one of the number again, but perhaps that may never be. It seems sad to have the Boarding school given up—does it not? Now let me tell you dear Emma and Eddie *I want to hear from you—from your own pen.* Now, write me soon as you can and let me know how you are situated—What sort of place you are in—how you like it—What are your privileges—What are your studies—how you get along with them—Do you find any hard steps when you would like an Aunt Abbie to help you out? I expect you think you could help her by this time—

What are your religious privileges? Do you enjoy them? Are you seeking the *one thing needed* more earnestly than anything else? May not I hope so?

Now Goodbye God bless you children—write me soon, both of you—and direct to Miss Abbie Spooner Athol Mass.

Kisagiin Nin Banque. Apigi—gaie Kin Ninanama—Bosho Bosho

On February 28, 1866, Harriet writes to inform Emma that she has an Indian namesake. The letter also makes clear that Harriet's example may inspire her children's easy cross-cultural relationships, for she casually mentions that Ojibwe join and even marry in the Wheeler household.

We rejoiced to learn that you were prospering so well in your studies, and was becoming more contented and happy. I would not bear this separation did I not feel that your best interests would be promoted by it. You say you wonder if we miss you. Oh my dear child, Mother misses you everywhere. It has been a dreary lonely winter to me. I am so glad spring is near. There has been a great deal of sickness since among the people and in the family since I wrote last. Martha Green is dead. She died about three weeks since. The circumstances connected with her sickness and death are very distressing. She left a little daughter. A short time before death your father asked her if she had any message she wished to send to you. She said, "Yes, tell her I name my little girl Emily for her." She spoke with great difficulty. She died a happy death; a few nights before her death she talked very freely about dying. She said she was not afraid to die. Her trust was in Jesus. She begged her mother not to weep for her. After talking some time, she prayed. Julia was watching with her at the end. She said her prayer made a deep impression on all present. The room was full. Her mother has been quite sick since the death but the babe is doing very well.

There are a great many sick now with the measles. The children had all had them. Wallie was quite sick. He is just recovering from them. Fred and Jean had their first in about a week after Hatie and Wallie came down with them. Before Fred and Jean were able to go out, your father came in one day with his arm broken. He was very faint and his hand was swollen badly. We called the Dr immediately after examining it. He said it broke close to the wrist joint. It pained him very much for a few days; it now seems to be doing well. We have not had the splint and bandage of yet + shall not be able to for two weeks to come. Leonard had started the morning before for St. Paul. In three days after he came back with knee badly injured. When I saw him brought in, it seemed as if it was more than I could bear. Hattie and Wallie were both quite sick at the time with the measles. Leonard is able to be about now some although he is still quite lame.

The Ashland mine has suspended operations.[47] Leonard and Rhoda have moved into the Boarding house. We find it very pleasant to have them near and there is great excitement in the country now about the Vermillion Lake gold mine.[48] Hundreds of people are flocking there. A delegation of Indians have gone on to Washington to sell the reserve. Hattie Green is with me. Mary Green[49] was *married* recently to Babo-ni-eish. The wedding was at our house. The children + Father all join me in much love to you—

Write often—

Your Affectionate Mother

H Wheeler

———————

Perhaps inspired by her father's successful missions to Washington, D.C., Julia apparently takes her protests on the road. Her Lowell grandmother reports on her visit in a letter dated March 1866.

*D*ear Harriet

You wish to know how Julia appeared when with us, I will say we enjoyed her visit *very much*. We did not think her insane but we did think she had altogether too much responsibility upon her for one *so young*. I told her I was fearful she would break down under it; I told her it seemed to me that in order to carry out her plans successfully she needed a most *perfect balance of character*. She seemed to me to be too young to be traveling around the country alone. She seemed *absent minded* but I did not think it strange. She took a severe cold while with us and as I bathed her throbbing brow, I could not but think how often I had stood thus over her mother in days that are past. I told her I felt she was capable of doing much good in the world if she could only take the right course. I do not wonder you are anxious about her. I do hope the Lord will hear the *prayers* that I have *been offered for her*.

The Woods have finally reconciled with their Shaker daughter, Mary.

*Y*ou ask if we hear from Mary often. She writes occasionally and has visited us twice within a year and we have visited her. We all spent the fourth of July with her last year. She has the same *good loving heart as ever*. Deacon Wetherby family are about as usual. Mrs. W. [Wetherbee] is getting quite feeble. She does not go out, but little Susan is the same as ever. I carried your letter down and read it to them. They were much interested. They all send love. Susan is in often. She was here this morning and spent an hour; she was here to tea last wed. They have been *very kind* since we have been so *lonely*.

We are very sorry to hear of Mr. Wheeler's feeble health and hope the spring may revive him. Also to hear of Willy's disappointment; I hope he may yet be permitted to go on with his studies and become a *faithful Minister* of the *Gospel*. So Leonard is married; well, I hope his wife will be indeed a blessing to *him* and *to you* all. Please give my love to her and tell her I would love to hear from her.

And little Emily is *teaching school* with Eddy. I hope they will do much good. The others I suppose you will not expect much help from just yet.

———————

Julia Wood hopes that their trials have made the Wheelers better human beings.

*Y*ou say you have learned some useful lessons in *these years* of *trial*. How many will have reason to thank God when they get home for the *discipline of earth* Bonnar says, "The morning cometh—that bright morning when the dew drops collected during earth's *night* of *weeping* shall sparkle in its beams. When in one blessed *moment* a lifelong experience of *trial* will be effaced and forgotten." Yes, if we are his children we know that our trials will be *just* what we need no *more* and no *less*. I hope and pray that the great afflictions through which you are called to pass may be so *notified* to you + I hope your Husband may be spared to you yet many years and that you may have felt *love* and *confidence* of *all* your children that no *root* of *bitterness* may be permitted to throw a shadow over your long days and may you have the unspeakable happiness of seeing them all . . . walking in the *road* to *heaven* is the prayer of your affect Mother J. M Wood

P.S. give much love to all

———————

Julia Wood's letter of July 6, 1866, reports that the Lowell churches, like the American Board of Commissioners for Foreign Missions, have lost interest in the Wheelers.

*A*s the box is almost ready to send. I set down to tell you something about it. In the first place, it is not as large as I hoped it would be. I did finally hope that we should be able to do something in our society after receiving your letter stating your wants. I mentioned it to some of the ladies. They thought favorably of our making up a box of shirts and gave me almost two dollars in money to purchase cloth for the next meeting. I bought the blue striped for one pair of shirts and dark calico for three which I cut out and supposed they would be made, but when I arrived at the meeting, I found the Ladies all engaged in making a half a dozen nice shirts for the pastor with his *twelve hundred a year* and I knew by the time those were done, it would be too late for the box and I brought home my bundle with the intentions of making them myself, but have not had the time to do it. Harriet, there is about as much of a missionary spirit in our church as there was when you was there.

I must close. I was over to spend the afternoon with Dea Wetherby's family for the first time in their new house on Kirk Street yesterday; had a very pleasant time we talked about you all; I love that family. I wish you could have one such family near you. And now will you kiss the little ones for me? I never wanted to see you all so much as at present. Give my love to all I know then do write as often as you have an opportunity. Pray for us much, for we *greatly need your prayers; wickedness abounds* and it almost seems as though this city was given over to destruction and what is most alarming is the stupidity that prevails in the churches. We have one of the most faithful ministers that any church ever had and yet it seems to make no impression and we are led to see how vain is everything without the Spirit of God

in haste

From your affectionate mother

7.

Life Without a Mission

After the Wheelers leave Bad River for Beloit, they put on optimistic faces when dealing with their children, as the letters they write to Julia on November 2, 1866, show. Leonard begins:

We are pretty settled in a house about a mile from College North on the Janesville road. It is a large two story home 60 feet by 22 with a cellar under the whole of it. And also a barn, good cistern, a work house with six acres of good land. The whole is held at $2800 dollars which is thought to be very cheap. But I couldn't see any way to purchase + so have a conditional promise to rent it till spring. This will give us a chance to look around. Our stuff came safely to hand—horses and all. My health is improving. I consulted Dr. Taggart[1] who examined me, and said I did not need medicine but a good vigorous diet + *plenty of whiskey*.

We have no reason to think otherwise than that we made a wise choice in coming here for a home.

Uncle Artemus,[2] I supposed, has returned from Lake Superior laden with the spoils of trade and bringing the latest edition of news from Odanah. What is it? We have not heard from there since leaving. Did Uncle Artemus bring my

Buffalo overcoat? If not he did, ask him to please send it on to me. It will be good for me to wear often in riding out here.

*D*ear Julia

I am in the midst of house cleaning and washing but must add one line. We have had a great time house hunting. Yesterday we got permission to remove here for the present and probably for the winter. People are very kind and I think I shall like here very much. Dr. T [Taggert] has examined your father's lungs. He told me that tubercles had formed in the upper part of the left lung and was now in the process of suppuration. I requested the Dr. before the examination if the result was unfavorable not tell him. He is not now aware of the state of his lungs.

The letter Harriet writes to her parents on February 12, 1867, shows that despite her happiness with Beloit, she feels deep sadness about leaving the mission and worries about her husband's health and how her large family would survive without him.

*I*t is late and I am very tired, but I feel that I shall rest better tonight if I have a letter ready for the morning mail. I fully intended to write on board the Steamer on our way down but Mr. W was so feeble and our little Wallie required so much care that I found it impossible to write.

It was a bitter, bitter trial for us to leave our dear old home and our poor people. But we felt that it was a case of life or death. Mr. Wheeler had an attack of lung fever in July from which he did not rally as usual and we feared that there was hardly a probability that he would live two months if he remained. He was so feeble, that we were obliged to remove him to the Boarding house while Lenny and I packed up. It was a sad weary time for me, I assure you.

Oh, it did seem as if my heart would break at times as we dismantled the old home. It was the only home my children had ever known and could we ever learn to love another as we had that. There was one thing for which I think I felt truly thankful. We left no little *graves* behind. Just as we were ready to leave, our people assembled in the larger dining hall of the boarding house. One of the members of our church had her little babe to be baptized. The child was named Edward Payton for our Eddy.

After the ceremony, Mr. W. committed them all to the care of the Great Shepard and then came our parting. Husband bore it better than I feared he would. But the Good Byes were not all said when we left Odanah; at every point on the Lake where the boat stopped, kind friends came on board with expressions of sympathy and offers of aid. It was quite an undertaking for me to take so long a journey with my invalid husband + many children, all our freight and a span of horses, but at every change some friend was by to relieve us of care and responsibility.

When we reached here we found that Professor Blaisdell, Professor Emerson + Mrs. Lathrop[3] had made arrangements to take us all into their families until we could get settled in our new home. Beloit is a beautiful place has excellent schools—Most delightful Christian privileges and contains some of the best people I ever knew.

Soon after we came, Mr. W had an examination of his lungs by an eminent physician here. He gave us the result of his examinations that the tubercles has formed in the upper part of the left lung and was in the process of suppuration. The lower part has been out of use for four years. The right lung is somewhat affected. I was somewhat unprepared for this announcement and yet I had feared the worst. I feel that our Heavenly Father has been very merciful in sparing him to us so long and I know he will do all things well. Yet there are times when I can not help looking forward shudderingly into the dark future. The question often arises what will become of the *little ones* without their father to guide them You will, I know, my dear parents pray for us—

I am dreading the months of March and April. Should he live through them, I think he may be comfortable through the summer. The Dr told me that this disease usually made much slower progress in a man of his age than it did in a younger person. He has seemed to be improving slowly for the last three weeks, coughs and raises less. Is able most of the time to mingle with the family and take his meals with us except in the morn. He has been troubled with Diarrhea this winter. His appetite is more variable than usual. The Dr told him he must live high + drink all the whiskey he could bear.

We were very much affected on hearing of the death of Dea Wetherbee. Dear Man, he has gone to his reward—How you must all miss him. Give our warmest love our tenderest sympathy to Susan and all the family. Please write the particulars about mother's health when you write. Do write soon. your Affect Daughter Harriet

———————

Harriet writes to console her father on June 15, 1867, when she hears of her stepmother's final illness; her letter reveals that her family, too, struggles with ailments, especially Willie.

My Dear Father,

Your letter reached us this noon. I was wholly unprepared for its contents. I felt quite alarmed about Mother when she had the attack winter before last and feared she might have a repetition of it but you have all written so hopefully and so long a time had passed that I had hoped the danger had passed.

My dear precious father my heart aches for you and could I fly, I would soon be with you. I have felt this afternoon as if I *must* come to you; I should feel it a privilege to aid in the care of dear Mother if she is still a sufferer here, but I can only commit you and her to the care of our kind loving father. He can and will comfort you, my dear father, and will sustain dear mother even though she should be called to pass through the valley of the shadow of death. You say in your letter that she has been a good wife to you. She has indeed. And she has been a *good mother* to me. I can truly say that as far as it as possible for another to do it, she has filled the place of my own Mother to me. If she is still conscious, give much love to her from us all. Tell her it is my constant prayer that she may be sustained and comforted in this trying hour.

We too have been much afflicted with sickness. I last wrote Walter was very sick with lung fever for a number of weeks. Before he fully recovered Willie was laid aside with inflammation of the eyes. He has suffered fearfully for the last two months. He has been at the eye Infirmary for six weeks in Chicago. He had an ulcer form in the eye. It broke twice and he had two operations performed on the eye. We have feared total blindness, but the probability now is that he will be able to see enough to get about comfortably, not enough to read common print. He had never fully recovered from the effects of the southern fever contracted in the army. The Dr says the poison is still in his system and is the cause of the difficulty with his eyes. It is a biter trial to us all. The poor boy bears it as well as could be expected. The Dr. says it will be two months before his eye will heal up. His general health is improving. Now, my dear father, I must close. Trust in the Lord and he will sustain you. Cast all your care upon him for he careth for you.

Your Affct Daugh

Harriet

Lowell June 24/67

My Dear Children,

I recvd your kind and sympathizing letter this morn. I find by that that you had not heard of the Death of your loving Mother. She died last Monday, one-half past four o'clock in the morning. I think she was conscious till the last. Willy[4] went up to the bed about two minutes before her last breath + took his grandmother's hand + said, "Good bye, Grandmother." She opened her eyes + smiled. She was the most pleasant corpse I ever saw. She was dressed in her silk gown + she looks just as if she was asleep with a smile on her face. The funeral was large + she was laid besides your Dear Mother. She has been a growing Christian + this last year more so. I have been for a year back very desponding + she was all hope. This past fall + winter, her health been very good + when I came home at night, I would have word of Cheer. She would kneel with me and pray to God for all the Children + Children's Children that not one of them be left from this Christian land. When she was taken lame a great many times, she said, "Mr. Wood, we are blessed that we have a comfortable home." She appeared to be full of thankfulness.

About 7 weeks ago, she had a large washing a noonday + of course she must have a large ironing. The wind blowed through the kitchen + she took a violent cold. Rev. Winn's + wife was in + after they went away, I got some hot water + soaked her feet + she went to bed, but could not sleep. She ached all over + had a high fever on her. She got up in the morn, but had to come back to the bed again. Willy + I got breakfast + after awhile she got up + in a few days got about house again, but the next attack involved her knees + brought pain. You could not come near her without her screaming. Her hands were swollen + at great pain. At last, she consented to have the Dr come + said it was inflammation Rheumatism. He wanted to have her take her bed, but she must be on her feet for two days more. When she took her bed, we brought a bed down into the Parlor. In the front of the Rheumatism, she had the palpitation of the heart which never left her till she died. After a few days on, her pains seemed better + Friday, the swelling seemed to go down. Sunday morn, she sat up in bed + drank some Tea + ate a soda biscuit + seemed very happy.

I went to meeting in the morn + at noon she seemed bright + so at night after supper I went in to the Parlor + sat down. She says, "Mr Wood, had you not better read?" I says, "Yes." I took the Bible + read a Chapt + got up + says, "Shall I call Elisa to come in? The girl's in kitchen." No answer. I went to her. She could not speak + even though she was dying, we called + the Doct was there soon. He gave her some medicine which relieved her. In the morning he said he did not expect her alive, but she could speak so that we could understand her. Hope was bright to the last. And now, my dear Children, pray for me daily. My soul is cast down. Write me every week. Some of the dear ones in your family, write. Tell Willy I am very sorrowful for him that he is so affected. Mr. Wheeler, please write to me as soon as convenient.

Your sister Mary is at my house. She goes home tonight. She sends her love to you. Love to all the dear ones this from your Affectionate Dearest Father S. Wood

Beloit July 2, 1867

*M*y Dear Father,

I received your letter a few days since. I was fully prepared for the intelligence it contained. I felt from the first that there was no hope. I was glad to learn so many particulars of her last sickness and death. What a comfort to feel that she was so fully prepared for the event. We know that our loss is her unspeakable gain. Would we selfishly wish if we could to call her back from the joy and brightness of heaven to the toils and trials of earth? You, my dear father, will miss her so sadly. Everything must seem dark and desolate to you now, but God still lives—you can confide in him and feel that although he has so sorely afflicted you, he has done it in love. We love to commit you daily to his care and keeping—and we do trust you will be sustained.

What arrangements have you made? You did not say anything in your letter about your plans. I wish it was so you could come and stop with us for a while.

JULY 12 We were expecting to cultivate twenty acres of land—but were obliged to give it up. We have a little more than two acres under cultivation. Edward leaves us tonight to work on a farm about two miles from here during the two months vacation. Freddy will probably leave next week. Little Eugene has work engaged for some time to come. Julia and Emma are very busy in making cone and cross work. They send it to Chicago for sale. So you see we are all trying to do what we can for our support. How I would love to see you and tell you how mercifully God has dealt with us and how he has supplied our wants thus far.

All join in much love.

Your Affec

On August 28, 1867, Abigail Spooner continues her correspondence with young Wheeler children, writing from Athol, Massachusetts, to Frederick Wheeler.

*M*y darling Freddie Boy,

Must I write you again without hearing a word from you? Have you forgotten about Abbie or are you so busy with your work, and your studies, and your play with your new acquaintances that you can't find time to write her *one* letter in a *year?* How do I know how you feel and how you like your new home and how you get along, if you don't tell me? Oh, how much I want to know about you—and all of you—won't you come and see me? Oh—how many times I think of you, and the other children, and want to save something for you—give you something—do something for you. How I wish I could *mend your stockings* as I used to—and take care of your things. Have you lost all the pretty things I gave you? I have got the same white handled jack knife which you used to whittle with so much. I wish you would come here and whittle with it again—and have it for your own. I will send you another picture of myself. It is *not* a very *nice* one but I think it is *natural. Can't* you *send* me *your picture? Send* me *yours + Genie's* together + tell me how much they cost; I would be glad to pay for them and *more* than pay. Write me *soon,* Freddy—tell me lots. Does my Freddie love *Jesus?* Does he go to Him when he is in *temptation* and *trouble?* Jesus *loves you*—so does Aunt Abbie.

Beloit Jan 3, 1868

*D*ear Grandfather,

As it is a new year and I have learned to write. I thought I would write you a letter. And first, I would wish you a happy new year. I had a very pleasant time new year's day. I was invited to three places. We were all invited to dine at Lathrop's; my mother had to stay at home because Walter was sick with the croup. We had a great deal of fun. First, we skated for about one hour then we took off our skates and played around for a time. After this, we had a good supper. After supper we played a few games. I had fun until nine o'clock.

We are all well and we like the Beloit people very well. They are very kind to us. We have very good society. Do not laugh at this, Grandfather, for it is my first letter. Please give my love to all my cousins.

Eugene

Harriet's note of January 6, 1868, first mentions the windmill Leonard Wheeler developed in northern Wisconsin. He hopes this invention will provide his family with financial security. It eventually did, but the letters show that reaching this goal required a long, discouraging process.

Eugene has left a little space for me to add a line, and wish you a happy New Year. Mr. W's health has been better this winter then it was last. The windmill is progressing slowly but surely. Leonard left at Christmas. He put up a mill in Michigan.

Your Affect Daughter
Harriet

On April 5, 1868, Susan Wetherbee writes after a silence she attributes to despair.

Lowell April 5, 68

Dearest Harriet,
Our correspondence has ceased but not our Love; oh no, you remember even in our first sorrow. Your dear departed Mother came in one evening and read an interesting letter on the occasion of your leaving your missionary home. Your dear husband has surely been spared to you beyond our expectations. If his health can be comfortable, may he long remain a blessing to his family—

Dear Harriet, I am thinking of days gone bye, of South St and Chapel Hill, memory and the religious element was usually the predominating one in our intercourse. Right principle was ever in some way the guiding motive of your action. I believe I have never engaged a friendship that was so precious as ours, so whole souled and blessed, and prolonged.

My dearest, Father had a long and distressing illness, often laboring for breath, in much weakness, yet so patient, and sweet, and the savior, whom he had so devotedly loved, so faithfully served, was with him to bless and comfort till the last. At one time he said, "Christ has done the great work, and I believe it, and there is no more that I can do, and now if he call, I hope to say, here I am Lord, again. I can leave all I see, Friends will follow, riches and honors, what are they; if I can only have one of the least of these crowns." If I could see you, I could tell you more.

Dear Mother had been growing increasingly feeble but was sick only two hours at last with an attack like Cholera Morpheus—for the last hour, laid quiet, got up, and died in my arms. The agony of that night, and the months that followed. God grant you may never know my experience. As we look back upon the few months preceding her death, and see how perfect her patience, and *hopefulness* in regard to our future here, how undisturbed her always sweet spirit.

After months of agony and darkness, looking upon the past with *remorse*, seeing no light here, feeling no cheer in the future, light gradually, dawned until one morning early I was *blessed*, felt that God was "too wise to err, too good to be unkind"—Felt that he had won my Love, and never have I known as much of the joy of penitence, confidence, and so much of submission as I now do—God be praised. Now dearest—I would like a real confiding letter from you. Can't you find time and heart to write it?

I miss your dear Mother very much. She often came in to see us, and whenever I had an inclination to go and spend a day with her, I was always welcomed by her and your Dear Father. I often call there, more often than I should, but I shall ever go to see them because he likes to have me, and his time must be short, although he is well for one of his years. He has treasure in Willie and Susie[6] who are everything to him.

Our family are well. It is pleasant, but I feel that no earthly arrangement is permanent. How I wish I could sit by your side in my little room here, this sun shining morning and have a kiss, too.

Susan M. Wetherbee.

Julia still struggles to support herself teaching and attends to Indian matters despite her difficult health. Her letter of October 19, 1868, places her in Lansing, Iowa.

My dear father,

Your letter with the $5 was received last week for which I am much obliged. I should have written back to you and to mother before this had I been able to do so, but I have been on the invalid list for a few days past. I took a severe cold about a month ago while visiting the Winnebago Indian camp on one of the Islands in the Mississippi above Lansing and have had a hard cough ever since. I suppose I was not as careful as I should be; at all events, I took an additional cold, the first of last week and have been quite miserable ever since. My head ached so bad in the day time and I slept so little nights through the week that it was with difficulty I got through the week and Friday night when I came home from school, I was about used up. Since then I have kept my room pretty lonely. I am better now as my fever as left me; but my cough still remains.

I'm glad to hear of the success of the windmill. Your circulars are got up in nice style. My school is the most pleasant one I ever taught. But I must close. Much love to all.

Julia

Beloit, Wis. Dec. 15th 1868

*D*ear Grandfather

It has been long since I have written you and as I have a few minutes, I thought I would improve. I have a good deal of studying to do as examination is coming on. First we are to have a written examination then a public examination. I am to be examined in five studies. I am in my last year in the Grammar Department. Junior Exhibition is coming off on Tuesday and we expect our cousins from Rockford and Fon du lac. Edward is one of the speakers and there is to be a string band and we expect fine music. Willie has got back from Iowa. It is very hard times in Iowa now; the farmers could not get their wheat to market before it fell. They like our Wind Mill very much, but cannot afford to buy the rights. Father is getting along very well here. He is introducing it into Tennessee. An Agricultural Warehouse man from Chattanooga has bought a mill and thinks he can sell a good many more. We are all very busy here and have but little time to play. It is either work or study. Vacation is coming in a week. I wished that I lived near enough so that I could make you a visit. I must now close. We all send love from your Affectionate Grandson Eugene Wheeler

Beloit wis Dec 15 1868

*D*ear Grandfather,

Eugene has left a page so I thought I would write a few lines. Weeks before last the first congo church had their Fair and festival two nights and one day. The last night they made tableaux. Emily made a mass bushel and mass roll and a flower wreath. The mass basket was sold for $7 and the cross $2; they cleared 900$ which was to pay the debt of the church. We have had very cold weather for 10 days; the snow is about 4 inches deep. As I am not very well and it is getting quite late, I must close.

From your Affectionate Grandchild
Hattie Wheeler

Beloit March 30/69

*M*y Dear Father,

We received your letter on Saturday. We were very glad to hear from you again and yet your letter made me feel a little guilty. I really intended to write you before this but I find it almost impossible to find time to write letters and I write so seldom that it is becoming quite a task.

We were glad to hear that your health was so good, but worry to learn that you were so desponding. I know my dear Father that you must have many lonely hours and I often wish I could be near you, but this does not seem to be the will of our Heavenly Father. We can only commit you to His care and keeping. This we love to do. We feel that he can and will comfort and sustain you and do *infi*nitely more and better for you than we could were we with you. Try, my dear Father, to cast *all* your cares and sorrows upon Jesus. He can and will fill you with joys unspeakable.

We have all suffered from the prevailing influenza but are better now. Mr. W has been very unwell and I was quite anxious about him for a time, but he is out again now. We received a letter from Leonard and Rhoda last night. They were well but L has worked very hard this winter. He has drawn to the beach over two hundred cord of wood this winter. He says it is the hardest work he ever did. He is now getting out timbers for a new house. His post office address is "Omena Leenenaw Co Mich."[7] He would be very glad to get a letter from you. Willie is working very hard in the Windmill business. Edward has left College for one term to help him. He thinks he will be able to keep up with his class so as to graduate next year. Emily may teach this summer. Fred is going to a farm to work Thursday; he gets fifteen dollars a month. Jean, Hattie and Walter will stay at home and help Father and mother. Our children have all done very well in school this winter. I was very glad to hear so particularly about Mary. I am so glad she has left the Shakers. I shall try to write her before long. Give much love to her when you see her. Write as often as you can. Mr. W and the children all join me in much love to you. Your Affectionate Daughter Harriet Wheeler Much love to Susy and Willie.

Beloit Oct 12/69

My very dear Father
The children are all busy with their lessons. Mr. W is resting. I have been writing Leonard and thought I would finish the evening by writing you.

We received your letter a few weeks since and was glad to hear of your continued health. We are all usually well with the exception of Mr. W. He has been absent most of the time for a month past attending fairs and exhibiting his Windmill. He is feeling very much exhausted and worn. He has also a little cough.

Our mill took the first prize at three county fairs and also the first prize a silver medal for "the best windmill and pump in actual operation" at the State fair Madison. Mr. W. fully intended to exhibit at Decatur, Ill, but the fair there was held at the same time as the one at Madison. The Mill is attracting considerable attention and has given perfect satisfaction to all purchasers.

In a few days it will be three years since we came to Beloit. We were homeless, houseless and among strangers. My poor husband was so feeble that it seemed impossible for him to live but a few months at most. These three years have been years of trials and of great mercies. Fine friends have been raised up for us; husband's health has very much improved, but it has been a constant struggle to get a living. It was quite an undertaking for a man in feeble health and with no means to get up such a machine as Mr. W has and it takes time and money to get it before the public. In the meantime, we must live. We are making slow but steady progress and I have no doubt but that it will soon give us a comfortable support.

You say in your last that you do not think I know what affliction is. Oh my dear father, I feel at time as if I had all I could bear up under. How true it is that every heart knoweth its own bitterness but is it not sweet to feel that it is the same loving Father that appoints the sorrows as well as the joy? If we are now faithful and trustful, it will soon be all rest and joy for us my dear father.

The children and Mr. W join me in much love to all. Where is Mary now? I hope to hear from her soon.

From Your Affectionate Daughter
Harriet

Beloit March 1 /70

*D*ear Father
I have done a large washing to day and am consequently very tired but I feel as if I must not delay writing you any longer. We were very glad to receive your last.

I was very sorry to learn that Mary's health was so poor. It made me sad to read her letter. O wish it was in my power to aid her. Please write me how and where she is in your next letter.

Husband has been laid aside a number of days with it but is a little better today. He has been very busy for a few weeks past in getting out his rotary mill for driving machinery. They hope to get it running this week. William has gone up north putting up Windmills. Emily is running a sewing machine. She is making up clothes for a house in Chicago. She has fifty dollars worth of sewing in the house now. Fred is in the preparatory department of the [Beloit] College; he does chores night and morning for one of our neighbors for which he receives fourteen shillings a week. Eugene is in the high school. During the recess at noon and Saturdays he goes to the shop and paints windmills. Our children are all doing well in school and are industrious out of it, but some of them lack the one thing needed.

Please write us often.
Harriet

In 1871, the indefatigable Julia moves to Chicago, apparently in hopes of making a living from her art.

Feb 1871

*M*y dear mother

I suppose you are looking for a letter from me about this time and wondering how I have succeeded in my plans. I have no doubt myself that somewhere is some interesting garret in this city—where mice are plenty—and the melody of musical cockroaches is heard—that room exists for me, but I have not found it yet. I reached Chicago last Thursday about three o'clock as we were delayed on the way by snowdrifts. Went straight to the Eagle House, combed my hair and started for the Art Stores to see what my prospects were for selling my paintings. It is but fair to say that said prospects were not at all *dazzlingly bright*. They would all be very happy to sell my work on commission since I might bring in any amount of it—and though they could not probably sell much just now—still it would go sometime—the money pressure could not last forever &c &c. I thought over the subject a few moments and concluded I had better go and see some of the ladies I had sewed for—and try and get a sewing job. So I stepped on board a State Street car and started for Michigan Avenue. The lady I went to see had a seamstress in the house already, but gave me the names of some of her friends—and one of these engaged me at once for three weeks. She told me I might commence the next day if I chose. Of course, I did choose and came here bag and baggage Friday morning.

I am sewing way down ever so far on the South Side on Wabash Avenue in an awfully genteel family—and find it very pleasant. My room is warm at all hours. The house is heated by a *furnace* and I am very comfortably fixed generally. I do not get very large pay—four dollars a week besides my board and washing—but it is all I can get anywhere these hard times—and is better than an uncertainty. If times are not better when my three weeks are out, I shall get another place to sew for two or three weeks until the busy season commences again. I am pretty tired at night or I should write more. I hope to hear from you soon. Shall go to the Post Office twice a week.

Julia

As this letter Harriet writes Julia on March 17, 1871, reveals, Julia's health once again has deteriorated; her worried parents urge her to leave Chicago and come home, where they can attend to her.

My Dear Daughter

I had begun to feel quite anxious about you and was intending to write you this evening again. I am very sorry to hear that you are so unwell. I have been fearful that this damp weather would affect you unfavorably. Now my poor child pack up and come right home. It is suicidal for you to stay any where in the vicinity of Chicago. I think you should find it much pleasanter here now than it was in the winter. The snow is all gone and it is much warmer and dryer. We have sold our place at Odanah—The American Board gave us this place and the Presbyterian Board paid us 14 hundred dollars. They pay five hundred this spring, so you must not feel that you will be a burden. They will pay nine hundred more at the end of this year. The ground and road is about dry. The people are beginning to plow and get in their grain. I want you to help me about our flower garden. I do feel my dear child that if you will come home and be careful you may have a chance to get well.

Willie goes in a few days to work for Mr. Olmstead[8] and we think Edward may go to the Madison co in the same evening. They are expecting to take hold of our mill for Minnesota and part of Iowa—

Come immediately; every day's delay makes it worse for you. If you are unable to come along, we will come for you. Wallie says tell Julia to come home quick. He wants to see you. Don't fail to write as soon as you get this. All send love.

Your affectionate Mother

H. Wheeler

Beloit, Wis. March 17, 1871

*D*ear Daughter Julia,

I can write but little this morning. My message is this. Pack up your trunks + come straight home—Chicago is no place for a consumptive. I was there two weeks ago—felt the chill damp wind from the lake before I got out of the cars. I hurried round, left part of my business undone + started for home. Wanted to see you much, but knew not where to look for you. Have sold our land at Odanah to Pres Board. Shall have several hundred dollars this spring— with it we shall try to make invalids more comfortable. We shall have horse + buggy of our own. Now don't think you will be a burden to us. All the family say come. All our snow is gone—the ground is getting dry the air is good—and I feel some better. We shall do something at the garden this week. Come + help us in the flower garden. Our windmill business is taking a hopeful turn. Now don't delay an hour to start for home. Let us know when you will be in Beloit + we will be ready to give you a comfortable ride home.

Your Affectionate father

L. H. Wheeler

Beloit March 19/71

*M*y Dear Daughter,

I was very glad to hear that you were so comfortably situated. You did not write us where you are.

I am very sorry to hear that you are troubled with female troubles. I was afraid that was the cause when you was at home. You will have to be careful about taking long walks. Do you cough much now? You must find it expensive boarding. I hope to be able to send you a little money in a few days. I hope you will not disappoint us about coming home in April. The wind flowers are already budded and the grass is turning green. I want you here to help me plan the flower beds this spring.

The contract with the Madison Manufacturing Co. for selling the wind mill was signed last week and they are making preparations to do a large business. Mr. Olmstead gave them the northern part of this state; they take also Minnesota and part of Iowa. They pledge themselves that the royalty shall amount to twelve hundred per year at least.

Write us soon as you receive this and let me know just how you are. Father and the children send much love. Fred is out with Ed putting up mills.

Your Affectionate Mother

H. Wheeler

———————

In the fall of 1871, Harriet and Leonard make another trip east to visit family. Their son Fred writes his mother from Beloit on September 10.

I received your letter last week and was glad to hear that you were enjoying your visit and that father is better. Tell him not to worry about the business for it is going on very well. The new mill with the iron pivot and shut off looks grand. We are getting ready to attend the Janesville Fair. We went up there yesterday and found the Batavia mill up and running.[9] It is represented by Blair. We have not got our mill up yet and have to work night and day to get it up. It looks as though we're going to have fair play this time. We are also going to attend the Rockford fair so you see I cannot go to school this fall and if I did not have to go to the fairs, I could not go to school for my script is clear. Did think I can get a job of Olmsted & Co to put up mills for them where they have no agent. I can put mills up as soon as anybody. Thank you muchly for the money you sent me; it was very acceptable for my garment is in a very dilapidated condition. I suppose by this time you are in Lowell having a grand time. I can imagine you on the street meeting first one friend and then another and finally crowding around so that you have to go into the street to give them room. Well, have a good time and don't let money hinder you, for the royalty is coming.

Week before last I spent the week with four other boys on the shores of Lake

Koshkonong.[10] We started on Monday with our team and reached the Lake at night finding the Lake full of ducks and shining over. We had a grand time the first two days, but the third while we were all off hunting, a drove of hogs broke into our tent devouring all our eatables and tearing our tent all to bits. When we reached the tent, it looked as though it was going to fly; the hogs had eaten the ducks and were not very careful with the feathers. The three days we remained after our hog disaster we almost starved. We had plenty of ducks and salt but were minus all things else. But at last the joyful day is come: Ana Miller came to take us home. But as it was we shot 75 ducks thinking we had been well paid for our trip.

All are well and send much love

Lowell Sept 15/71

Dear Emma,

Tell Fred his letter was better than medicine. Your father and Grandfather both had a hearty laugh over the "hog disaster." Every few minutes I would hear your father breaking out anew in a loud laugh over it.

How I wish I could step in and see you this morning. It is clouding up for the equinoctial storm and I feel a little blue and homesick. Sister Mary is here and went with us. We had a nice visit. Aunt is the same dear good aunt she always was. I do think she is one of the best women I ever knew.

Tues eve

I have just returned from a visit to the Wetherbees. Met there some old friends. All our family were invited yesterday. We rode up on to Dracut Heights to see Grandfather's old place. But the dear ones that used to greet me so lovingly have all gone to a better home I trust.

I suppose the boys are busy attending fairs. I want to hear from home very much. Have you received the money from Madison yet?

Your father walked from the Wetherbees home tonight, but he was quite tired. I think he is improving slowly. Tell the children mother thinks of them every hour of the day. Have Wallie go to school every day. Give my love to all the family, also to Mary. Your Affec

Mother

Beloit Oct 17/71

*M*y Dear Father

We reached home in just one week and two hours from the time we left Lowell. Found the family all well and glad to see us.

Nov 17

*D*ear Father

I had written thus far and have not been able to resume it again until now. We have had company most of the time and Mr. Wheeler has been very sick. Yesterday he had a Hemorrhage from the lungs. He is now very feeble and I am feeling very anxious about him. I feel that he is going down slowly but surely to the grave. Pray for us my dear father.

Leonard has been at home with us for two weeks. He has had a great deal of trouble. He has found that the man he was in partnership with was not a reliable man. And he has left him. The setting up the business has troubled and embarrassed him very much. I have felt so troubled about him I could not write nor do anything else. His wife is with us now and we expect him here next week. They will probably spend the winter here. He will work for the manufacturing com on a salary for the present.

I cannot tell you, my dear father, how very pleasant is the memory of my visit East. It was such a rest. It seems to me that I can never have another such a one this side of the grave. I often think of you all. I can imagine just how you look and just what you are doing. Where is sister Mary now? Give much love to her. Husband joins much love to all

Your Affect Daughter
Harriet

Mary Warren's letter of December 12, 1871, from the Red Cliff Reservation in northern Wisconsin, suggests that although grateful to hear from the Wheelers, she misses them.

My Dear Mrs. Wheeler—
The box containing the cloak you were so kind to purchase for me came all safely on one of the last boats. I had become quite anxious about it and was very much afraid it would not come at all. I was very much pleased with it, and have made it up and have worn it two or three times already; it is a perfect fit. Enclosed you will find the amount of the bill.

I was happy to hear that you had such a pleasant visit east and hope it may be repeated again at some future day not far distant. I suppose you are all busy as ever and the boys all attending school. I should love dearly to spend Christmas with you in Beloit; I hope it will be a happy season to you all.

I shall in all probability spend my holidays in Bayfield.

Mrs. Vaughn[11] intends on having a Christmas tree for the benefit of her numerous friends and acquaintances. I presume it will be a pleasant affair—

My school is in good and prosperous condition, and I have been remarkably well this season though we have had a great deal of sickness in this place, and many of the children have been very sick. The weather is now very cold and the lake partly frozen over. I often wish that Emma was here with me this winter; I think she would enjoy herself and it would be so splendid for me. You can well imagine I get very lonely sometimes when up here alone. But still I have no great occasion for complaint. I have many comforts, and a great deal to be thankful for. The friends at Bayfield are all so very kind and thoughtful for me. I always look forward with a great deal of pleasure to the close of each week which usually finds me in good quarters.

I will send some copies of the Press[12] which will give you an idea of our railroad question. I expect Ashland will be the centre of much attraction and excitement by next spring and of course Odanah will come in for a share. Much love to all and each of the family.

Affectionately,

Mary W.

Finally, on January 14, 1872, Harriet's much-discussed Shaker sister, Mary, writes. Given everyone's concern about her, the letter seems surprisingly articulate, intelligent, and kind. She seems more self-possessed and confident than when she wrote her sister Harriet on May 30, 1841, the only other letter from Mary that survives. In sum, her time with the Shakers seems to have done her good. According to Shaker records, she left in the 1860s, presumably to take care of her father until his death, then returned to the Shaker community at Harvard, where she died on March 10, 1914, at the age of ninety-six.

Lowell Jan 14th 1872

Dear Sister Harriet,

I will write you a few lines as I feel quite ashamed that we have not written you ere' this, but it cost me such an effort now to write that I postpone it as long as possible. *Do pardon* this seeming negligence and be assured you have our *heartfelt sympathy* and *prayers* in your great affliction and it may be bereavement of your beloved husband and father to your children. May God grant you strength to endure it with resignation to the divine will, knowing and believing He doeth all things well and for our *best good.* You probably have anticipated the final result of Mr. Wheeler's illness for some time and may be better prepared for the stroke. Yet when the last hope is crushed and the last tie is sundered that binds him to earth, the heart will bleed and nothing but divine grace can heal the wound and pour consolation into the bruised spirit. We feel assured that you have long ere this learned where to cast your *every burden* and *trial* and let past and deliverances comfort and strengthen you in our present affliction. With you, we will mingle our prayers and tears that we may help you in some measure bear this *great sorrow*. We were glad to her that Sister Hannah was with you and hope she is with you now as you must be very much worn down with anxiety. I fear we shall hear that you are wholly prostrated but will hope that you will get some rest. Wish I could be with you and give a helping hand. We were also very much pleased to receive a few lines from Julia and to learn that she was at home. Please remember me to her in *much love*. I am waiting for work which I hope to get soon. I am desirous of stopping here as I feel that father needs me with him. He seems to grow infirm very fast—and I do not feel that it is safe to leave him alone. He felt your departure keenly and was very much depressed for some time but seems to be getting over it now. He often speaks of your visit with great satisfaction. Indeed we all enjoyed it very much.

Remember me in *much love* to Mr. W if living and accept a large portion for *yourself* and family also sister H if with you.

Please write us *soon*. Your affectionate sister

Mary

Red Cliff Wis Jan 28 /72

My Mrs. Wheeler—

I received your fine letter the other day. And I assure you I was very grateful to hear from Beloit. I had heard through Henry Blatchford that Mr. Wheeler was not expected to live, and you can imagine how very anxious I have been. I wondered why Emily did not write to me even a few lines. You did not mention whether she was at home or not. Did she ever receive my last letter? I had requested her to buy some insertion[13] and enclosed a dollar. It was for Mrs. Haynard, an acquaintance of mine, or I should not mind it at all.

What a time of trouble and anxiety you have had; But how true it is, that the Lord give us the strength to endure and bear all our trials and burdens. If we do not realize it at the time, we do in after days. I have had many occasions to look back to such times and could only be thankful + feel humbled. I trust and pray that Mr. Wheeler is better and daily improving, I was very much affected by your account of his illness and of the state of his mind. May we all ever be prepared for "the Master's call."

Are the boys all at home? Is Leonard with you? And where is Julia? If Emily is at home, I hope she will write to me immediately. I am in hope there is a letter for me on the way. I expect you are all completely tired out.

I have not been able to visit the mission as yet. I hope to do so before Spring. It is a very successful operation, but they have not sufficient help. In regard to my visiting this spring, that has been my intention all along, but now I do not know whether I can afford it at present, for I have been investing and buying land at Ashland. If I should make my fortune by the speculation, I do not know what I may be induced to do.

I expect Ashland will be the great centre of attraction by next season. Mr. Whittlesey tells me that I can double my money now if I was disposed to sell.

It will be decided by Spring where the Terminus of the Wisconsin Central R.R. will be. The contention is between Ashland + Bay City. I almost expect to see you back at Odanah one of these days. They have an excellent farmer at Odanah and the Indians are making great improvements. May God lend a helping hand to all this change and progress.

Let me hear from you soon if only for a few lines. My love to all the family. Remember me particularly to Mr. Wheeler.

Yours Truly—
Mary

Beloit Feb 23/72

My Dear Father,
    I fear my precious husband is going rapidly down to the grave. Pray for us. Pray that he may be sustained to the last; and that he may be spared protracted suffering. It seems to me I *cannot bear* to see him suffer. I cannot tell you how dark and desolate the future looks to me without him. But I know the Lord can make it all light.

How are you and all the dear ones in Lowell? Give much love to all. How precious and comforting would be their sympathy and presence now. Tell Mary I shall try to answer her letter before long. Husband says, "Give a great deal of love to Father and all the dear friends."

Your Affectionate
Daughter Harriet

Monday Morn

My Dear Father, Brother and Sisters,
My precious Husband has gone home to his rest. He died last night at nine o'clock.

Pray for us.
Your Affectionate
Daughter
Harriet

Lowell March 3/72

My Dear Dear Daughter Harriet,
I received the letter Thursday morn giving the account of the Death of your dear beloved husband. Your father can sympathize with you; there is nothing in this world that is so trying in this world as when your dear mother was taken from me. I had six dear Children to care for + it seemed I must give up all. But the Lord I do believe sent one to help take care of them.

You are left with nine Children, but they are all grown up except Harriet + Walter and, my dear daughter, you know where to go for help that you may guide them right.

I hope you will write me about Mr Wheeler's death. He told me when he was here that when he got home that he should make his will. Did he do it? I feel that your dear children will take care of you.

Mary has gone to M A Richardson to live. There is four of them in the family + Mrs. Richardson is a worker. They had a fine house on the hill, north side of the south Common. I should give her a home if I had one but I have not.

When you was here, I meant to have some talk with Mr. Wheeler upon some subject on religion but his health was so poor + he was so weak that I didn't say so much as I meant to. I see things somewhat different than I used to + I hope plainer but I find I am a poor creature. Nothing can I do aright without the Holy Spirit leading me to my savior's atoning blood. I do feel very lonely. When my Dear wife was alive, I had somebody to converse with on the subject of religion, but now I have none. Willy and Susan are kind to me, but they don't want to talk about the subject. But we have family prayers + Susan always sings with me. And now I want you to write me. Love to all the Dear Children. Willy + Susan send their love to you + to all their cousins. Tell Julia to write me. Remember me in your Prayers. This from your affectionate Father
S Wood

Lowell March 5/72

Dear Harriet,

MONDAY A.M. At the missionary concert last eve Rev. Mr. Foster spoke of the decease of dear Mr. Wheeler. Mr. Elbridge Richardson[14] spoke of his early coming to Lowell as other Andover students came, of his labors here on the Sabbath, of his acquaintance in our family and subsequent marriage, told of his birth place, college graduation spoke highly of his qualification for the work on which he entered. Mr. Foster referred to meeting him some years since—and also to his recent conversation with him last fall. He was surprised at his knowledge of history, not only of his own country—spoke of his isolation from society, and felt that the power of religion had made him what he was—said that some of our missionaries who had come from these fields of labor are so eloquent. He seemed to have fathomed Mr. Wheeler's mind and I wish I could repeat his *language concerning him*. He referred to the windmill as one of the fruits of his sanctified + consecrated bones. Mr. Brooks corroborated Mr. R's words, and prayed for the children, and should I say it, widow. Let me say Mr. R said Mr. Wheeler had a helpmate, spoke of your missionary character and services, while Superintendent of the Infant Sabbath School &c. I suppose there were not many there who could shed a tear over the reminiscences of the past, but there was one!

Yes, Oh yes, dear Harriet, I have felt that I could I personally have shared in your society, I should have been a better person than I have. Let then the thought of the service you have been enabled to render your dear One in the chosen business of his life comfort you now.

You will be glad to know that for the last week my health has been better; my sight is stronger, my spirit better than for a year—and more. If you have never suffered depression of spirits for months, accompanied by a great want of energy you could not have sympathized with me—but thank God the gloom has opened. Had I been as I now am, I should have enjoyed your visit so much more—

Oh Harriet, how my heart yearns to see you. If I could fly, I would soon be at your side. How the closing of a life brings back the past, but I hope it is not so with you. I know it is not, but my wrongdoing is sometimes so prominent in my mind, that more remorse than clear sweet grief fills my heart.

Your Susan M. Wetherbee

Beloit March 9/72

My Dear Father,

I cannot tell you how glad I was to receive a letter from you. In this hour of my trial and bereavement, my heart turns to you as of old for sympathy and comfort. You say truly that you know how hard it is to bear. But my dear father, how much we have to be thankful for. How could we bear these trials if we mourned as those without hope—If we felt that this separation was the final one. Dear ones are gone to their home and are at rest. Of their happiness we have not the tremor of a doubt. I cannot tell you what a comfort this is to me. My dear husband suffered so long from sickness and pain that it is a comfort to me to think of his rest. During his last sickness he suffered so much from restless and wakefulness. If at any time he slept an hour or two, he would say to me, "Oh help me, my dear, thank our heavenly Father for this sweet rest." It seemed to me the morning after his death as I went down to the sitting room, as if I could almost hear him say to me, "Thank God for this blessed release." Tuesday morning before he died, he said to me, "I have had some very refreshing sleep. And now to commemorate it, I want you to bring your breakfast in here; and eat it with me." I set a little table up to his bedside and we took one last meal together.

The few last weeks of his life he was unwilling to have me leave him even to sleep and so all the rest I got I took on the bed by his side. It is a great comfort to me that I was able to take care of him to the last. During all the thirteen years of his feebleness I have always been able to take care of him when he needed care.

We had some precious seasons of prayer together during his sickness. He had such a sweet childlike trust in his Heavenly Father such a calm resting upon the promises of God, that it was delightful to hear him. His mind seemed to dwell particularly on those passages of scripture which represent Christ as the only ground of hope for salvation. Once he said we have peace with God through our Lord Jesus Christ, Here is *my peace*; I a poor, wretched, guilty, sinner have peace through our Lord Jesus Christ.

He sent his love and good bye to all his friends.

He was much respected here and many followed as mourners to the grave. Last Sabbath pastor preached his funeral sermon. It was a beautiful and truthful delineation of his character. The Text was "Behold an Israelite indeed in whom is no guile." Give much love to all. The children all send love.

Your Affectionate Daughter

Harriet

Wally wants me to tell his dear Grandpa that he does like his papers very much. I wish you could have seen him yesterday when the papers came you sent this week. He kissed them so charmingly, "Oh, my dear, my darling Grandpa, he sent me more paper."

Red Cliff Wis—
Mar 14, 1872

*M*y Dear Mrs. Wheeler—
Your letter containing the sad intelligence of the "going home" of our dear one reached me this morning—It is with heavy and sorrowful heart, that I have followed the usual routine and duties of the day.

The earlier years have come back to me with an appeal which touches my heart and moistens my eyes. The good old home by the peaceful river, the plans, the labors and the thousand associations of those past scenes and of that home, which was a home indeed to the orphan and homeless.

The memory of the one who has gone to a better home is so fully associated and mingled with the recollections of my own past life, that it will ever remain fresh, dear and sacred. I can truly say, that his duties toward me were ever faithful, thoughtful and kind.

The poor Indians of Odanah will truly mourn and sympathize with us in our affliction, and also the many, old and tried friends of the country.

Only last Sabbath evening, I was at Mr. Whittlesey's and Dr Ellis who had arrived the day before from Ontonagon was also there—we all had a very pleasant conversation in speaking of the present prospects of the country, and in recalling the good old times at Odanah, and of that home that was ever free, hospitable, impartial.

Little did we dream of the sad truth, that even then, that dear household was plunged into deep sorrow and the good, kind friend and father had passed to the "mansions above?"

I will write again soon—Give much love to all the family and may God bless and comfort you all.

Very Affectionately
Mary Warren

Beloit June/72

My Dear Father

You say you are sad and lonely. Well, my dear father I can sympathize with you as I never did before. I never realized before what a dreary desolate blank earth must be to you now. We may have all our families about us but they cannot take the place of the dear ones that are gone. I have had some very sad and trying days since I last wrote you. The last week in May we had a Missionary convention here. Mr. Treat was here from Boston; two young men Smith and Porter were ordained as Missionaries to China.[15] It was a very interesting occasion but a very painful one to me. It brought back so vividly to my mind the past—the time when my dear husband was set apart to the same work. At the close of the ordination services they sang the same hymn and tune that was sung at his ordination in Lowell thirty years ago. "Ye Christian Heralds go Proclaim." Oh, how distinctly it brought back to my mind that occasion—the parting from our friends—the long journey and then our life among the Indians. It seemed as if I lived them all over again. It was not only giving up my dear husband again, but giving up our poor people and the mission work. For a few days I was almost overwhelmed with grief. But I do feel that the Lord's ways are all good and right—that he can give us peace and comfort when earthly joy is taken from us.

How is your health this hot weather? Fred is putting up mills. The younger children are in school.

My garden has occupied my time this spring. I have a large good garden. We shall have new potatoes next week. We have radishes, lettuce and green peas now. Our fruits are looking unusually well this year. We shall have an abundance of currants—and raspberries and some strawberries. Eugene does most of the work in the garden out of school hours. Please give much love to all.

Your Affectionate
Daughter
H Wheeler

Harriet's letter to her father of October 8, 1872, indicates that she struggles financially after her husband's death, even resorting to renting out her home and moving in with her oldest child, Leonard, and his wife.

I have seated myself this beautiful morning to write you a few lines. You have been much in my thoughts the past few weeks. I have in imagination lived over the scenes of last year at this season. It seems at times as if I could almost see my dear husband lying on the lounge in your sitting room and you at his side, trying to talk with him. I cannot tell you how much I miss my dear husband. I feel so desolate and alone in the world. I can sympathize with you as I never did before.

I have had a very trying and anxious summer. We have been making some changes in our business which has added to my cares. Besides I have had a large garden to superintend. Everyone has done most of the work in it. I found myself very much worn this fall. I broke up house keeping the first of Sept and am now boarding with Leonard and wife. They live much nearer school and it is better for the children on that account. Hattie has entered the high school and this is Eugene's last year there. He will at the end of the year be fitted for College—

The children are all doing well in school. We have boarding with us the two lady teachers in the High school both devoted Christian women and also the Presbyterian minister. He is a very excellent man and his influence over the children will be good.

Emily is helping Rhoda do the work. Leonard has been quite sick with fever.

Where is Mary now? Give love to them all. What a comfort it would be to me to stop in and see you all this morning. I have not for many years felt such a longing to see you all as I have for the past few months.

Lowell Oct 25/72

*M*y Dear Harriet,

You wrote me of your loneliness. How I feel for you. I suffer much from my loneliness. One night I didn't go to sleep till twelve o'clock, but in all my trials of sickness I have not a minute of regret that I married. I had happy wives + I believe they are with their Savior. You write me that you broke up housekeeping and board with your son Leonard + Rhoda. May I ask if Eugene, Harriet + Walter board with you? Do you think you will like to Board out? I know you are with a kind hearted son.

Mr. Wheeler when he was here to Lowell [said] that when he should got home he should will the house and land to you. Was he sick that he could not do it? I don't know but I am doing wrong in asking those questions, but I feel anxious about the welfare of my children.

All my Grand children that I have seen + I have seen them all except five + they are all good looking. O if I had money I would have all three of my Western daughters come to Lowell at my expense but I have none. Your Brother N [Newell] wants to get into his new house to eat his turkey in at Thanksgiving. N is thin in flesh + he grows old faster than you do. Mary comes over to see me once a week; she was here Monday night. She appears happy; she is putting her money into the bank. Willy + Susie appear very happy. The Wetherbees are all well, send their love to you. As for me, my health bodily is about the same; I grow weaker; I go to meeting every Sunday.

And now my Harriet won't you write me soon + tell me how you get along. Remember me in your prayers. Give my love to all your dear Children + take a large share to yourself. From your affectionate Father *S. Wood.* You must excuse my bad spelling; I never had much schooling when I was a boy.

Susan + Willy send Love to you all

Harriet's letter of February 14, 1873, to her ailing daughter Julia in Chicago reveals that after Leonard Wheeler's death, business problems develop with the windmill. All the same, Harriet will move back home with her children.

I received your letter yesterday and was sorry to learn that you had been so unwell.

You must have suffered terribly. You will have to be very careful about taking cold again. I think we shall all be glad when this dreadful winter is over.

Walter is counting the days now till we go home. He thinks Feb goes off very slowly. I have been much more comfortable here than I should have been at home this winter, but still I shall be glad when I once more get settled at home. It will be much better for Walter to be there. I would like very much to visit you at Chicago before I move, but I have not the means to go.

I am hoping there will be some changes in the business before spring. Parties are expected to meet here next Monday to see about forming a Stock co. for the Windmill. Mr. S. T Merrill[16] will be the Pres of the Co., if one is formed. It may all fall through as a great many other plans have done. I have not received a dollar in money from the Madison Co or the Co here since your father's death. We have taken back the lease from the Madison Co. We miss your dear father everywhere. I think the boys feel his loss much more than they supposed they would.

Emma is expecting to go East to Conn. the second Tuesday in March. She is going to live with cousin Rollin Allen. Mrs. Allen is quite an invalid and wants Emma to help in the care of the household. I am sorry to have her go, but he can do better for her than I can. He has sent her money to pay her expenses. Rhoda has paid her two dollars per week this winter. We received a letter from Mary Warren a few days since. She expects to make us a visit in March. She will probably stay until the opening of navigation. I will try and send you an Ashland paper soon. The mission is in quite a prosperous condition. Hattie Green has become a Christian and is quite a help to the teachers.

Write me often and tell all your plans. It is very trying to me that I cannot aid any more just now, but my dear child go to Jesus with all your care and troubles commit all your ways to him. And He will direct you. Walter was disappointed you did not say anything about coming home. He says he is going to fix up the yard + everything about this place + then he says you will stay.

Your Affectionate
Mother

Harriet's letter to Julia of April 1, 1873, suggests that Julia's health has so deteriorated that she missed a planned meeting with her sister Emma in Chicago. While the Wheelers clean and repair the home they've returned to, Willie travels to Washington, D.C., in an attempt to secure the patent for the windmill that people have attempted to steal from them.

I am just getting ready to go up to the house but I cannot bear to have this mail go out without a letter to you. Hattie and I have been cleaning house for two days past. And we have a long job before us yet. I was obliged to have the sitting room plastered. I hope to get settled at home this week. I expect to find it very lonely there.

I do not see how you could miss Emily. She went from the Chicago Depot to the Pittsburgh + Fort Wayne—She waited there till the five o'clock train. She was very much disappointed in not seeing you. Willie has not yet returned from Washington. We do not know what our fate is to be yet. All we hear is encouraging: our lawyer there thinks we should get the reissue.

The past few months have been very trying ones and were it not that I do believe the Lord will plead the cause of the Widow and the fatherless, I should despair.

Apr 6

I am now at home. All is confusion as we are not settled yet. The children and I are all cleaning and we find it very hard. The house has been occupied this winter—and everything thing is out of order. I received a letter from Emily last eve. She is very homesick. She says she has written you but gets no answer. Willie is still in Washington. Our Windmill case was probably decided upon last week; he has appealed the pump case to the Commissioner. I expect him home; I shall write you as soon as soon as I know the results. Walter sends love. He culled the first wind flower yesterday.

Your Affet

Mother

Beloit June 9/73

*M*y Dear Father

The past few months have been important and anxious ones to us. Willie left here the first of March for Washington. He was there for six weeks. He found that as the venture of our windmill principle became known, but particularly after my husband's death, there were many ready to rob us of our rights. Willie laid our case before the Patent office and succeeded in getting a patent which we think will protect us. Since then, we have put the business into the hands of a limited Stock Co. of fifty thousand dollars. We have rented a large Stone Mill. They expect to commence the work of manufacturing our own mill this week. While East, Willie opened up quite a trade in the business. We have an agent for Boston and vicinity. He sold a number of mills last month. Leonard and Willie are both very busy and have a great deal of care pressing upon them. They are now fairly launched into the whirl of business. Oh, pray for them that our dear Father in heaven will guide and keep them. Fred has been in school the past six months but will be out the first of July. He will then go right into the business.

Eugene will graduate from the high school the last of this month. He is hard at work at his graduating speech. His subject is the Indian question. Eugene will go with the shop to work for year. He has been a close faithful student and I think a change will do him good. Hattie and Wally are both in school. I wish you could see how pleased Wally was with the papers you sent him.

Write me dear Father and tell me your trials. If I can help you in no other way, I can pray for you Your Affect. Daughter Harriet Wheeler

All send love.
Dear sister Mary, tell her I have not forgotten her.

On July 24, 1873, Julia writes her grandfather after she has come home to die. Her letter reveals that her mother raises money by selling berries and currants from her garden.

We were very glad to receive your very welcome letter. I came home about three weeks ago. I have been in consumption for many months past, and am now in a very feeble condition. My left lung is gone and my right lung is considerable diseased. I feel very thankful to be at home—and under mother's care. I find her a very tender and faithful nurse. She is trying very hard to get time to write you, and will do so just as soon as she can. She has me to take care of—besides doing her own house-work just now, as her girl has gone home to assist her own family during the harvest season. Our garden has been very unusually prolific in the line of small fruits. Our purple-cane raspberries have yielded an abundance of the most delicious fruit. We had it for a month on our table three times a day. Mother sold a good many at high rates—in fact all she could spare—and put down the first in jam for the coming winter. Our white + red currents are beautiful. Mother sold most of them, after making all the jelly she wanted. I wish you were right in this room here just now. Our vines screen it from the glaring sun and we have the windows and doors all open. The fresh-pure-morning air comes softly in—and wherever the eye turns towards door or window it rests on a dense mass of green. Then we could have a good long talk which would be so much more agreeable than conversing through pen and paper.

CHAPTER SEVEN

Julia died in September 1873. On November 6, 1873, Harriet writes her father of Julia's passing.

*J*have been passing through the deep waters, my dear father. You have doubtless heard before this something about Julia's death. She failed very rapidly after her return. She seemed to make a great effort to keep about until she could get home. She had no wish or expectation of getting well for three months before she died. She said to me that her only hope of salvation was that Jesus had died for her. She frequently asked us to read to her the 53rd chapter of Isaiah and the hymn, "Just as I am without one plea." She said to me one day that it seemed to her that this hymn expressed the whole gospel.

I have hope that she is now at rest with her dear father in the better land. Oh, my dear father, I can not tell you what a comfort it is to me, in my bereavements and loneliness, to feel that they are at rest. Earth seems so changed to me, and heaven *so much nearer.*

After all these losses, the few letters surviving from the rest of Harriet's life focus on practicalities, giving little indication of the intense emotional and spiritual life that pervaded her earlier writings. She writes the following letter to her daughter Hattie in January 1874 from Fond du Lac, Wisconsin, where her sister Hannah Hoagland lived.

*M*y Dear Hattie,
I was very sorry I did not see you again the morning before I left. I had a good many "last directions to give" but I presume you will get along just as well without them. I cannot help feeling a little anxious about the house; I left it in such a flight. I wish you would take the boiler and wash it out clean and have Fred take it down to Mr. Waterman and have a new bottom put in it.

The one I think was left outside. It had better be put into the house. I hope you will not fail to put something up to all the windows. I would like to have Jean buy a bushel of Shell Corn at the feed store for the chickens. They will deliver it at the barn. I will enclose a dollar and if there is any left you can pay Mrs. Hinney for my bonnet. I suppose you and Jean are enjoying yourself very much. I hope you will make Rhoda just as little trouble as possible. You will have time to make up your studies which I hope you will improve. Has Leonard got home yet? Tell him I wish he would write me. My appetite is better but I do not gain strength very fast. Write me as soon as you receive this. Give much love to Mrs. Lathrop family. And any who may inquire for me.

Your Affectionate

Mother

H Wheeler

Give a great deal of love to Leonard Rhoda and Mary. Tell them I should be glad to hear from any of them. Hattie, I wish you would you would take the exact length and width of the pillow I sent to Rhoda. I want to make some pillows.

The Wheelers' religious commitment persists in their son, Edward Payton, but his writing lacks the ease and genuineness of his parents. He writes his mother from Andover Theological Seminary on February 12, 1874.

My thoughts have been of and with you in your sickness of late. While I am waiting to hear about you, I thought I would relieve my anxiety in this way. My last letter was addressed to you at Fon du lac. I hoped your visit there might prove of permanent advantage to your health. Yet your thoughts were doubtless much with the children at home and you soon desire to return. I can not help associating with your stay at aunt's, her generous table and fat pies. After another year's experience at the club, I cannot think of Aunt without tears.

You have doubtless profited much from her sympathy and encouragement. It was always our misfortune never to know much about our friend, yet Aunt seemed to me to possess the bright side of things. The children are doubtless full grown and doing much to help themselves. Hattie still lingers with her letter. I begin to fear she is not setting her aims very high in life. That degenerate Beloit Society is very apt to stifle the noblest ambition. Do I speak too hastily? My fears arise from the great lack of religious earnestness among the young people. It is a growing conviction that all true interest in self improvement has its roots in deep religious conviction. I should be contented with their prospects in education if I knew they were earnest Christians. You will pardon me if I speak freely on this subject. My own experience has led me to extreme conclusions. It is whenever my purpose has been most single that my earnestness for study has been greatest. My own feeling is the need of more wholehearted consecration to God. The selfishness + ingratitude of my life appear more and more. As I linger on the threshold of preparation for the work, the heart of culture seems too much wanting. Last Sabbath I went over to preach. Had some views of the greatness of the work. My audience had other views far from the truth. My sermon was on love of God to sinners. Some were somewhat moved; others seemed to consider it an ideal talk. Your affectionate son

E. P. Wheeler

A letter to the Wheelers' youngest daughter, Hattie, from Ellen Ainslee, a missionary to Turkey from Beloit, reveals a different attitude than that the Wheelers took to La Pointe. While they worked with the Ojibwe, Ellen Ainslie stands apart, watches, and judges.

Midyear Oct 16 1883

*D*ear friend Hattie:—
I see in the papers about your family doings + "goings" and business so I keep more track of you than you do of me. Your Georgia trip must have

been delightful. Did you see many queer negroes? Or was not that the part of the population you associated with? When you write please tell me how you are and your mother and the things that do not appear in the papers.

This country is so different from America that no description of it could give an idea of it. The people at first seemed very wild because they looked so queer in their foreign dress, but now they do not seem so to me. They are always interesting to watch. When I first came to the country I thought I had a pretty correct opinion of the natives but the longer I stay I can see how I was prejudiced for or against them in this or that direction and now I have come to the conclusion that my opinion cannot be given. If I judge the natives, it must be by my American ideas and an oriental cannot be made to conform to occidental ideas.

When your brother comes this way to put a windmill on Jacob's well you can come and stay with me and I will show you all the queer people and things I can. Machinery doesn't seem to be adapted to the oriental. A civil engineer from Germany is employed by the govt. on roads etc. He was telling me of an ice machine he brought to Diarbeki and set up and he made good ice several times. He went away and the owner thought he would make ice but he got out his cigarette and left his servant to run the machine. After a while a great noise was heard, and the machine had burst and also damaged the building. A great many dollars were thus thrown away.

Here in Midyat is a flour mill. It has been set up only a few months but is already broken. One of the stoves seemed to wobble a great deal and only very coarse flour is made, better can be made by little hand mills at which "two women shall be grinding." Every day + almost every night we hear this grinding in the field just back of our house. It is a pretty sight to watch two lively women as they make the stove spin round and continually putting in the wheat without hindering the movement of the stove. I could write a book (if I were able) about the ways, means, manners + customs of this part of the world and then one minute of seeing with the eye is worth all + more than all that can be written.

I must say Good Night. With love to you, your mother + Emily. Ainslie (Ellen)

At the start of a letter written on January 30, 1889, to her son Eugene, the woman who survived twenty-five winters in northern Wisconsin with few complaints has little positive to say about anything or anyone, but by its end, Harriet's compassion resurfaces.

 y Dear Jean
We did not miss a train after leaving Detroit. The scenery along the road was tame and uninteresting. Gradually things began to take on a shiftless seedy appearance. Corn still standing in the field. Some of it still standing husked lying in piles of the snow. It was raining when we reached Kankakee. There the negroes began to swarm. It was dark when we went into Cincinnati, but we were in time to get some stewed Oyster before the train started.

Here we left all traces of snow behind. The air became perceptibly warmer.

Soon after leaving C, the Porter made up our bed and we went to bed but not to sleep. The car was heated to furnace heat. It seemed impossible to breathe the close air.

The perspiration started from everyone.

I felt in the morning as though I had taken a Turkish bath. There was no stopping for breakfast or dinner and had it not been for our lunch basket we should have suffered.

I feel that we have great occasion for thankfulness for the comfortable + pleasant circumstances of the journey. The weather was hourly growing warmer. At night a full moon illumined the way so that we could distinguish objects almost as well as by daylight.

The weather since we came has been simply delightful. Last Sunday, it was so warm that the people were sitting on their verandahs without hats or wraps. Doors and windows open. Ladies tell me it was exceptionally warm even for this climate. Since this it is has not been quite as warm but the children are out playing in the yard without wraps every day.

But enough of this. How are you getting along at home? My thoughts are with you much of the time. I never realized as I have since I left what a hard time you have had this winter. Don't feel that your unselfishness, kindness has not been appreciated. I trust you have been laying up some treasure in heaven + will have your reward. Write me soon. Much love to all. Tell Walter I shall write him in a few days and tell him some of the funny sights we see here. I think I am gaining slowly. I have been out to ride on the street once. Hat wishes you to enquire very tenderly for her cat.

Affect Mother

Harriet's letter of December 30, 1890, shows her once more lost in sadness.

*M*y Dear children

Your letters have been received. I cannot express to you how grateful I am for your kind remembrance. Christmas day was bright and pleasant outside, but within all was gloom. We did not feel able to invite the family to our house. We would not exchange presents as usual except the children, a few little ones among themselves. Even the stockings were not hung up. About three o'clock the express Wagon drove up with your beautiful present. It seemed to break the spell. I think I never saw Hattie enjoy anything more than she did this present.

The grandchildren came in from three to five to have some games.

Emily and Mr. Leonard came up in the afternoon. They bought me a pair of kid gloves. William and his two little ones were also with us.

In July 1892, Harriet returns to Ashland, Wisconsin, just down the road from Odanah, for a conference on the area organized by her son Edward Payton, who has returned to serve as the first president of Northland College, then called North Wisconsin Academy. Breathing Lake Superior air brings Harriet back to life.

*D*ear Eugene + All

We reached here Saturday at ten o'clock and have been in one whirl ever since.

The two days of conference closed yesterday and Edward's hopes and expectations have even more than realized. Crowds have attended and the papers that have been read have been remarkable.

The weather has been perfect; had it been ordered for the occasion it could not have been improved. How I wish I could give you all a picture of the day—as the Boats moved out with the Band playing, Flags floating in the breeze and loaded down to the gunwale with a happy enthusiastic crowd.

The wind was strong enough to ripple the water, but not enough to make us seasick. I shall not attempt to tell you about the meetings on the island until I see you. The interest culminated yesterday at the laying of the corner stone of the Academy.

Our old friends have all been very kind. [Dr.] Ellis + Mrs. called the first day I came + have called most every day since. We have invitations now which would keep us [busy] a long time if we could accept them all.

Wish you could be with us.

Very Affectionately

Mother

In 1894, in the hope of once more recovering her energies at Ashland, Harriet Wheeler returns. Unfortunately, she suffers a fatal fall.

August 16, 1894, *Beloit Free Press* (reprint of an article written by Augusta S. Kennedy for the *Ashland Daily Press*).[17]

*T*he people of Ashland remember with sadness the announcement about three weeks ago that Mrs. Harriet Wheeler fell and sustained injuries from which it would be impossible for her to recover. She had but lately arrived from their home at Beloit to spend the remainder of the summer visiting with her son, Rev. E. P. Wheeler. The dear heart bore up bravely in her last days, and at the very end, her soul passed from the earthly temple so quietly, so peacefully, that those at her bedside do not know the exact time when the spirit took its flight.

Mrs. Harriet Wood Wheeler was born in Lowell, Mass., Dec. 9, 1816. She was of Puritan descent on both sides, her ancestors having been among the earliest non-conformists of Eastern England. Her birth occurred at a time when New England was being stirred by the first foreign missionary movement inaugurated in this country. Her parents fully sympathized with the "new departure" in religious undertakings. She was accordingly named after the first woman missionary to the heathen, Harriet Newell. Her education was completed under Mary Lyon, of educational fame. At the age of 25 years, married Rev. L. H. Wheeler, then under appointment of the American board of foreign missions, as missionary to the Ojibwa Indians of Lake Superior. They made their bridal tour from New England to La Pointe on Madelaine, in the summer of 1841. They were six weeks on the way alternating on their journey with stage coaches, canal boats, sailing crafts and bateau. They reached the Island just fifty-three years ago the 1st of this month. Here and at Odanah Mrs. Wheeler shared in the labors and privations of her husband's work among the Indians for twenty-five years. Owing to Mr. Wheeler's failing health, the family moved to Beloit in the southern part of the state, on account of the college advantages of the town. Mr. Wheeler survived the change but a few years.

Mrs. Wheeler shared with her husband in an unflagging interest and faith in the future of this region. It is to her solicitation that her son, Rev. E. P. Wheeler, was led to come back to Ashland,—the scene of his boyhood days and associates. It is intimated also that other sons may yet return to add the influence of their matured business experiences to the forces that are at work to build up our city. It was a trial to her to be obliged to end her days away from many who have become near and dear by the residence in Beloit. Yet she was also thankful that her last hours could be spent under the shadow of our Academy, which from the outset she has looked upon as a continuation of her early missionary labor.

The blow falls heavily upon Dr. Ellis and his wife and other friends of early days. She will be mourned by many in this city and vicinity as one who occupied a nearer place than even that of the closest kinship. "Blessed are the dead that die in the Lord, yea, saith the Spirit and their works do follow them."

When we who know her so well looked at her fragile physique, it seemed as if she must have been crushed beneath her load, but love and faith buoyed up her flagging health and carried her on. For the last few months, however, she has been very feeble and her one thought has been that she must have Lake Superior air or die.

How hard and mysterious it seems to us that she should have left her home and come here to met her fate. Only two days before she had gone with a merry party to the christening of a steamer, and seemed as happy and delighted as any of the throng. Little did we think that it was to be her last time with us. Mercifully are the times and seasons hidden from our eyes. An alarm of fire being sounded she rushed out in the quick way so natural to her, but missed her footing and fell to be picked up, bruised and broken. For three long weeks she suffered physical torture, but whenever a gleam of consciousness shone upon her, she lamented that she must be a trouble to others, entirely forgetting herself.

Attended by her devoted children she lay ill Sunday night, August 12, when just as the gates of sunset shut out the dying day the golden portals beyond swung open and our beloved friend passed through. Life's long, weary day ended. She bade good-night to the world to wake in the arms of Him whose loving mercies she had so long trusted, and whom she had so faithfully served.

Truly a mother in Isreal has fallen. Never till the books are made up at the end of time will she know of all the good she has done.

The years of utter self-abnegation which had been hers are something wonderful when viewed in the light of these days when so much worldliness infuses itself into the best efforts.

From the east and the west, from the north and the south, will they rise up and call her blessed.

None were too lowly or too poor for her kind ministration.

She did not give money alone but the pressure of the hand, the comforting word and the sympathetic tear which told so eloquently the burden was shared by her. After all perhaps she would have chosen to die here, so near the place where her heart has always been. And in a conversation with her before the delirium came upon her she said to me, "It has always been my prayer that Dr. Ellis might be with me in my last sickness," and thus it came about.

When asked to write this notice I accepted the trust gladly as the last tribute I could pay to a loving friend, but my heart fails me when I think how feeble is my best effort to do justice to her memory.

Her words and her deeds are her best monument. Her life was a constant praise service and her death comes like the benediction that follows after prayer.

Notes

Chapter One. PREPARATION FOR THE JOURNEY

1. Zilpah Polly Grant Bannister (1794–1874). John F. Ohles, ed., *Biographical Dictionary of American Educators* (Westport: Conn.: Greenwood Press, 1978), reports that at Grant's school, "grades were not stressed, and there were no academic prizes or honors. Students were taught to love the pursuit of knowledge. They received a formal and systematic preparation for careers as teachers. Interested in the needs of the West, she entered into a loan program designed to prepare Ipswich students to serve as missionary teachers" (84–85).

2. Shortly after Maria Cowles and Harriet Wheeler studied under her in Ipswich, Mary Lyon (1797–1849) founded Mount Holyoke College, the first institution of higher education for women. She wanted to make Mount Holyoke affordable, so students did the domestic work. After attending laboratory classes taught by Amos Eaton at Amherst, she insisted that science play an important role in the Mount Holyoke curriculum. Marilyn Ogilvie and Joy Harvey, eds., *The Biographical Dictionary of Women in Science: Pioneering Lives to the Mid-20th Century* (New York: Routledge, 2000), 815.

3. LD 7093.38 I6 MS 0556 Ipswich Female Seminary Collection, Series 2, Box 1, Folder 4: Ipswich Female Seminary pamphlet, 8–9, quoted by permission of Mount Holyoke College Archives and Special Collections.

4. Quote in J. N. Davidson, *In Unnamed Wisconsin: Studies in the History of the Region Between Lake Michigan and the Mississippi to which is appended A Memoir of Mrs. Harriet Wood Wheeler* (Milwaukee: Silas Chapman, 1895), 232.

5. This letter is addressed "Dear Brother and Sister," but a note at the top explains that it was written to Rev. Henry Cowles and that the original was given to Oberlin College by Cowles's

granddaughters. The Oberlin College Archives has no record of the letter, however. It is quoted here by permission of the Mount Holyoke College Archives and Special Collections, which retains a copy of it in LD 7093.38 16 MS 0556 Ipswich Female Seminary Collection, Series 7, Box 1, Folder 12: Maria Cowles Letter, March 29, 1831. After attending the Ipswich Female Seminary, Maria Cowles served as an assistant teacher at Oberlin College from 1837 to 1838. In 1835, the Oberlin Collegiate Institute was the first American college to allow women on their faculty. Lucille Addison Pollard, *Women on College and University Faculties* (New York: Arno Press, 1977), 108–109. In 1837, four young women were admitted to the freshman class at Oberlin; in 1841, three of them received bachelor degrees, "the first recorded women to accomplish this task and receive this award." Frances Juliette Hosford, *Father Shipherd's Magna Carta: A Century of Coeducation in Oberlin College* (Boston: Marshall Jones, 1937), 31. The Reverend Henry Cowles was a professor at Oberlin. His wife, Alice Welch Cowles, another former student of Mary Lyon's, was "the first president of the Oberlin Female Moral Reform Society" and in this capacity urged women at Oberlin to dress modestly and avoid public speaking. Linda L. Geary, *Balanced in the Wind: A Biography of Betsey Mix Cowles* (Lewisburg, Pa.: Bucknell University Press, 1989), 38.

6. Mary Holiday was born in 1812 to a white trader, John Holiday, and the Ojibwe woman he married. Her intelligence also impressed her teachers at the Mackinaw Mission School on Mackinac Island. Keith R. Widder, *Battle for the Soul: Métis Children Encounter Evangelical Protestants at Mackinaw Mission, 1823–1837* (East Lansing: Michigan State University Press, 1999), 114. Mary Holiday's religious orientation also seems compatible with those of Lyon and Grant; Caroline Williams Rodgers reports that Mary told her, "We must pray from our hearts as we felt, if we hoped to have God hear us." Quoted in Widder, *Battle for the Soul*, 159.

7. Benita Eisler, ed., *The Lowell Offering* (New York: W. W. Norton, 1998), 16.

8. Records indicate that Betsey Chamberlain lived in Lowell as early as 1831, alternating between there and Newmarket. She joined Lowell's First Congregational Church on March 6, 1831. Judith A. Ranta, *The Life and Writings of Betsey Chamberlain Native American Mill Worker* (Boston: Northeastern University Press, 2003), 7. She contributed essays to the *Offering* that argued that the mill workers deserved better working conditions. Eisler, *Lowell Offering*, 208–210.

9. Eisler, *Lowell Offering*, 32.

10. Burnap was pastor of the Appleton Street (Orthodox) Congregational Church from 1837 until 1852. Crowley, *Illustrated History of Lowell*, 91.

11. Lucy Larcom was such a fine poet that she counted John Greenleaf Whittier, first as an admirer, then as a lifelong friend. She published her first book in 1855 and followed it with fourteen others, most famously, *A New England Girlhood*. Bernice Selden, *The Mill Girls* (New York: Atheneum, 1983), 39–40, 52–63.

12. Susan Moore Wetherbee Diary, National Park Service, Lowell National Historical Park, Lowell, Mass., a gift from Mr. and Mrs. Clarence Forbes. According to the records in the Lowell National Historical Park Archives, she was born on November 15, 1811, in Harvard, Massachusetts, the daughter of Asa Wetherbee, a carpenter, and Polly Wetherbee. She died on December 22, 1881. She introduces herself at the start of her journal with these words: "Our family consists of Parents and Children eight in number—Grandmother—and two boarders."

13. This is probably Edward Beacher Wood, the second child of Samuel and Julia, who died of consumption when he was a year old.

14. William T. Boutwell, like Harriet and Leonard Wheeler, began his mission work at La Pointe in 1831, and like Leonard Wheeler, he had graduated from Andover Theological Seminary. Willard A. Rowell, *The Story of Old Mission on Madeline Island in Lake Superior. Written for the One Hundredth Anniversary of Old Mission* (n.p.: n.p., 1932), 9.

15. The Andover Theological Seminary was the first graduate theological school in the United States. When the school was founded at the beginning of the nineteenth century, it sought to adhere to high standards; this made it unusual among the professional institutions of that time. Nelson B. Henry, ed., *Education for the Professions* (Chicago: University of Chicago Press, 1962), 61–62. The institution was committed to "a fixed body of eternally valid truths" until a number of faculty retired between 1879 and 1882, and the school shifted in a more liberal direction. George M. Marsden, *Fundamentalism and American Culture* (New York: Oxford University Press, 1980), 25.

16. The Reverend Benjamin C. Meigs and his wife were in the second group of missionaries sent out by the American Board of Commissioners for Foreign Missions. John James Currier, *History of Newburyport, Massachusetts* (Newburyport, Mass.: author, 1909), 2:532. According to William Cothren, *History of Ancient Woodbury, Connecticut* (Baltimore: Genealogical Publishing, 1977), Meigs was a missionary in Ceylon (471).

17. Caleb Cushing, a native of Newburyport, impressed Daniel Webster when Cushing argued his first case before the Supreme Judicial Court of the Commonwealth with Webster as opposing counsel in 1825. Claude M. Fuess, *The Life of Caleb Cushing* (New York: Harcourt, Brace, 1923), 62.

18. President of the Massachusetts Senate, 1831; first mayor of Salem, 1836; and congressman from Massachusetts, 1838. Josiah Quincy, *The History of Harvard University* (Cambridge, Mass.: John Owen, 1840), 505.

19. Webster was a noted speaker. At the time of this dinner, he also represented Massachusetts in the U.S. Senate. Harold D. Moser, ed., *Daniel Webster: A Bibliography* (Westport, Conn.: Praeger, 2005), xxiii.

20. Rev. Stedman W. Hanks served as the first pastor of the John Street Church from 1840 until 1853. Charles Crowley, *An Illustrated History of Lowell* (Boston: Lee and Shepard, and Lowell, Mass.: B. G. Sargeant and Joshua Merrill, 1868), 95.

21. La Pointe is a village on Madeline Island, Wisconsin.

22. Candidate Department of the Papers for American Board of Commissioners for Foreign Missions, ABC 6, Vol. 17. Used by permission of the Houghton Library, Harvard University, and the United Church of Christ.

23. Candidate Department of the Papers for American Board of Commissioners for Foreign Missions, letter from Leonard Wheeler to Rufus Anderson, ABC 6, Vol. 17. Used by permission of the Houghton Library, Harvard University, and the United Church of Christ.

24. William Lloyd Garrison (1805–1879) was a fervent abolitionist and editor of the *Liberator*, which he founded in 1831. It persisted thirty-five years, or until after the Civil War ended. He was also interested in religious change. John L. Thomas, *The Liberator: William Lloyd Garrison a Biography* (Boston: Little, Brown, 1963).

25. Mrs. Fox is undoubtedly the mother of Amanda Fox, who, like Harriet and her sister Mary, taught in the Lowell primary schools. *Lowell Directory*, 1837, 1838, 1839, 1840.

26. "Cars" refers to a train.

27. The John Street Church was established on May 9, 1839. Crowley, *Illustrated History of Lowell*, 95.

28. Amos Blanchard was pastor of the Worthen Street Baptist Church and then of the Kirk Street Church. Crowley, *Illustrated History of Lowell*, 91–92.

Chapter Two. THE REALITY OF MISSION LIFE

1. Keith Widder presents a history of the La Pointe mission in "Founding La Pointe Mission, 1825–1833," *Wisconsin Magazine of History* 64 (Spring 1981): 181–201.

2. Wheeler Family Papers, Wisconsin Historical Center and Archives, Ashland, Box 3, Folder 8.

3. Quoted in Davidson, *In Unnamed Wisconsin*, 234–235.

4. Quoted in Davidson, *In Unnamed Wisconsin*, 236–238.

5. Sherman Hall ran the mission at La Pointe from 1831 until the government made plans to remove the Ojibwe to Minnesota. In 1853, he moved to Crow Wing, Minnesota, where he thought he would run a manual training school for the removed Ojibwe. In 1854, the American Board of Commissioners for Foreign Missions decided to abandon the project, and Hall found himself unemployed. He purchased a farm in Sauk Rapids, Minnesota, where he stayed until his death in 1879. "Notes and Documents," *Minnesota History* 7 (1926): 62–63.

6. "Ojibwas," *Missionary Herald* 38 (1842): 203–204.

7. "Documents," *Wisconsin Magazine of History* 16 (1932): 199–201. Granville T. Sproat was a teacher at the La Pointe Agency beginning in 1837. *Missionary Herald* 33 (1837): 25–26.

8. The Millerites believed the Second Coming would occur in 1844, ending the world.

9. The Congregational Church sat at the epicenter of the first settlement of Andover, Massachusetts.

10. This refers to what is now the Fond du Lac Reservation in northeastern Minnesota, an area inhabited by the Ojibwe since A.D. 800, not the city of Fond du Lac, Wisconsin.

11. Edmund F. Ely, another missionary for the American Board of Commissioners for Foreign Missions, worked at several Ojibwe missions besides Fond du Lac, including Pokeguma, Red Lake, and La Pointe. In 1849, he was released from his service with the board. Rev. Steven R. Riggs, "Protestant Missions in the Northwest," *Collections of the Minnesota Historical Society* 6 (1894): 119–149.

12. There was also an Ojibwe mission at Sandy Lake Minnesota; Edmund Ely also served as a missionary there. Davidson, *In Unnamed Wisconsin*, 58.

13. Quoted in Davidson, *In Unnamed Wisconsin*, 238–239.

14. Boutwell served at a number of Ojibwe missions for the American Board of Commissioners for Foreign Missions, settling at Leech Lake in Minnesota. Davidson, *In Unnamed Wisconsin*, 160. In 1834, he married Hester Crooks, the daughter of Ramsay Crooks and part Indian, and then they began missionary work together at Leech Lake. Rev. Stanley Edwards Lathrop, *A Historical Sketch of the "Old Mission"* (Ashland, Wis.: S. E. Edwards, 1905), 27.

15. The president of the United States at this time was John Tyler, who served from 1841 to 1845.

16. The American Seaman's Friends Society maintained a home for sailors, and, as a result, the *Merchants' Magazine and Commercial Review* claims that it is doing "more for the *protection, comfort,* and *moral* improvement of seamen, than any of the means directed to this object." As

of October 1843, the home had received 4,755 boarders (since May 1842). *Merchants' Magazine and Commercial Review* 9 (July–December 1843): 583.

17. The Sabbath School Society was established to encourage Sabbath schools and "to form depositories for supplying Sabbath schools with suitable books, on the lowest terms possible." It also sent books to missionaries in the West. By 1850, the Massachusetts Sabbath Society had 986 publications, 572 of them books. *A Brief History of the Massachusetts Sabbath School Society: And of the Rise and Progress of Sabbath Schools In the Orthodox Congregational Denomination in Massachusetts* (Boston: Massachusetts Sabbath School Society, 1850), 8, 23, 36.

18. Quoted in Davidson, *In Unnamed Wisconsin*, 241. Davidson gives no date for the letter, but describes it as "an extract from a letter written to the Young People's Missionary Society of Lowell, Massachusetts."

19. Quoted in Davidson, *In Unnamed Wisconsin*, 240–241. Davidson presents this quotation with no context, and the original is apparently lost, leaving its date uncertain.

20. Quoted in Davison, *In Unnamed Wisconsin*, 240. Davidson presents this quotation with no context, and the original is apparently lost, so the date is uncertain. Davidson does say that she is writing "with regard to the Odanah enterprise," meaning the Wheelers' conviction that they had to help the Ojibwe establish a settlement, which they did in 1845; they called it Odanah.

21. Abigail Spooner.

22. Harriet's brother.

23. In his *History of the Ojibway People* (Minneapolis: University of Minnesota Press, 1984), William Warren identifies Charles H. Oakes as a "prominent" trader "among the Ojibways during the early part of the nineteenth century" (384). According to W. H. C. Folsom, *Fifty Years in the Northwest* (St. Paul, Minn.: Pioneer Press, 1888), Oakes was born in 1803, started trading with the Indians in 1824, and joined the American Fur Company in 1827, where he stayed until 1850, with his headquarters usually at La Pointe (572). In 1850, he began the St. Paul banking firm Borup & Oakes.

24. Quoted in Davidson, *In Unnamed Wisconsin*, 239–240.

25. *Gashkendam* means "lonely." *A concise Dictionary of Minnesota Ojibwe*, edited by John D. Nichols and Earl Nyholm (Minneapolis: University of Minnesota Press, 1995).

26. I am unable to identify Mrs. Bright, but Mrs. Grant is probably Judith Grant Perkins, author of *The Persian Flower: A Memoir of Judith Grant Perkids of Oroomiah Persia*, published in 1853.

27. The Ojibwe would be in the sugar bush harvesting maple sugar.

28. David Greene was a corresponding secretary for the American Board of Commissioners for Foreign Missions. He "represented the board in its supervision of mission activities among the western and southern tribes." Charles M. Gates, "The Lac Qui Parle Indian Mission," *Minnesota History* 16 (1935): 134. Greene served as corresponding secretary for twenty years. Herbert Hunt and F. C. Kaylor, *Washington West of the Cascades* (Chicago: S. J. Clarke, 1917), 2:358.

29. Letter from Sherman Hall to David Greene, June 10, 1846, Papers of the American Board of Commissioners for Foreign Missions, ABC 18.4.1, vol. 1 (65). Used by permission of the Houghton Library, Harvard University, and the United Church of Christ.

Chapter Three. BUILDING A HOME ALONE IN THE FOREST

1. John D. Nichols, ed., *"A Statement Made by the Indians": A Bilingual Petition of the Chippewa of Lake Superior, 1864* (London, Ont.: Centre for Research and Teaching of Canadian Native Languages, University of Western Ontario, 1988), 13.

2. Nichols, *"Statement Made by the Indians,"* 15.

3. A. L. Brooks taught a Bible class to a large group of young men at the John Street Church in Lowell. Pamphlet entitled *Observance of the Semi-Centennial John-Street Church in Lowell* (1889), 53. This pamphlet can be found in the Lowell Historical Society, Lowell, Mass.

4. According to the 1850 and 1860 federal censuses, Hannah was married to Benjamin R. Smith, a farmer. They lived in Fond du Lac, Wisconsin, until his death in the Civil War.

5. Frederick Ayer founded the mission on La Pointe in 1830 after the trader Lyman Warren invited him. Ayer moved on to several Ojibwe missions, including those at Sandy Lake, Yellow Lake, Pokeguma, Fond du Lac, and Red Lake. In 1849, the American Board of Commissioners for Foreign Missions released him. Riggs, "Protestant Missions in the Northwest."

6. William Whipple Warren (1825–1853), author of the *History of the Ojibway People*, the earliest attempt to preserve stories told by Ojibwe elders. Theresa M. Schenck, *William W. Warren: The Life, Letters, and Times of an Ojibwe Leader* (Lincoln: University of Nebraska Press, 2007), vi.

7. As later letters in this collection indicate, Mary Warren English remained in contact with the Wheelers throughout her life. Born in 1835, she died in 1925. Schenck, *William W. Warren*, 10. She helped Frances Densmore with her research into Ojibwe culture for fifteen years. Brenda J. Childs, introduction to Frances Densmore, *Strength of the Earth: A Classic Guide to Ojibwe Uses of Native Plants* (St. Paul: Minnesota Historical Society Press, 2005), viii.

8. Mary Cadotte, the eldest unmarried daughter of the influential trader Michel Cadotte Sr. and the daughter of Waub-ij-e-jauk (White Crane). Schenck, *William W. Warren*, 4.

9. Lyman Warren began trading at Lac du Flambeau with his brother Truman in 1819, but in 1822 they sold their business to the American Fur Company. Schenck, *William W. Warren*, 3–4. Warren sought, successfully, to have a mission established at La Pointe. Davidson, *In Unnamed Wisconsin*, 49, 157.

10. Charles Pulsifer was sent to the LaPointe mission as a teacher by the American Board of Commissioners for Foreign Missions in 1849. He moved to Crow Wing with Sherman Hall in 1853 to work at a boarding school that was to be established. When this plan fell through, he returned to Bad River to work with Leonard Wheeler in 1854. Riggs, "Protestant Missions in the Northwest," 149, 151, 176–177.

Chapter Four. STANDING WITH THE OJIBWE AGAINST REMOVAL AND SMALLPOX

1. Ronald N. Satz, *Chippewa Treaty Rights: The Reserved Rights of Wisconsin's Chippewa Indians in Historical Perspective* (Madison: Wisconsin Academy of Sciences, Arts and Letters, 1991), 56, 61.

2. Alexander Ramsey, territorial governor of Minnesota. Schenck, *William W. Warren*, 69.

3. *Missionary Herald* 49 (1853): 312.

4. Davidson, *In Unnamed Wisconsin*, 170.

5. That agent is John S. Watrous, who "was removed from his position as Chippewa subagent in 1853." Schenck, *William W. Warren*, 174. Both William Warren and Leonard Wheeler had complained about him for years, particularly when he forced the Ojibwe to collect their payment at Sandy Lake. Wheeler stated that Watrous had "neither education or ability, nor personal morality nor integrity enough to command respect without it." Schenck, *William W. Warren*, 161. When Chief Buffalo traveled to Washington, D.C., in 1852, he also complained about Waltrous to President Millard Fillmore. Satz, *Chippewa Treaty Rights*, 67.

6. Henry Blatchford, who was half Ojibwe, began studying in the mission school at Mackinac when he was ten years old. Licensed to preach in 1860, he worked with the Ojibwe until his death at the age of ninety-three (1901). Widder, *Battle for the Soul*, 130, 138. He undoubtedly moved to Crow Wing because he anticipated removal.

7. Junius Welton previously lived at La Pointe, but then moved south to build a sawmill on the White River. Hamilton Nelson Ross, *La Pointe: Village Outpost on Madeline Island* (Madison: State Historical Society of Wisconsin, 2000), 116.

8. Edwin Hall is Sherman Hall's son.

9. Henry C. Gilbert, the Indian Agent in Detroit from 1853 until 1858. Silas Farmer, *History of Detroit and Wayne County and Early Michigan* (Detroit: Silas Farmer, 1890), 324.

10. Asaph Whittlesey, a member of the state legislature and also an Indian Agent. *History of Northern Wisconsin* (Chicago: Western Historical, 1881), 67. On June 2, 1877, he drove the last spike in the Ashland Line establishing a rail connection between Ashland and the rest of the United States. Ross, *La Pointe*, 131.

11. A whitlow is a painful inflammation near the end of a finger or toe.

12. This letter has apparently not survived.

Chapter Five. STRUGGLING AGAINST SICKNESS

1. Lewis Cass served as governor of the Michigan Territory from 1813 to 1831, when he moved onto the national scene after President Andrew Jackson named him secretary of war in 1831. He had an intense interest in American Indian culture, so he energetically advocated and sought fair treatment for Indians. Willard Carl Klunder, *Lewis Cass and the Politics of Moderation* (Kent, Ohio: Kent State University Press, 1996), 52–56.

2. Grace Greenwood is the pen name of Sara Jane Clarke Lippincott (1823–1904). She was a journalist and editor who also traveled the lecture circuit "speaking in favor of suffrage and pay equity for women, fair treatment of the American Indian, prison reform, and an end to slavery and capital punishment." Sam G. Riley, *Biographical Dictionary of American Newspaper Columnists* (Westport, Conn.: Greenwood Press, 1995), 185–186.

3. Probably the Honorable D. B. Stevens, who served three terms in the Wisconsin General Assembly and was associated with lumbering interests in northern Wisconsin. Ellis Baker Usher, *History of Wisconsin 1848–1913* (Chicago: Lewis, 1914), 8:2340.

4. She may be referring to the caning of Massachusetts senator and abolitionist Charles Sumner on May 22, 1856, by Preston Brooks. Brooks, a South Carolina congressman who favored slavery, was outraged by Sumner's language in a speech attacking fellow Southerners, especially Brooks's uncle, Senator Andrew P. Butler of South Carolina. "Sumner's caning, rather than the sack of Lawrence [Kansas], provided the Republicans with their most effective image of Southern arrogance." Richard H. Abbott, "Caning of Sumner," in *Encyclopedia of the Confederacy*, ed. Richard N. Current (New York: Simon and Schuster, 1999), 4:1561. Brooks's action also generated sympathy for Sumner, whose injuries prevented him from returning to the Senate until December 1859. Abbott, "Caning of Sumner," 4:1560–1562.

5. Eden B. Foster, pastor of the John Street Church from 1853 until 1861, when he resigned. But he returned to the pulpit there in 1866. Crowley, *Illustrated History of Lowell*, 85.

6. They will attend school in Ohio.

7. In the King James version of the Bible, these verses read: "And no man hath ascended up to heaven, but he that came down from heaven, *even* the son of Man which is in heaven" (13). "And as Moses lifted up the serpent in the wilderness, even so must the Son of man be lifted up" (14).

8. Western Reserve College, which later became a part of Case Western Reserve University, was founded in Tallmadge, Ohio, in 1826. Since no public high schools existed, it also had a preparatory school. Known as a center of abolitionism, the College admitted African American students in the 1830s. Carol Summerfield and Mary Elizabeth Devine, eds., *International Dictionary of University Histories* (Chicago: Fitzroy Dearborn, 1998), 69.

9. According to Harriet's father's autobiography, Henry died of typhoid in Mexico. Wheeler Family Papers, Box 3, Folder 3.

10. Phillips Academy in Andover, Massachusetts, is a residential high school established in 1778. From the beginning, it focused on its students' moral education, and its principal from 1838 until 1871, Samuel Harvey Taylor, was a strict disciplinarian. Frederick S. Allis Jr., *Youth from Every Quarter: A Bicentennial History of Phillips Academy, Andover* (Hanover, N.H.: University Press of New England, 1979), 49, 144.

11. Richard E. Morse is the author of "Chippewas of Lake Superior," *Wisconsin Historical Collections* 3 (1856): 338–369. "Morse was present at the annuity payments to Chippewa bands in 1855 at La Pointe." Barbara Dotts Paul and Justus F. Paul, *Wisconsin History: An Annotated Bibliography* (Westport, Conn.: Greenwood, 1999), 45.

12. Edwin Ellis, a medical doctor who helped found the city of Ashland, Wisconsin, in 1855. Folsom, *Fifty Years in the Northwest*, 49. In 1861, after Ashland declined, he taught until 1866 in the mission school Leonard Wheeler established at Bad River. *History of Northern Wisconsin*, 70.

13. Charles E. Mix, commissioner of Indian Affairs, wrote the following on November 6, 1858, about the government's Indian policies: "Experience has demonstrated that at least three serious, and, to the Indians, fatal errors have, from the beginning, marked our policy towards them, viz: their removal from place to place as our population advanced: the assignment to them of too great an extent of country, to be held in common; and the allowance of large sums of money as annuities, for the lands ceded by them. These errors, far more than the

want of capacity on the part of the Indian, have been the cause of the very limited success of our constant efforts to domesticate and civilize him." In Wilcomb E. Washburn, comp., *The American Indian and the United States: A Documentary History* (New York: Random House, 1973), 1:68.

14. John Waldo, the purchasing agent for the American Board of Commissioners for Foreign Missions in Boston. Benjamin Woodbridge Dwight, *The History of the Descendents of John Wright of Dedham, Massachusetts* (Boston: J. F. Trow & Son, 1874), 2:837.

15. Rev. D. Irenaeus Miner, who, with his wife, Jennie Cooley, began teaching at Bad River in 1859. But life at Odanah proved too challenging for the Miners to endure; they left in 1861. Davidson, *In Unnamed Wisconsin*, 171.

16. J. H. Nourse, who originally came to Indian Territory to teach at the Spencer Academy, Choctaw Nation, but illness forced him to settle in Bayfield. In 1858, he ran a hotel called the Bayfield House, which burned down. Later, he taught and served as county treasurer, town clerk, and collector of the port and receiver in the U.S. Land Office. *History of Northern Wisconsin*, 85.

17. Cyrus K. Drew, an Indian Agent at Bayfield, Wisconsin, from 1858 until 1861. http://www.wisconsinhistory.org.

18. Morgan Lewis Hewitt, who was born January 20, 1807, in Hartford, New York. He settled in Cleveland, but moved to Marquette, Michigan, in 1854, lured by the iron mines opening west of Marquette. In fact, he gave up the practice of medicine. Ernest H. Rankin, "The Mathers of Marquette and Cleveland, 1857," *Inland Seas Quarterly Journal of the Great Lakes Historical Society* 24 (Fall 1968): 195. Hewitt was founder of the Cleveland Iron Company and "chiefly interested in mining iron ore for shipment to blast furnaces." George P. Merk, "The Legacy of Peter White," *Michigan History Magazine* 83 (May–June 1999): 50.

19. J. W. Edwards, who represented the Marquette County Republicans at the Houghton Convention. John S. Burt. *They Left Their Mark: William Austin Burt and His Sons, Surveyors of the Public Domain* (Rancho Cordova, Calif.: Landmark, 1985), 143. According to the *Portage Lake Mining Gazette* of July 13, 1876, he "lost his life last Sunday on Lake Superior, by the burning of the propeller St. Clair." He "was on his way to Ontonagon county, where he had been examining the property of the Cleveland silver mine in the Iron River district."

20. At 2:30 A.M. on September 8, 1860, the schooner *Augusta* rammed the *Lady Elgin* in Lake Michigan, offshore from Winnetka, Illinois. The *Lady Elgin* then sank, leaving hundreds of its passengers clinging to pieces of wreckage and struggling toward shore. A total of 297

people perished, making the sinking of the *Lady Elgin* the second worst disaster to take place on the Great Lakes. William Ratigan, *Great Lake Shipwrecks and Survivals* (Grand Rapids, Mich.: Wm. B. Eerdmans, 1969), 44–49.

Chapter Six. HARRIET'S CHILDREN

1. In 1845, the government established an Indian Agency at Long Prairie and brought 400 to 700 Winnebago from Illinois to Long Prairie. Www.longprairie,com. Theresa Schenck confirms that Long Prairie was the site of a Winnebago Agency run by Jonathan Fletcher. Schenck, *William W. Warren*, 52.

2. The first set of laws developed for the state of Minnesota included the formation of volunteer companies composed of men between the ages of eighteen and forty-five who served five years, dealing with riots or insurrections. *General Laws of the State of Minnesota* (St. Paul, Minn.: Earle S. Goodrich, State Printer, 1858), 235–242.

3. Fort Snelling was established to guard "the frontier when it stopped at the Mississippi." Evan Jones, *Citadel in the Wilderness: The Story of Fort Snelling and the Old Northwest Frontier* (New York: Coward-McCann, 1966), 12. By 1857, the fort was surrounded by civilization, and so Franklin Steele bought it from the war department. After Steele made a profit from charging rent, the army resumed control of it until 1946. Jones, *Citadel in the Wilderness*, 230–231.

4. There are only two males named Cam in the Minnesota territorial and state censuses 1849–1905 identified as living in Dakota County. The most likely subject of Mary Warren's reference is Sath Cam, who was born in New York in 1807.

5. Captain John P. Ward of the boat *Planet*. *Portage Lake Mining Gazette*, August 4, 1862.

6. Senator Henry Mower Rice from Minnesota, who also served as a congressman. "Through his personal influence secured the consent of the objecting Sioux Indians to confirmation of the treaty of 1851 whereby all of Minnesota west of the Mississippi River and south of Ojibway County was open to white settlers." *Biographical Directory of the United States Congress*, bioguide.congress.gov.

7. She is living in the home of Stephen C. Cleaves, who works at the Franklin Stamping Mill associated with the Franklin Mine. He and his wife later had a fourth son, but three of their sons drowned. According to the *Portage Lake Mining Gazette*, June 22, 1871: "Last Thursday afternoon, Frank S., son of S. E. Cleaves, of Ripley, was drowned in Portage Lake by the upsetting and sinking of a small sailboat.... This is the third son that Mr. and Mrs. Cleaves have lost by drowning, and it is only about six months ago that Neddy, their youngest boy,

lost his life by going through the ice near Dollar Bay." In the May 4, 1871, issue of the *Portage Lake Mining Gazette*, Stephen Cleaves thanked people for their concern.

8. Sarah Cleaves's maiden name was Sarah Morrel. She was born in Windham, Maine, and married at Lowell in 1850. She moved to Portage Lake in 1859. She died in January 1888, and her funeral took place at the Hancock Congregational Church. *Portage Lake Mining Gazette*, January 19, 1888.

9. Carlo Bassini, *Art of Song* (Boston: D. L. Balch, 1856).

10. Nathan Richardson, *Modern School for the Pianoforte* (Boston: Oliver Ditson, 1859).

11. *McGuffey Eclectic Readers* were published from 1836 until 1920, so it is impossible to determine which one Julia Wheeler owned.

12. I. B. Woodbury, ed., *The Chorus Glee Book, Consisting of Glees, Quartets, Trios, Duets, and Solos* (New York: F. J. Huntington, Mason Brothers, 1855). Since there are also earlier editions, it is impossible to say which one Julia Wheeler owned.

13. The only Whittier collection with two volumes is *The Poetical Works of John Greenleaf Whittier Complete in Two Volumes*, ed. Stephen Alonzo Schoff (Boston: Ticknor and Fields, 1857, 1861).

14. I could locate no such book, but the *Annual Report of the Board of Education* published by the Massachusetts Board of Education in 1857 mentions Farquelle's *Le Grand pere* (26).

15. Thomas Kerchever Arnold and Jesse Ames Spencer, *A Practical Introduction to Latin Prose Composition* (New York: D. Appleton, 1850), although it is also possible that she owned an earlier edition published in 1846.

16. There are several kinds of Latin books to which Ethan Allen Andrews and Solomon Stoddard contributed, but the only book that they alone produced is *First Lessons in Latin Or, An Introduction to Andrews and Stoddard's Latin Grammar* (Boston: Crocker and Brewster, 1858).

17. Elijah Hinsdale Burritt, *Geography of the Heavens and Atlas Designed to Illustrate the Geography of the Heavens* (Hartford, Conn.: Huntington and Savage, 1845).

18. With such a vague description, one cannot confidently identify the book, but *A System of Natural Philosophy* by J. L. Comstock (New York: Pratt, Woodford, Farmer and Brace, 1854) is a possible candidate.

19. Probably *Elementary Geology* by Edward Hitchcock; there are four editions that she could have owned, but the one published by M. H. Newman of New York in 1847 seems a good possibility.

20. John Wilson, *A Treatise on English Punctuation* (Boston: Crosby, Nichols, 1856).

21. The 1860 federal census lists only one Livermore family in Houghton, that of John S.

Livermore, who had a daughter named Martha. Someone named John S. Livermore was also an Indian Subagent at La Pointe from 1848 to 1850. Anthony Godfrey, *A Forestry History of the Ten Wisconsin Indian Reservations under the Great Lakes Agency* (Salt Lake City: U.S. West Research, 1996), n.p.

22. Probably Richard M. Smith, Indian Agent who was lost on Lake Huron in 1871. According to the *New York Times* of October 23, 1871, "Mr. Smith was honest, upright and an exceedingly energetic and faithful man and officer." He died trying to deliver funds to Indians; he left most of the payments he had to make behind because he knew he might perish because of the lake's rough waters. In *In Unnamed Wisconsin*, Davidson reports that Agent Richard Smith visited the Wheelers at their mission (235).

23. Ann Brigham is probably Mrs. E. F. Brigham, who is active in the Ladies Aid Society. According to the *Portage Lake Mining Gazette* of November 19, 1864, she is a member of the Tableaux and Charade Committee, and the Tableaux Committee will meet at her home. According to the same issue of the paper, she is also on the Table Committee.

24. Luther E. Webb, an Indian Agent at the La Pointe Agency from 1861 to 1868. http://www.wisconsinhistory.org.

25. The Honorable H. Q. McKernan represented Houghton in the Michigan legislature, which convened in Lansing, Michigan. *Portage Lake Mining Gazette*, February 18, 1865.

26. J. J. Blaisdell, professor of rhetoric and English literature at Beloit College from 1859 to 1864; from 1864 to 1869 he was superintendent of city schools in Beloit. In 1854, he was chaplain of the Fortieth Wisconsin Volunteers. *History of Rock County, Wisconsin* (Chicago: Western Historical, 1879), 735.

27. William R. Merriman, president and professor of mental and moral sciences at Ripon College when it was founded in 1863. David P. Mapes, *History of the City of Ripon* (Milwaukee: Aikens and Cramer, 1873), 254.

28. Clarissa Tucker Tracy, a matron and instructor in biology at Ripon College. Mapes, *History of the City of Ripon*, 255.

29. Franklin Woodbury Fisk, professor of rhetoric and English at Beloit College from April 1854 until July 1859. He left to take a job at Chicago Theological Seminary. C. C. Lord, *Life and Times in Hopkinton, N.H.* (Concord, N.H.: Republican Press Association, 1890), 368.

30. Joseph Emerson, who on May 24, 1848, was invited to assume control of Beloit College, along with J. J. Bushnell. He first taught Latin and Greek and then Greek alone. *History of Rock County, Wisconsin*, 745.

31. In less than one week in August 1862, the Minnesota Sioux went on the rampage, killing hundreds of whites: the precise number is unknown; 260 women, children, and mixed-bloods were also held in brutal captivity for forty days. Almost 40,000 settlers fled their homes. Duane Schultz, *Over the Earth I Come: The Great Sioux Uprising of 1862* (New York: St. Martin's Press, 1992).

32. Henry Benjamin Whipple, bishop of Minnesota's Episcopal Church. He traveled to Washington, D.C., and passionately explained to President Lincoln why the Sioux attacked, pointing out that they had long suffered abuse. Schultz, *Over the Earth I Come*, 258.

33. She refers here to the treaty of 1851, when, after each chief signed the agreement with the government, "he was given another paper to sign and told it was simply an extra copy of the treaty. Actually, it was an agreement acknowledging certain debts to the traders and agreeing to repay them." As a result, traders claimed "most of the $495,000 promised the Indians as compensation for their removal from 24 million acres of their former land, which they had sold for a ridiculously low amount." Also Alexander Ramsey, the territorial governor, and his secretary, Hugh Tyler, took a 15 percent fee for arranging the treaty; Tyler got another $55,000 "for arranging Senate approval." Schultz, *Over the Earth I Come*, 9–10.

34. Henry Hastings Sibley, "a fur trader, soon to be governor, congressman, and the man chosen to quell the Sioux uprising." He also claimed the Sioux owed him $145,000 as a result of the 1851 treaty. Schultz, *Over the Earth I Come*, 10.

35. Contemporary historians call him Wabasha. Although seen as a Sioux chief who exerted moderating influence, he had a sharp reaction to the final version of the 1851 treaty: "There is one thing more which our great father can do, that is gather us all together on the prairie and surround us with soldiers and shoot us down." Quoted in Gary Clayton Anderson, *Kinsman of Another Kind: Dakota-White Relations in the Upper Mississippi Valley, 1650–1862* (St. Paul: Minnesota Historical Society Press, 1997), 192–193. But he did refuse to participate in the Sioux uprising and approached Sibley with an offer to help free the hostages held by Little Crow.

36. Anderson spells his name "Taopi" in *Kinsman of Another Kind* (273), while Schultz calls him "Taopee." He was a chief who, along with Wabasha, signed a letter to Sibley offering to help free the hostages Little Crow held. Schultz, *Over the Earth I Come*, 220–222.

37. Although Little Crow had persistently argued for accommodation with the whites, he was persuaded to lead the Sioux uprising and take white hostages. Schultz, *Over the Earth I Come*, 183–199.

38. A missionary to the Dakota (Sioux), author of the *English-Dakota Dictionary*, and the son

of another missionary to the Dakota, the Reverend Thomas Smith Williamson, M.D. After the Sioux uprising, both father and son "did not, for one moment yield to hesitation, but pushed their work with redoubled zeal." Nelson W. Evans and Emmons B Stivers, *A History of Adams County, Ohio from Its Earliest Settlement to the Present Time* (West Union, Ohio: E. B. Stivers, 1900), 641–642. J. P. Williamson worked with the Sioux at Fort Snelling and traveled with them when they were removed, protesting the conditions they had to endure during the trip. Schultz, *Over the Earth I Come*, 280–282.

39. Samuel Dutton Hinman (1839–1890), a missionary at the Lower Sioux Agency in Redwood County, Minnesota, at the time of the Sioux uprising. After this event, he continued to work with the Sioux at Fort Snelling and supervised their removal to near Fort Randall. In 1866, he was assigned to the Santee Agency, Nebraska. Http://www.nebraskahistory.org/lib-arch/research/manuscripts/family/samuel-hinman.htm. Because of his willingness to work with the Indians at Fort Snelling, he was beaten unconscious by a group of white men. Schultz, *Over the Earth I Come*, 278.

40. The firm Hubbell and Hawley was also called the North Western Fur Company. In 1863, Hubbell and Hawley received a contract to deliver supplies to the Sioux and Winnebago at the Fort Thompson reservation. In supposed fulfillment of this obligation, they gave the starving Indians tons of rotten food and frozen cattle: "The contractors demonstrated a wholesale contempt for law, humanity, and the welfare of famished Indians." Barton H. Barbour, *Fort Union and the Upper Missouri Fur Trade* (Norman: University of Oklahoma Press, 2001), 220. But they still made a great deal of money and were given another contract. Barbour, *Fort Union and the Upper Missouri Fur Trade*, 216–218.

41. This refers to Fond du Lac, Wisconsin, where Harriet's sister Hannah lived, as opposed to the Fond du Lac Reservation in Minnesota.

42. Emma is away at school, probably at Ripon, Wisconsin. Ripon College was preceded by a secondary school that continued to function after the college was established in 1863. Mapes, *History of the City of Ripon*, 247.

43. "Me-she-naw-way or the disciple, 2d chief his X mark" signed the 1854 treaty on behalf of the La Pointe band. Satz, *Chippewa Treaty Rights*, 184.

44. "Naw-waw-ge-waw-nose, or the Little Current, 2d chief, his X mark" is a signatory on the 1854 treaty as a representative of the La Pointe band. Satz, *Chippewa Treaty Rights*, 184.

45. George Warren was born to Mary Warren English's aunt and uncle, Charlotte and Truman Warren, in 1823. He had a twin brother, Edward. Schenck, *William W. Warren*, 4.

46. Dr. Edwin Ellis. In 1865, Ellis took charge of the boarding school Wheeler established. Riggs, "Protestant Missions in the Northwest," 179.

47. People in Ashland had hopes of mining iron ore from the Penokee Range. Instead, Ashland served as a port for mines located other places.

48. In 1865, Henry H. Eames claimed to have found gold in the Vermillion Lake region of Minnesota, and so various gold mining companies quickly formed and established themselves in the area, but found little gold. In 1868, an expert sent into the area by private parties said there was no gold there. William Watts Folwell, *A History of Minnesota* (St. Paul: Minnesota Historical Society Press, 1969) 4:4–7.

49. Mary Green is one of the fifteen people listed as members of Leonard Wheeler's church at Bad River when he left it. Another member identified as Babomigorhigehwa may be her husband. Ross, *La Pointe*, 125.

Chapter Seven. LIFE WITHOUT A MISSION

1. The *Beloit Directory* for 1857–1858 lists C. J. Taggart as a physician at the corner of School and Pleasant.

2. There are two listings in the 1860 Wisconsin census for Artemus Wheeler. The Artemus Wheeler that is the most likely candidate for the person Leonard Wheeler speaks of here is Artemus Clayton Wheeler, a sixty-one-year-old farmer in Winnebago, Wisconsin, who, like Leonard Wheeler, was born in Vermont. The other Artemus Wheeler is a clerk who lives in Fond du Lac. There is no likely candidate named Artemus Wheeler or Artemus Wood in the 1850 Wisconsin census.

3. Martha Lathrop was the widow of Stephen Pearl Lathrop, a professor at Beloit College and later at the University of Wisconsin in Madison. She was also William Wheeler's landlady when he attended Beloit College and later became his mother-in-law.

4. Harriet's brother William Henry Wood, whom she called "Henry," died of the typhoid in Mexico. His wife had died earlier, and so his father, Samuel Wood, and his stepmother, Julia Wood, raised his son, William, whom they called "Willy."

5. D. D. Winn, pastor of the Worthen Street Baptist Church in Lowell from 1853 until 1855. Crowley, *Illustrated History of Lowell*, 91.

6. Susie is William Wood's wife, Susan.

7. Leonard Wheeler built a retirement home in Omena, Michigan, which he called Sunset Lodge. It now functions as a bed and breakfast.

8. O. B. Olmstead & Company was another windmill company in Rock County. Http://www. usgennet.org/usa/wi/county/rock/Bus/HistBus008.html.

9. The United States Wind Engine and Pump Company was established in Batavia, Wisconsin, in 1857. Http://www.bataviahistoricalsociety.org/vannort.htm.

10. A lake in the Rock River valley from which the Winnebago were removed in 1840 and to which small groups of Winnebago returned until 1895. Web site, "Lake Koshkonong History Part I—Native Americans." Http://www.webpages.charter.net/jsill/Koshkonong/History-Native American.html.

11. Emeline Vaughn, founder of the Vaughn Library in Ashland and the wife of Sam Vaughn, one of Ashland's founders. Sam Vaughn was a businessman and politician, serving in the state assembly and as chairman of the county board. *History of Northern Wisconsin*, 73–74.

12. *Bayfield Press.*

13. Lace embroidery.

14. Elbridge G. Richardson was the overseer of the No. 1 Mill for the Hamilton Corporation in Lowell. Henry Adolphus Miles, In Lowell, *As It Was as It Is*, 2nd ed. (Lowell, Mass.: N. L. Dayton, 1846), 168.

15. Henry D. Porter and Arthur H. Smith. Both graduated with the class of 1867 at Beloit College, and both began mission work at Pang Chuang, China, in 1872. Porter became a medical missionary, and Smith served as a general missionary. Porter believed that medical work could be a vehicle for spiritual healing, while Smith became a world-famous missionary who suggested reforms in American diplomacy after the Boxer Rebellion in China. "Beloit's International History: The Foundation Period 1847–1898," http://www.beloit.edu/oie/campus_internat/history_1847.html.

16. S. T. Merrill came to Beloit to teach at Beloit College, but soon involved himself in business, building the first paper mill on the Rock River in 1851. In 1872, he invested in O. E. Merrill & Company's iron works and became treasurer and then president while he was also president of the Eclipse Wind-Mill Company. Starting in 1876, he represented Beloit in the state legislature and was also appointed commissioner to the international expositions at Vienna and Paris. *History of Rock County, Wisconsin*, 758.

17. Augusta S. Kennedy. Davidson, *In Unnamed Wisconsin*, 265–266.

Selected Bibliography

MANUSCRIPTS

American Board of Commissioners for Foreign Missions Archives, Houghton Library, Harvard University, Cambridge, Mass.

Ipswich Female Seminary Collection, Mount Holyoke Archives and Special Collections, Mount Holyoke College, South Hadley, Mass.

Wetherbee, Susan, Diary, National Park Service, Lowell National Historical Park, Lowell, Mass.

Wheeler Family Papers, Northland Mss 14, Wisconsin Historical Center and Archives, Ashland.

PUBLICATIONS

Anderson, Gary Clayton. *Kinsmen of Another Kind: Dakota-White Relations in the Upper Mississippi Valley, 1650–1862*. St. Paul: Minnesota Historical Society Press, 1997.

Baraga, Bishop Frederic. *The Diary of Bishop Frederic Baraga*. Ed. Regis M. Walling. Detroit: Wayne State University Press, 1990.

Bunge, Nancy. "Redeeming the Missionary: Leonard Wheeler and the Ojibwe." *ATQ* 14 (December 2000): 265–277.

———. "Straddling Cultures: Harriet Wheeler's and William W. Warren's Renditions of Ojibwe History." *ATQ* 16 (March 2002): 31–43.

Davidson, J. N. *In Unnamed Wisconsin: Studies in the History of the Region Between Lake Michigan and the Mississippi to which is appended A Memoir of Mrs. Harriet Wood Wheeler*. Milwaukee: Silas Chapman, 1895.

Kugel, Rebecca. *To Be the Main Leaders of Our People: A History of Minnesota Ojibwe Politics, 1825–1898*. East Lansing: Michigan State University Press, 1998.

Moran, William. *The Belles of New England: The Women of the Textile Mills and the Families Whose Wealth They Wove*. New York: St. Martin's Press, 2002.

Morrison, Eliza. *A Little History of My Forest Life: An Indian-White Autobiography*. Ed. Victoria Brehm. Tustin, Mich.: Ladyslipper Press, 2002.

Porterfield, Amanda. *Mary Lyon and the Mt. Holyoke Missionaries*. New York: Oxford University Press, 1997.

Robert, Dana L. *American Women in Mission: A Social History of Their Thought and Practice*. Macon, Ga.: Mercer University Press, 1997.

Ross, Hamilton Nelson. *La Pointe: Village Outpost on Madeline Island*. Madison: State Historical Society of Wisconsin, 2000.

Satz, Ronald N. *Chippewa Treaty Rights: The Reserved Rights of Wisconsin's Chippewa Indians in Historical Perspective*. Madison: Wisconsin Academy of Sciences, Arts and Letters, 1991.

Schenck, Theresa. *William W. Warren: The Life, Letters, and Times of an Ojibwe Leader*. Lincoln: University of Nebraska Press, 2007.

Schultz, Duane. *Over the Earth I Come: The Great Sioux Uprising of 1862*. New York: St. Martin's Press, 1992.

Warren, William. *History of the Ojibway People*. St. Paul: Minnesota Historical Society Press, 1984.

White, Richard. *The Middle Ground: Indians, Empires and Republics in the Great Lakes Region, 1650–1815*. Cambridge: Cambridge University Press, 1991.

Widder, Keith R. *Battle for the Soul: Métis Children Encounter Evangelical Protestants at Mackinaw Mission, 1823–1837*. East Lansing: Michigan State University Press, 1999.

———. "Founding La Pointe Mission, 1825–1833." *Wisconsin Magazine of History* 64 (Spring 1981): 181–201.

Zimm, John. "Wisconsin's Historic Windmills." *Wisconsin Magazine of History* 92 (Spring 2009): 28–34.

Index

INDEX

Wood, Patience (Harriet's biological mother), 3, 206

Wood, Samuel (Harriet's father), 69, 193, 225; letters by, 42–43, 55–56, 73–74, 76–77, 86–87, 117–118, 185–186, 206–207, 213; relationships with children and grandchildren of, 86–87, 125, 126, 132, 204, 213

Wood, Samuel Newell (Harriet's brother; Newell), 3, 55–56, 64–65, 76, 111

Wood, Susan (wife of Harriet's nephew William Wood; Susie), 190, 213

Wood, William (son of William Henry Wood; Willie, Willy), 127, 185, 186, 190, 213

Wood, William Henry (Henry), 3, 87, 118, 120, 122, 245 (n. 4)